MTTC Mathematics (Secondary)
22
Teacher Certification Exam

By: Sharon Wynne, M.S.
Southern Connecticut State University

"And, while there's no reason yet to panic, I think it's only prudent that we make preparations to panic."

XAMonline, INC.
Boston

Copyright © 2008 XAMonline, Inc.
All rights reserved. No part of the material protected by this copyright notice may be reproduced or utilized in any form or by any means, electronic or mechanical, including photocopying, recording or by any information storage and retrievable system, without written permission from the copyright holder.

To obtain permission(s) to use the material from this work for any purpose including workshops or seminars, please submit a written request to:

> XAMonline, Inc.
> 21 Orient Ave.
> Melrose, MA 02176
> Toll Free 1-800-509-4128
> Email: info@xamonline.com
> Web www.xamonline.com
> Fax: 1-781-662-9268

Library of Congress Cataloging-in-Publication Data

Wynne, Sharon A.
  Mathematics (Secondary) 22: Teacher Certification / Sharon A. Wynne. -2nd ed.
  ISBN 978-1-58197-645-8
    1. Mathematics (Secondary) 22.   2. Study Guides.   3. MTTC
    4. Teachers' Certification & Licensure.   5. Careers

Disclaimer:
The opinions expressed in this publication are the sole works of XAMonline and were created independently from the National Education Association, Educational Testing Service, or any State Department of Education, National Evaluation Systems or other testing affiliates.

Between the time of publication and printing, state specific standards as well as testing formats and website information may change that is not included in part or in whole within this product. Sample test questions are developed by XAMonline and reflect similar content as on real tests; however, they are not former tests. XAMonline assembles content that aligns with state standards but makes no claims nor guarantees teacher candidates a passing score. Numerical scores are determined by testing companies such as NES or ETS and then are compared with individual state standards. A passing score varies from state to state.

Printed in the United States of America   œ-1

MTTC: Mathematics (Secondary) 22
ISBN: 978-1-58197-645-8

TEACHER CERTIFICATION STUDY GUIDE

About the Subject Assessments

MTTC™: Subject Assessment in the Mathematics examination

Purpose: The assessments are designed to test the knowledge and competencies of prospective secondary level teachers. The question bank from which the assessment is drawn is undergoing constant revision. As a result, your test may include questions that will not count towards your score.

Test Version: There are two versions of subject assessment for Mathematics in Michigan. The Mathematics (Secondary) exam emphasizes comprehension in Mathematical Processes and Number Concepts; Patterns, Algebraic Relationships, and Functions; Measurement and Geometry; Data Analysis, Statistics, Probability, and Discrete Mathematics. The Mathematics (Elementary) exam emphasizes comprehension in Mathematical Processes and Number Concepts; Patterns, Algebraic Relationships, and Functions; Measurement and Geometry; Data Analysis, Statistics, Probability, and Discrete Mathematics. The Mathematics (Secondary) study guide is based on a typical knowledge level of persons who have completed a *bachelor's degree program* in Mathematics.

Time Allowance, Format and Scoring: You will have 4½ hours to finish the exam. There are approximately 100 multiple-choice questions in the exam.

Weighting: Approximately 22% of the total content consists of Mathematical Processes and Number Concepts; 28% consists of Patterns, Algebraic Relationships, and Functions; 22% consists of Measurement and Geometry; 28% consists of Data Analysis, Statistics, Probability, and Discrete Mathematics.

Additional Information about the MTTC Assessments: The MTTC series subject assessments are developed by *National Evaluation Systems.* They provide additional information on the MTTC series assessments, including registration, preparation and testing procedures and study materials such topical guides that have about 30 pages of information including approximately 20 additional sample questions.

TEACHER CERTIFICATION STUDY GUIDE

Table of Contents

PG #

SUBAREA I.   MATHEMATICAL PROCESSES AND NUMBER CONCEPTS

Competency 1   Understand principles of mathematical reasoning and techniques for communicating mathematical ideas 1

Competency 2   Understand problem-solving strategies, connections among different mathematical ideas, and the use of mathematics in other fields 11

Competency 3   Understand number systems and equivalent ways of representing numbers 16

Competency 4   Understand number theory and operations on number systems 21

SUBAREA II.   PATTERNS, ALGEBRAIC RELATIONSHIPS, AND FUNCTIONS

Competency 5   Describe, analyze, and generalize mathematical patterns 52

Competency 6   Use symbolic expressions to describe and analyze patterns of change and functional relationships 59

Competency 7   Understand properties and applications of linear and quadratic functions, and solve related equations and inequalities 68

Competency 8   Understand properties and applications of polynomial, rational, radical, exponential, logarithmic, and trigonometric functions, and solve related equations and inequalities 105

Competency 9   Understand principles and applications of differential and integral calculus 136

MATHEMATICS (Secondary)

TEACHER CERTIFICATION STUDY GUIDE

SUBAREA III.   MEASUREMENT AND GEOMETRY

Competency 10   Understand attributes of measurement and measuring units 176

Competency 11   Apply measurement principles to analyze the spatial characteristics of two- and three-dimensional shapes 187

Competency 12   Apply geometric principles of points, lines, angles, planes, congruence, and similarity to analyze the formal characteristics of two- and three-dimensional shapes 205

Competency 13   Apply properties of geometric transformations and coordinate and vector methods to describe geometric objects in two and three dimensions 231

SUBAREA IV.   DATA ANALYSIS, STATISTICS, PROBABILITY, AND DISCRETE MATHEMATICS

Competency 14   Understand methods of collecting, organizing, and displaying data 245

Competency 15   Understand methods of describing, analyzing, and interpreting data 250

Competency 16   Understand methods of making prediction and inferences based on data 259

Competency 17   Understand the theory of probability and probability distributions 268

Competency 18   Understand principles of discrete mathematics 276

Answer Key to Practice Problems 279

Sample Test 286

Answer Key 299

Rationales for Sample Questions 300

TEACHER CERTIFICATION STUDY GUIDE

Great Study and Testing Tips!

What to study in order to prepare for the subject assessments is the focus of this study guide but equally important is *how* you study.

You can increase your chances of truly mastering the information by taking some simple, but effective steps.

Study Tips:

1. Some foods aid the learning process. Foods such as milk, nuts, seeds, rice, and oats help your study efforts by releasing natural memory enhancers called CCKs (*cholecystokinin*) composed of *tryptopha*n, *choline*, and *phenylalanine*. All of these chemicals enhance the neurotransmitters associated with memory. Before studying, try a light, protein-rich meal of eggs, turkey, and fish. All of these foods release the memory enhancing chemicals. The better the connections, the more you comprehend.

Likewise, before you take a test, stick to a light snack of energy boosting and relaxing foods. A glass of milk, a piece of fruit, or some peanuts all release various memory-boosting chemicals and help you to relax and focus on the subject at hand.

2. Learn to take great notes. A by-product of our modern culture is that we have grown accustomed to getting our information in short doses (i.e. TV news sound bites or USA Today style newspaper articles.)

Consequently, we've subconsciously trained ourselves to assimilate information better in neat little packages. If your notes are scrawled all over the paper, it fragments the flow of the information. Strive for clarity. Newspapers use a standard format to achieve clarity. Your notes can be much clearer through use of proper formatting. A very effective format is called the *"Cornell Method."*

Take a sheet of loose-leaf lined notebook paper and draw a line all the way down the paper about 1-2" from the left-hand edge.

Draw another line across the width of the paper about 1-2" up from the bottom. Repeat this process on the reverse side of the page.

Look at the highly effective result. You have ample room for notes, a left hand margin for special emphasis items or inserting supplementary data from the textbook, a large area at the bottom for a brief summary, and a little rectangular space for just about anything you want.

3. Get the concept then the details. Too often we focus on the details and don't gather an understanding of the concept. However, if you simply memorize only dates, places, or names, you may well miss the whole point of the subject.

A key way to understand things is to put them in your own words. If you are working from a textbook, automatically summarize each paragraph in your mind. If you are outlining text, don't simply copy the author's words.

Rephrase them in your own words. You remember your own thoughts and words much better than someone else's, and subconsciously tend to associate the important details to the core concepts.

4. Ask Why? Pull apart written material paragraph by paragraph and don't forget the captions under the illustrations.

Example: If the heading is "Stream Erosion", flip it around to read "Why do streams erode?" Then answer the questions.

If you train your mind to think in a series of questions and answers, not only will you learn more, but it also helps to lessen the test anxiety because you are used to answering questions.

5. Read for reinforcement and future needs. Even if you only have 10 minutes, put your notes or a book in your hand. Your mind is similar to a computer; you have to input data in order to have it processed. *By reading, you are creating the neural connections for future retrieval.* The more times you read something, the more you reinforce the learning of ideas.

Even if you don't fully understand something on the first pass, *your mind stores much of the material for later recall.*

6. Relax to learn so go into exile. Our bodies respond to an inner clock called biorhythms. Burning the midnight oil works well for some people, but not everyone.

If possible, set aside a particular place to study that is free of distractions. Shut off the television, cell phone, pager and exile your friends and family during your study period.

If you really are bothered by silence, try background music. Light classical music at a low volume has been shown to aid in concentration over other types. Music that evokes pleasant emotions without lyrics are highly suggested. Try just about anything by Mozart. It relaxes you.

7. Use arrows not highlighters. At best, it's difficult to read a page full of yellow, pink, blue, and green streaks. Try staring at a neon sign for a while and you'll soon see that the horde of colors obscure the message.

A quick note, a brief dash of color, an underline, and an arrow pointing to a particular passage is much clearer than a horde of highlighted words.

8. Budget your study time. Although you shouldn't ignore any of the material, *allocate your available study time in the same ratio that topics may appear on the test.*

TEACHER CERTIFICATION STUDY GUIDE

Testing Tips:

1. Get smart, play dumb. Don't read anything into the question. Don't make an assumption that the test writer is looking for something else than what is asked. Stick to the question as written and don't read extra things into it.

2. Read the question and all the choices *twice* before answering the question. You may miss something by not carefully reading, and then re-reading both the question and the answers.

If you really don't have a clue as to the right answer, leave it blank on the first time through. Go on to the other questions, as they may provide a clue as to how to answer the skipped questions.

If later on, you still can't answer the skipped ones . . . *Guess.* The only penalty for guessing is that you *might* get it wrong. Only one thing is certain; if you don't put anything down, you will get it wrong!

3. Turn the question into a statement. Look at the way the questions are worded. The syntax of the question usually provides a clue. Does it seem more familiar as a statement rather than as a question? Does it sound strange?

By turning a question into a statement, you may be able to spot if an answer sounds right, and it may also trigger memories of material you have read.

4. Look for hidden clues. It's actually very difficult to compose multiple-foil (choice) questions without giving away part of the answer in the options presented.

In most multiple-choice questions you can often readily eliminate one or two of the potential answers. This leaves you with only two real possibilities and automatically your odds go to Fifty-Fifty for very little work.

5. Trust your instincts. For every fact that you have read, you subconsciously retain something of that knowledge. On questions that you aren't really certain about, go with your basic instincts. **Your first impression on how to answer a question is usually correct.**

6. Mark your answers directly on the test booklet. Don't bother trying to fill in the optical scan sheet on the first pass through the test.

Just be very careful not to miss-mark your answers when you eventually transcribe them to the scan sheet.

7. Watch the clock! You have a set amount of time to answer the questions. Don't get bogged down trying to answer a single question at the expense of 10 questions you can more readily answer.

MATHEMATICS (Secondary)

THIS PAGE BLANK

SUBAREA I. MATHEMATICAL PROCESSES AND NUMBER CONCEPTS

Competency 1   **Understand principles of mathematical reasoning and techniques for communicating mathematical ideas.**

Conditional statements are frequently written in "**if-then**" form. The "if" clause of the conditional is known as the **hypothesis**, and the "then" clause is called the **conclusion**. In a proof, the hypothesis is the information that is assumed to be true, while the conclusion is what is to be proven true. A conditional is considered to be of the form:

If p, then q

p is the hypothesis. q is the conclusion.

Conditional statements can be diagrammed using a **Venn diagram**. A diagram can be drawn with one circle inside another circle. The inner circle represents the hypothesis. The outer circle represents the conclusion. If the hypothesis is taken to be true, then you are located inside the inner circle. If you are located in the inner circle then you are also inside the outer circle, so that proves the conclusion is true.

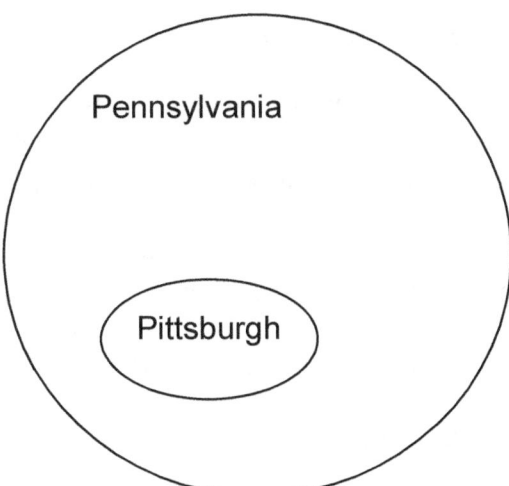

Example:
If an angle has a measure of 90 degrees, then it is a right angle.

In this statement "an angle has a measure of 90 degrees" is the hypothesis.

In this statement "it is a right angle" is the conclusion.

Example:

If you are in Pittsburgh, then you are in Pennsylvania.
 In this statement "you are in Pittsburgh" is the hypothesis.
 In this statement "you are in Pennsylvania" is the conclusion.

Inverses, converses, and contrapositives of conditionals

Conditional: If p, then q p is the hypothesis. q is the conclusion.

Inverse: If ~p, then ~q. Negate both the hypothesis (If not p, then not q) and the conclusion from the original conditional.

Converse : If q, then p.   Reverse the 2 clauses. The original hypothesis becomes the conclusion. The original conclusion then becomes the new hypothesis.

Contrapositive: If ~q, then ~p. Reverse the 2 clauses. The If not q, then not p original hypothesis becomes the conclusion. The original conclusion then becomes the new hypothesis. THEN negate both the new hypothesis and the new conclusion.

Example: Given the **conditional**:

If an angle has 60°, then it is an acute angle.

Its **inverse**, in the form "If ~p, then ~q", would be:

If an angle doesn't have 60°, then it is not an acute angle.

> NOTICE that the inverse is not true, even
> though the conditional statement was true.

Its **converse**, in the form "If q, then p", would be:

If an angle is an acute angle, then it has 60°.

> NOTICE that the converse is not true, even
> though the conditional statement was true.

Its **contrapositive**, in the form "If ~q, then ~p", would be:

If an angle isn't an acute angle, then it doesn't have 60°.

> NOTICE that the contrapositive is true, assuming
> the original conditional statement was true.

TIP: If you are asked to pick a statement that is logically equivalent to a given conditional, look for the contra-positive. The inverse and converse are not always logically equivalent to every conditional. The contra-positive is ALWAYS logically equivalent.

Find the inverse, converse and contrapositive of the following conditional statement. Also determine if each of the 4 statements is true or false.

Conditional: If $x = 5$, then $x^2 - 25 = 0$.   TRUE
Inverse: If $x \neq 5$, then $x^2 - 25 \neq 0$.   FALSE, x could be $^-5$
Converse: If $x^2 - 25 = 0$, then $x = 5$.   FALSE, x could be $^-5$
Contrapositive: If $x^2 - 25 \neq 0$, then $x \neq 5$.   TRUE
Conditional: If $x = 5$, then $6x = 30$.   TRUE
Inverse: If $x \neq 5$, then $6x \neq 30$.   TRUE
Converse: If $6x = 30$, then $x = 5$.   TRUE
Contrapositive: If $6x \neq 30$, then $x \neq 5$.   TRUE

Sometimes, as in this example, all 4 statements can be logically equivalent; however, the only statement that will always be logically equivalent to the original conditional is the contrapositive.

Conditional statements can be diagrammed using a **Venn diagram**. A diagram can be drawn with one figure inside another figure. The inner figure represents the hypothesis. The outer figure represents the conclusion. If the hypothesis is taken to be true, then you are located inside the inner figure. If you are located in the inner figure then you are also inside the outer figure, so that proves the conclusion is true. Sometimes that conclusion can then be used as the hypothesis for another conditional, which can result in a second conclusion.

Suppose that these statements were given to you, and you are asked to try to reach a conclusion. The statements are:

All swimmers are athletes.
All athletes are scholars.

In "if-then" form, these would be:
If you are a swimmer, then you are an athlete.
If you are an athlete, then you are a scholar.

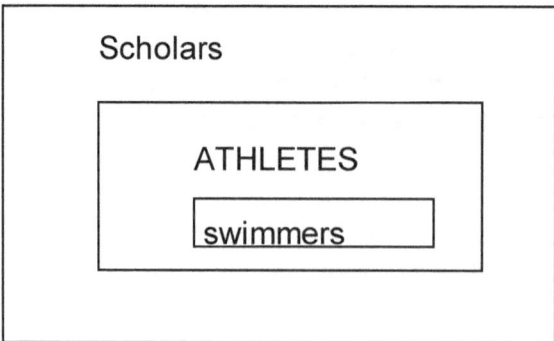

Clearly, if you are a swimmer, then you are also an athlete. This includes you in the group of scholars.

Suppose that these statements were given to you, and you are asked to try to reach a conclusion. The statements are:

All swimmers are athletes.
All wrestlers are athletes.

In "if-then" form, these would be:
If you are a swimmer, then you are an athlete.
If you are a wrestler, then you are an athlete.

Clearly, if you are a swimmer or a wrestler, then you are also an athlete. This does NOT allow you to come to any other conclusions.

A swimmer may or may NOT also be a wrestler. Therefore, NO CONCLUSION IS POSSIBLE.

Suppose that these statements were given to you, and you are asked to try to reach a conclusion. The statements are:

All rectangles are parallelograms.
Quadrilateral ABCD is not a parallelogram.

In "if-then" form, the first statement would be:
If a figure is a rectangle, then it is also a parallelogram.

Note that the second statement is the negation of the conclusion of statement one. Remember also that the contrapositive is logically equivalent to a given conditional. That is, **"If ⌐ q, then ⌐ p"**. Since" ABCD is NOT a parallelogram " is like saying **"If ⌐ q,"** then you can come to the conclusion **"then ⌐ p"**. Therefore, the conclusion is ABCD is not a rectangle. Looking at the Venn diagram below, if all rectangles are parallelograms, then rectangles are included as part of the parallelograms. Since quadrilateral ABCD is not a parallelogram, that it is excluded from anywhere inside the parallelogram box. This allows you to conclude that ABCD can not be a rectangle either.

```
┌─────────────────────────┐
│  PARALLELOGRAMS         │     quadrilateral
│   ┌──────────────┐      │     ABCD
│   │  rectangles  │      │
│   └──────────────┘      │
└─────────────────────────┘
```

Try These:

What conclusion, if any, can be reached? Assume each statement is true, regardless of any personal beliefs.

1. If the Red Sox win the World Series, I will die.
   I died.

2. If an angle's measure is between 0° and 90°, then the angle is acute.
   Angle B is not acute.

3. Students who do well in geometry will succeed in college.
   Annie is doing extremely well in geometry.

4. Left-handed people are witty and charming.
   You are left-handed.

Inductive thinking is the process of finding a pattern from a group of examples. That pattern is the conclusion that this set of examples seemed to indicate. It may be a correct conclusion or it may be an incorrect conclusion because other examples may not follow the predicted pattern.

Deductive thinking is the process of arriving at a conclusion based on other statements that are all known to be true, such as theorems, axiomspostulates, or postulates. Conclusions found by deductive thinking based on true statements will **always** be true.

MATHEMATICS (Secondary)

Examples :

Suppose:
  On Monday Mr.Peterson eats breakfast at McDonalds.
  On Tuesday Mr.Peterson eats breakfast at McDonalds.
  On Wednesday Mr.Peterson eats breakfast at McDonalds.
  On Thursday Mr.Peterson eats breakfast at McDonalds again.

Conclusion: On Friday Mr. Peterson will eat breakfast at McDonalds again.

This is a conclusion based on inductive reasoning. Based on several days observations, you conclude that Mr. Peterson will eat at McDonalds. This may or may not be true, but it is a conclusion arrived at by inductive thinking.

A **counterexample** is an exception to a proposed rule or conjecture that disproves the conjecture. For example, the existence of a single non-brown dog disproves the conjecture "all dogs are brown". Thus, any non-brown dog is a counterexample.

In searching for mathematic counterexamples, one should consider extreme cases near the ends of the domain of an experiment and special cases where an additional property is introduced. Examples of extreme cases are numbers near zero and obtuse triangles that are nearly flat. An example of a special case for a problem involving rectangles is a square because a square is a rectangle with the additional property of symmetry.
Example:

Identify a counterexample for the following conjectures.

1. If n is an even number, then $n+1$ is divisible by 3.

    $n = 4$
    $n + 1 = 4 + 1 = 5$
    5 is not divisible by 3.

2. If n is divisible by 3, then $n^2 - 1$ is divisible by 4.

    $n = 6$
    $n^2 - 1 = 6^2 - 1 = 35$
    35 is not divisible by 4.

Direct Proofs

In a 2 column proof, the left side of the proof should be the given information, or statements that could be proved by deductive reasoning. The right column of the proof consists of the reasons used to determine that each statement to the left was verifiably true. The right side can identify given information, or state theorems, postulates, definitions or algebraic properties used to prove that particular line of the proof is true.

Indirect Proofs

Assume the opposite of the conclusion. Keep your hypothesis and given information the same. Proceed to develop the steps of the proof, looking for a statement that contradicts your original assumption or some other known fact. This contradiction indicates that the assumption you made at the beginning of the proof was incorrect; therefore, the original conclusion has to be true.

In order to understand mathematics and solve problems, one must know the definitions of **basic mathematic terms and concepts**. For a list of definitions and explanations of basic math terms, visit the following website: http://home.blarg.net/~math/deflist.html

Additionally, one must use the language of mathematics correctly and precisely to accurately communicate concepts and ideas.

For example, the statement "minus ten times minus five equals plus fifty" is incorrect because minus and plus are arithmetic operations not numerical modifiers. The statement should read "negative ten times negative five equals positive 50".

Examples, illustrations, and symbolic representations are useful tools in explaining and understanding mathematical concepts. The ability to create examples and alternative methods of expression allows students to solve real world problems and better communicate their thoughts.

Concrete examples are real world applications of mathematical concepts. For example, measuring the shadow produced by a tree or building is a real world application of trigonometric functions, acceleration or velocity of a car is an application of derivatives, and finding the volume or area of a swimming pool is a real world application of geometric principles.

Pictorial illustrations of mathematic concepts help clarify difficult ideas and simplify problem solving.

Examples:

1. Rectangle R represents the 300 students in School A. Circle P represents the 150 students that participated in band. Circle Q represents the 170 students that participated in a sport. 70 students participated in both band and a sport.

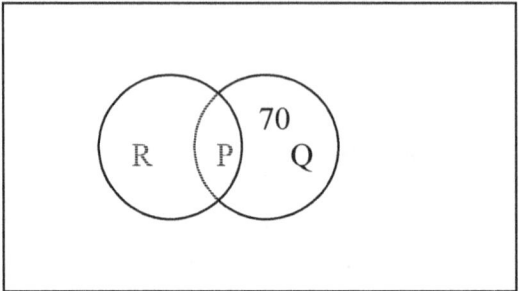

Pictorial representation of above situation.

2. A ball rolls up an incline and rolls back to its original position. Create a graph of the velocity of the ball.

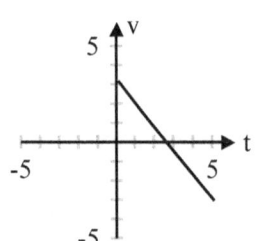

Velocity starts out at its maximum as the ball begins to roll, decreases to zero at the top of the incline, and returns to the maximum in the opposite direction at the bottom of the incline.

Symbolic representation is the basic language of mathematics. Converting data to symbols allows for easy manipulation and problem solving. Students should have the ability to recognize what the symbolic notation represents and convert information into symbolic form. For example, from the graph of a line, students should have the ability to determine the slope and intercepts and derive the line's equation from the observed data. Another possible application of symbolic representation is the formulation of algebraic expressions and relations from data presented in word problem form.

Recognition and understanding of the relationships between concepts and topics is of great value in mathematical problem solving and the explanation of more complex processes.

For instance, multiplication is simply repeated addition. This relationship explains the concept of variable addition. We can show that the expression 4x + 3x = 7x is true by rewriting 4 times x and 3 times x as repeated addition, yielding the expression (x + x + x + x) + (x + x + x). Thus, because of the relationship between multiplication and addition, variable addition is accomplished by coefficient addition.

Another example of a mathematical relationship is powers as repeated multiplication. This relationship explains the rules of exponent operations. For instance, the multiplication of exponential terms with like bases is accomplished by the addition of the exponents.

$$2^2 \times 2^5 = 2^7$$

$$(2 \times 2) + (2 \times 2 \times 2 \times 2 \times 2) = 2^{2+5} = 2^7$$

This rule yields the general formula for the product of exponential terms, $z^m \times z^n = z^{m+n}$, that is useful in problem solving.

Mathematical concepts and procedures can take many different forms. Students of mathematics must be able to recognize different forms of equivalent concepts.

For example, we can represent the slope of a line graphically, algebraically, verbally, and numerically. A line drawn on a coordinate plane will show the slope. In the equation of a line, y = mx + b, the term m represents the slope. We can define the slope of a line several different ways. The slope of a line is the change in the value of the y divided by the change in the value of x over a given interval. Alternatively, the slope of a line is the ratio of "rise" to "run" between two points. Finally, we can calculate the numeric value of the slope by using the verbal definitions and the algebraic representation of the line.

Students of mathematics must be able to recognize and interpret the different representations of arithmetic operations.

First, there are many different verbal descriptions for the operations of addition, subtraction, multiplication, and division.

The table below identifies several words and/or phrases that are often used to denote the different arithmetic operations.

Operation	Descriptive Words
Addition	"plus", "combine", "sum", "total", "put together"
Subtraction	"minus", "less", "take away", "difference"
Multiplication	"product", "times", "groups of"
Division	"quotient", "into", "split into equal groups",

Second, diagrams of arithmetic operations can present mathematical data in visual form. For example, we can use the number line to add and subtract.

The addition of 5 to -4 on the number line; -4 + 5 = 1.

Finally, as shown in the examples below, we can use pictorial representations to explain all of the arithmetic processes.

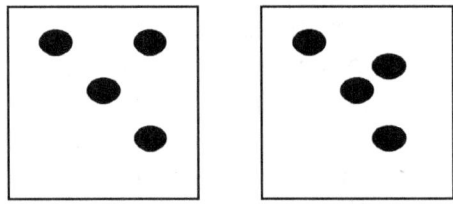

Two groups of four equals eight or 2 x 4 = 8 shown in picture form.

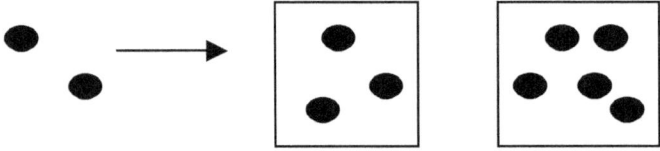

Adding three objects to two or 3 + 2 = 5 shown in picture form.

MATHEMATICS (Secondary)

Competency 2 **Understand problem-solving strategies, connections among different mathematical ideas, and the use of mathematics in other fields.**

Successful teachers are able to identify all types of student errors. Identifying patterns of errors allows teachers to tailor their curriculum to enhance student learning and understanding. The following is a list of common errors committed by algebra and calculus students.

Algebra
1. Failing to distribute:
   ex. $4x - (2x - 3) = 4x - 2x + 3$ (**not** $4x - 2x - 3$)
   ex. $3(2x + 5) = 6x + 15$ (**not** $6x + 5$)
2. Distributing exponents:
   ex. $(x + y)^2 = x^2 + 2xy + y^2$ (**not** $x^2 + y^2$)
3. Canceling terms instead of factors:
   ex. $\dfrac{x^3 + 5}{x} \neq x^2 + 5 \;=\; x^2 + \dfrac{5}{x}$ (**not** $x^2 + 5$)
4. Misunderstanding negative and fractional exponents:
   ex. $x^{\frac{1}{2}} = \sqrt{x}$ (**not** $\dfrac{1}{x^2}$)
   ex. $x^{-2} = \dfrac{1}{x^2}$ (**not** $\sqrt{x}$)

Calculus
1. Failing to use the product, quotient, and chain rules:
   $f(x) = (5x^2)(3x^3),$
   ex. $f'(x) = (10x)(3x^3) + (5x^2)(9x^2)$
   $= 30x^4 + 45x^4 = 75x^4$
   [**not** $(10x)(9x^2) = 90x^3$]
2. Misapplying derivative and integration rules:
   ex. $\int \dfrac{1}{x} = \ln x + C,$
   $\int \dfrac{1}{(x^2+1)} = \dfrac{1}{\tan x} + C$ (**not** $\ln(x^2+1) + C$)

Teachers also must not neglect multiple errors in the work of a student that may be disguised by a correct answer. For example, failing twice to properly distribute negative one in the following arithmetic operation produces a deceptively correct answer.

$4x - (2x+3) - (2x - 3) = 4x - 2x + 3 - 2x - 3 = -2x$ (incorrect distribution)
$4x - (2x+3) - (2x - 3) = 4x - 2x - 3 - 2x + 3 = -2x$ (correct distribution)

Successful math teachers introduce their students to multiple problem solving strategies and create a classroom environment where free thought and experimentation are encouraged. Teachers can promote problem solving by allowing multiple attempts at problems, giving credit for reworking test or homework problems, and encouraging the sharing of ideas through class discussion. There are several specific problem solving skills with which teachers should be familiar.

The **guess-and-check** strategy calls for students to make an initial guess at the solution, check the answer, and use the outcome of to guide the next guess. With each successive guess, the student should get closer to the correct answer. Constructing a table from the guesses can help organize the data.

Example:

There are 100 coins in a jar. 10 are dimes. The rest are pennies and nickels. There are twice as many pennies as nickels. How many pennies and nickels are in the jar?

There are 90 total nickels and pennies in the jar (100 coins – 10 dimes).

There are twice as many pennies as nickels. Make guesses that fulfill the criteria and adjust based on the answer found. Continue until we find the correct answer, 60 pennies and 30 nickels.

Number of Pennies	Number of Nickels	Total Number of Pennies and Nickels
40	20	60
80	40	120
70	35	105
60	30	90

When solving a problem where the final result and the steps to reach the result are given, students must **work backwards** to determine what the starting point must have been.
Example:

John subtracted seven from his age, and divided the result by 3. The final result was 4. What is John's age?

> Work backward by reversing the operations.
> $4 \times 3 = 12$;
> $12 + 7 = 19$
> John is 19 years old.

MATHEMATICS (Secondary)

Estimation and testing for **reasonableness** are related skills students should employ prior to and after solving a problem. These skills are particularly important when students use calculators to find answers.

Example:

Find the sum of 4387 + 7226 + 5893.

4300 + 7200 + 5800 = 17300   Estimation.
4387 + 7226 + 5893 = 17506   Actual sum.

By comparing the estimate to the actual sum, students can determine that their answer is reasonable.

Problem solving strategies are simply plans of attack. Student often panic when confronted with word problems. If they have a "list" of ideas, ways to attempt a solution, they will be able to approach the problems more calmly and confidently. Some methods include, but are not limited to, draw a diagram, work backwards, guess and check, and solve a simpler problem.

It is helpful to have students work in groups. Mathematics does not have to be solitary activity. Cooperative learning fosters enthusiasm. Creating their own problems is another useful tool. Also, encourage students to find more than one way to solve a problem. Thinking about problem solving after the solution has been discovered encourages understanding and creativity. The more they practice problems, the more comfortable and positive students will feel.

The use of supplementary materials in the classroom can greatly enhance the learning experience by stimulating student interest and satisfying different learning styles. Manipulatives, models, and technology are examples of tools available to teachers.

Manipulatives are materials that students can physically handle and move. Manipulatives allow students to understand mathematic concepts by allowing them to see concrete examples of abstract processes. Manipulatives are attractive to students because they appeal to the students' visual and tactile senses. Available for all levels of math, manipulatives are useful tools for reinforcing operations and concepts. They are not, however, a substitute for the development of sound computational skills.

Models are another means of representing mathematical concepts by relating the concepts to real-world situations. Teachers must choose wisely when devising and selecting models because, to be effective, models must be applied properly. For example, a building with floors above and below ground is a good model for introducing the concept of negative numbers. It would be difficult, however, to use the buildling model in teaching subtraction of negative numbers.

Finally, there are many forms of **technology** available to math teachers. For example, students can test their understanding of math concepts by working on skill specific computer programs and websites. Graphing calculators can help students visualize the graphs of functions. Teachers can also enhance their lectures and classroom presentations by creating multimedia presentations.

The **National Council of Teachers of Mathematics standards** emphasize the teacher's obligation to make mathematics relevant to the students and applicable to the real world. The mathematics need in our technological society is different from that need in the past; we need thinking skills rather than computational. Mathematics needs to connect to other subjects, as well as other areas of math.

Artists, musicians, scientists, social scientists, and business people use mathematical modeling to solve problems in their disciplines. These disciplines rely on the tools and symbology of mathematics to model natural events and manipulate data.

Mathematics is a key aspect of visual art. Artists use the geometric properties of shapes, ratios, and proportions in creating paintings and sculptures. For example, mathematics is essential to the concept of perspective. Artists must determine the appropriate lengths and heights of objects to portray three-dimensional distance in two dimensions.

Mathematics is also an important part of music. Many musical terms have mathematical connections. For example, the musical octave contains twelve notes and spans a factor of two in frequency. In other words, the frequency, the speed of vibration that determines tone and sound quality, doubles from the first note in an octave to the last. Thus, starting from any note we can determine the frequency of any other note with the following formula.

$$\text{Freq} = \text{note} \times 2^{N/12}$$

Where N is the number of notes from the starting point and note is the frequency of the starting note. Mathematical understanding of frequency plays an important role in the tuning of musical instruments.

In addition to the visual and auditory arts, mathematics is an integral part of most scientific disciplines. The uses of mathematics in science are almost endless. The following are but a few examples of how scientists use mathematics. Physical scientists use vectors, functions, derivatives, and integrals to describe and model the movement of objects. Biologists and ecologists use mathematics to model ecosystems and study DNA. Finally, chemists use mathematics to study the interaction of molecules and to determine proper amounts and proportions of reactants.

Many social science disciplines use mathematics to model and solve problems. Economists, for example, use functions, graphs, and matrices to model the activities of producers, consumers, and firms. Political scientists use mathematics to model the behavior and opinions of the electorate. Finally, sociologists use mathematical functions to model the behavior of humans and human populations.

Finally, mathematical problem solving and modeling is essential to business planning and execution. For example, businesses rely on mathematical projections to plan business strategy. Additionally, stock market analysis and accounting rely on mathematical concepts.

TEACHER CERTIFICATION STUDY GUIDE

Competency 3   **Understand number systems and equivalent ways of representing numbers.**

a. **Natural numbers**--the counting numbers, 1, 2, 3,...

b. **Whole numbers**--the counting numbers along with zero, 0, 1, 2...

c. **Integers**--the counting numbers, their opposites, and zero, ..., ⁻1, 0, 1,...

d. **Rationals**--all of the fractions that can be formed from the whole numbers. Zero cannot be the denominator. In decimal form, these numbers will either be terminating or repeating decimals. Simplify square roots to determine if the number can be written as a fraction.

e. **Irrationals**--real numbers that cannot be written as a fraction. The decimal forms of these numbers are neither terminating nor repeating. <u>Examples:</u> $\pi, e, \sqrt{2}$, etc.

f. **Real numbers**--the set of numbers obtained by combining the rationals and irrationals. Complex numbers, i.e. numbers that involve i or $\sqrt{-1}$, are not real numbers.

To **convert a fraction to a decimal,** simply divide the numerator (top) by the denominator (bottom). Use long division if necessary.

If a decimal has a fixed number of digits, the decimal is said to be terminating. To write such a decimal as a fraction, first determine what place value the farthest right digit is in, for example: tenths, hundredths, thousandths, ten thousandths, hundred thousands, etc. Then drop the decimal and place the string of digits over the number given by the place value.

If a decimal continues forever by repeating a string of digits, the decimal is said to be repeating. To write a repeating decimal as a fraction, follow these steps.

    a.   Let x = the repeating decimal
           (ex. $x = .716716716...$)
    b.   Multiply x by the multiple of ten that will move the decimal just to the right of the repeating block of digits.
           (ex. $1000x = 716.716716...$)

MATHEMATICS (Secondary)

c. Subtract the first equation from the second.
   (ex. $1000x - x = 716.716.716... - .716716...$)
d. Simplify and solve this equation. The repeating block of digits will subtract out.
   (ex. $999x = 716$ so $x = 716/999$)
e. The solution will be the fraction for the repeating decimal.

The **Denseness Property** of real numbers states that, if all real numbers are ordered from least to greatest on a number line, there is an infinite set of real numbers between any two given numbers on the line.

Example:

Between 7.6 and 7.7, there is the rational number 7.65 in the set of real numbers. Between 3 and 4 there exists no other natural number.

The **real number properties** are best explained in terms of a small set of numbers. For each property, a given set will be provided.

Axioms of Addition

Closure—For all real numbers a and b, $a + b$ is a unique real number.

Associative—For all real numbers a, b, and c, $(a + b) + c = a + (b + c)$.

Additive Identity—There exists a unique real number 0 (zero) such that $a + 0 = 0 + a = a$ for every real number a.

Additive Inverses—For each real number a, there exists a real number $-a$ (the opposite of a) such that $a + (-a) = (-a) + a = 0$.

Commutative—For all real numbers a and b, $a + b = b + a$.

Axioms of Multiplication

Closure —For all real numbers *a* and *b*, *ab* is a unique real number.

Associative—For all real numbers *a*, *b*, and *c*, *(ab)c = a(bc)*.

Multiplicative Identity—There exists a unique nonzero real number 1 (one) such that $(1 \bullet a) = (a \bullet 1) = a$.

Multiplicative Inverses—For each nonzero real number, there exists a real number 1/*a* (the reciprocal of a) such that a(1/a) = (1/a)a = 1.

Commutative—For all real numbers *a* and *b*, *ab = ba*.

The Distributive Axiom of Multiplication over Addition

For all real numbers *a*, *b*, and *c*, *a(b + c) = ab + ac*.

On a **number line** the number to the left is always smaller than the number on the right which is greater.

Example: Compare 15 and 20 on the number line.

Since 20 is further away from the zero than 15 is, then 20 is greater than 15, or $20 > 15$.

Example: Compare $\frac{3}{7}$ and $\frac{5}{10}$.

To compare fractions, they should have the same least common denominator (LCD). The LCD in this example is 70.

$$\frac{3}{7} = \frac{3 \times 10}{7 \times 10} = \frac{30}{70} \qquad \frac{5}{10} = \frac{5 \times 7}{10 \times 7} = \frac{35}{70}$$

Since the denominators are equal, compare only the denominators. $30 < 35$, so:
$$\frac{3}{7} < \frac{5}{10}$$

Sets

Set A -- $\{-5, -3, 0, 1, 2, 3, 5\}$

Set B -- $\{-7, -2, 0, 1, 3, 4, 5, 6\}$

Set C -- $\{-6, -4, -2, 4, 6\}$

The **Union** ($\cup$) of two sets is the set of all the numbers which are either in the first set or the second set or both sets.

$$A \cup B \text{ is } \{-7, -5, -3, -2, 0, 1, 2, 3, 4, 5, 6\}.$$

The **Intersection** ($\cap$) of two sets is the set of numbers that are in both sets.

$$A \cap B \text{ is } \{0, 1, 3, 5\}.$$

The **Null Set** is also called the empty set; it is the set that does not contain any numbers. The Null Set can be expressed two different ways: either { } or $\emptyset$. {0} is NOT the Null Set since it does have one element.

$A \cap C$ is the empty set, { }, since they do not share any elements.

Example:
Using tiles to demonstrate both geometric ideas and number theory.

Give each group of students 12 tiles and instruct them to build rectangles. Students draw their rectangles on paper.

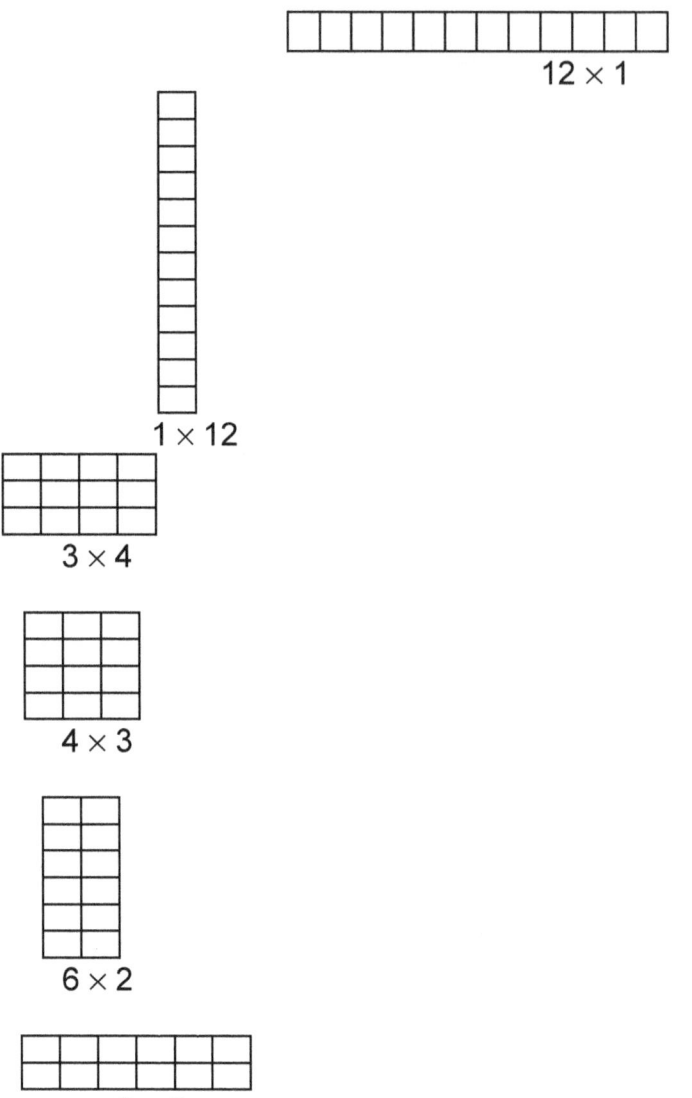

Encourage students to describe their reactions. Extend to 16 tiles. Ask students to form additional problems.

Competency 4   **Understand number theory and operations on number systems.**

Prime numbers are numbers that can only be factored into 1 and the number itself. When factoring into prime factors, all the factors must be numbers that cannot be factored again (without using 1). Initially numbers can be factored into any 2 factors. Check each resulting factor to see if it can be factored again. Continue factoring until all remaining factors are prime. This is the list of prime factors. Regardless of what way the original number was factored, the final list of prime factors will always be the same.

Example: Factor 30 into prime factors.

    Factor 30 into any 2 factors.
        $5 \cdot 6$ Now factor the 6.
        $5 \cdot 2 \cdot 3$ These are all prime factors.

    Factor 30 into any 2 factors.
        $3 \cdot 10$ Now factor the 10.
        $3 \cdot 2 \cdot 5$ These are the same prime factors even though the original factors were different.

Example: Factor 240 into prime factors.

    Factor 240 into any 2 factors.
        $24 \cdot 10$ Now factor both 24 and 10.
        $4 \cdot 6 \cdot 2 \cdot 5$ Now factor both 4 and 6.
        $2 \cdot 2 \cdot 2 \cdot 3 \cdot 2 \cdot 5$ These are prime factors.

This can also be written as $2^4 \cdot 3 \cdot 5$.

GCF is the abbreviation for the **greatest common factor**. The GCF is the largest number that is a factor of all the numbers given in a problem. The GCF can be no larger than the smallest number given in the problem. If no other number is a common factor, then the GCF will be the number 1. To find the GCF, list all possible factors of the smallest number given (include the number itself). Starting with the largest factor (which is the number itself), determine if it is also a factor of all the other given numbers. If so, that is the GCF. If that factor doesn't work, try the same method on the next smaller factor. Continue until a common factor is found. That is the GCF. Note: There can be other common factors besides the GCF.

Example: Find the GCF of 12, 20, and 36.
The smallest number in the problem is 12. The factors of 12 are 1,2,3,4,6 and 12. 12 is the largest factor, but it does not divide evenly into 20. Neither does 6, but 4 will divide into both 20 and 36 evenly.
Therefore, 4 is the GCF.

Example: Find the GCF of 14 and 15.
Factors of 14 are 1,2,7 and 14. 14 is the largest factor, but it does not divide evenly into 15. Neither does 7 or 2. Therefore, the only factor common to both 14 and 15 is the number 1, the GCF.

Multiples

LCM is the abbreviation for **least common multiple**. The least common multiple of a group of numbers is the smallest number that all of the given numbers will divide into. The least common multiple will always be the largest of the given numbers or a multiple of the largest number.

Example: Find the LCM of 20, 30 and 40.

The largest number given is 40, but 30 will not divide evenly into 40. The next multiple of 40 is 80 (2 x 40), but 30 will not divide evenly into 80 either. The next multiple of 40 is 120. 120 is divisible by both 20 and 30, so 120 is the LCM (least common multiple).

Example: Find the LCM of 96, 16 and 24.
The largest number is 96. 96 is divisible by both 16 and 24, so 96 is the LCM.

Divisibility Tests

a. A number is divisible by 2 if that number is an even number (which means it ends in 0,2,4,6 or 8).

1,354 ends in 4, so it is divisible by 2. 240,685 ends in a 5, so it is not divisible by 2.

b. A number is divisible by 3 if the sum of its digits is evenly divisible by 3.

The sum of the digits of 964 is 9+6+4 = 19. Since 19 is not divisible by 3, neither is 964. The digits of 86,514 is 8+6+5+1+4 = 24. Since 24 is divisible by 3, 86,514 is also divisible by 3.

c. A number is divisible by 4 if the number in its last 2 digits is evenly divisible by 4.

The number 113,336 ends with the number 36 in the last 2 columns. Since 36 is divisible by 4, then 113,336 is also divisible by 4.

The number 135,627 ends with the number 27 in the last 2 columns. Since 27 is not evenly divisible by 4, then 135,627 is also not divisible by 4.

d. A number is divisible by 5 if the number ends in either a 5 or a 0.

225 ends with a 5 so it is divisible by 5. The number 470 is also divisible by 5 because its last digit is a 0. 2,358 is not divisible by 5 because its last digit is an 8, not a 5 or a 0.

e. A number is divisible by 6 if the number is even and the sum of its digits is evenly divisible by 3.

4,950 is an even number and its digits add to 18. (4+9+5+0 = 18) Since the number is even and the sum of its digits is 18 (which is divisible by 3), then 4950 is divisible by 6. 326 is an even number, but its digits add up to 11. Since 11 is not divisible by 3, then 326 is not divisible by 6. 698,135 is not an even number, so it cannot possibly be divided evenly by 6.

f. A number is divisible by 8 if the number in its last 3 digits is evenly divisible by 8.

The number 113,336 ends with the 3-digit number 336 in the last 3 places. Since 336 is divisible by 8, then 113,336 is also divisible by 8. The number 465,627 ends with the number 627 in the last 3 places. Since 627 is not evenly divisible by 8, then 465,627 is also not divisible by 8.

g. A number is divisible by 9 if the sum of its digits is evenly divisible by 9.

The sum of the digits of 874 is 8+7+4 = 19. Since 19 is not divisible by 9, neither is 874. The digits of 116,514 is 1+1+6+5+1+4 = 18. Since 18 is divisible by 9, 116,514 is also divisible by 9.

h. A number is divisible by 10 if the number ends in the digit 0. 305 ends with a 5 so it is not divisible by 10. The number 2,030,270 is divisible by 10 because its last digit is a 0. 42,978 is not divisible by 10 because its last digit is an 8, not a 0.

i. Why these rules work.

All even numbers are divisible by 2 by definition. A 2-digit number (with T as the tens digit and U as the ones digit) has as its sum of the digits, T + U. Suppose this sum of T + U is divisible by 3. Then it equals 3 times some constant, K. So, T + U = 3K. Solving this for U, U = 3K - T. The original 2 digit number would be represented by 10T + U. Substituting 3K - T in place of U, this 2-digit number becomes 10T + U = 10T + (3K - T) = 9T + 3K. This 2-digit number is clearly divisible by 3, since each term is divisible by 3. Therefore, if the sum of the digits of a number is divisible by 3, then the number itself is also divisible by 3. Since 4 divides evenly into 100, 200, or 300, 4 will divide evenly into any amount of hundreds. The only part of a number that determines if 4 will divide into it evenly is the number in the last 2 places. Numbers divisible by 5 end in 5 or 0. This is clear if you look at the answers to the multiplication table for 5. Answers to the multiplication table for 6 are all even numbers. Since 6 factors into 2 times 3, the divisibility rules for 2 and 3 must both work. Any number of thousands is divisible by 8. Only the last 3 places of the number determine whether or not it is divisible by 8. A 2 digit number (with T as the tens digit and U as the ones digit) has as its sum of the digits, T + U. Suppose this sum of T + U is divisible by 9. Then it equals 9 times some constant, K. So, T + U = 9K. Solving this for U, U = 9K - T. The original 2-digit number would be represented by 10T + U. Substituting 9K - T in place of U, this 2-digit number becomes 10T + U = 10T + (9K - T) = 9T + 9K. This 2-digit number is clearly divisible by 9, since each term is divisible by 9. Therefore, if the sum of the digits of a number is divisible by 9, then the number itself is also divisible by 9. Numbers divisible by 10 must be multiples of 10 which all end in a zero.

To change a number into **scientific notation**, move the decimal point so that only one number from 1 to 9 is in front of the decimal point. Drop off any trailing zeros. Multiply this number times 10 to a power. The power is the number of positions that the decimal point is moved. The power is negative if the original number is a decimal number between 1 and -1. Otherwise the power is positive.

Example: Change into scientific notation:

4,380,000,000	Move decimal behind the 4
4.38	Drop trailing zeros.
$4.38 \times 10^?$	Count positions that the decimal point has moved.
4.38×10^9	This is the answer.

Change into scientific notation:

$^-.0000407$	Move decimal behind the 4
$^-4.07$	Count positions that the decimal point has moved.
4.07×10^{-5}	Note negative exponent.

If a number is already in scientific notation, it can be changed back into the regular decimal form. If the exponent on the number 10 is negative, move the decimal point to the left. If the exponent on the number 10 is positive, move the decimal point to the right that number of places.

Example: Change back into decimal form:

3.448×10^{-2}	Move decimal point 2 places left, since exponent is negative.
.03448	This is the answer.
6×10^4	Move decimal point 4 places right, since exponent is negative.
60,000	This is the answer.

To add or subtract in scientific notation, the exponents must be the same. Then add the decimal portions, keeping the power of 10 the same. Then move the decimal point and adjust the exponent to keep the number in front of the decimal point from 1 to 9.

MATHEMATICS (Secondary)

Example:

$$6.22 \times 10^3$$
$$+ 7.48 \times 10^3$$ Add these as is.
$$13.70 \times 10^3$$ Now move decimal 1 more place to the left and
$$1.37 \times 10^4$$ add 1 more exponent.

To multiply or divide in scientific notation, multiply or divide the decimal part of the numbers. In multiplication, add the exponents of 10. In division, subtract the exponents of 10. Then move the decimal point and adjust the exponent to keep the number in front of the decimal point from 1 to 9.

Example:

$(5.2 \times 10^5)(3.5 \times 10^2)$ Multiply $5.2 \cdot 3.5$

18.2×10^7 Add exponent

1.82×10^8 Move decimal point and increase the exponent by 1.

Example:

$$\frac{(4.1076 \times 10^3)}{2.8 \times 10^{-4}}$$ Divide 4.1076 by 2.8

Subtract $3 - (^-4)$

1.467×10^7

The visual representation of multiplication is present in an rectangular array of units represented as blocks.

Fractions can be clarified using pattern blocks, fraction bars, or paper folding.

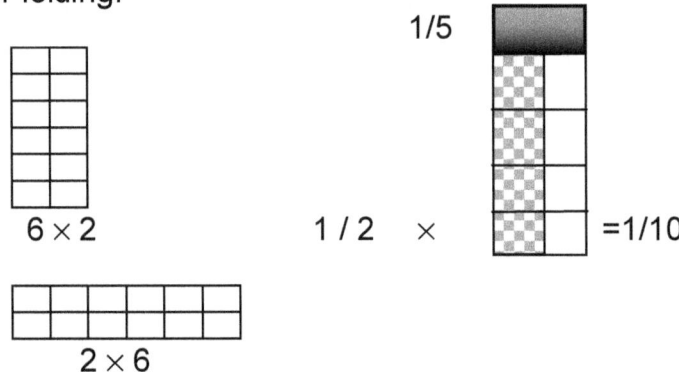

A **ratio** is a comparison of 2 numbers. If a class had 11 boys and 14 girls, the ratio of boys to girls could be written one of 3 ways:

$$11:14 \quad \text{or} \quad 11 \text{ to } 14 \quad \text{or} \quad \frac{11}{14}$$

The ratio of girls to boys is:

$$14:11, \; 14 \text{ to } 11 \text{ or } \frac{14}{11}$$

Ratios can be reduced when possible. A ratio of 12 cats to 18 dogs would reduce to 2:3, 2 to 3 or $2/3$.

Note: Read ratio questions carefully. Given a group of 6 adults and 5 children, the ratio of children to the entire group would be 5:11.

A **proportion** is an equation in which a fraction is set equal to another. To solve the proportion, multiply each numerator times the other fraction's denominator. Set these two products equal to each other and solve the resulting equation. This is called **cross-multiplying** the proportion.

Example: $\dfrac{4}{15} = \dfrac{x}{60}$ is a proportion.

To solve this, cross multiply.

$$(4)(60) = (15)(x)$$
$$240 = 15x$$
$$16 = x$$

Example: $\dfrac{x+3}{3x+4} = \dfrac{2}{5}$ is a proportion.

To solve, cross multiply.

$$5(x+3) = 2(3x+4)$$
$$5x + 15 = 6x + 8$$
$$7 = x$$

Example: $\dfrac{x+2}{8} = \dfrac{2}{x-4}$ is another proportion.

To solve, cross multiply.

$$(x+2)(x-4) = 8(2)$$
$$x^2 - 2x - 8 = 16$$
$$x^2 - 2x - 24 = 0$$
$$(x-6)(x+4) = 0$$
$$x = 6 \text{ or } x = {}^-4$$

Both answers work.

Fractions, decimals, and percents can be used interchangeably within problems.

→ To change a percent into a decimal, move the decimal point two places to the left and drop off the percent sign.
→ To change a decimal into a percent, move the decimal two places to the right and add on a percent sign.
→ To change a fraction into a decimal, divide the numerator by the denominator.
→ To change a decimal number into an equivalent fraction, write the decimal part of the number as the fraction's numerator. As the fraction's denominator use the place value of the last column of the decimal. Reduce the resulting fraction as far as possible.

Example: J.C. Nickels has Hunch jeans 1/4 off the usual price of $36.00. Shears and Roadkill have the same jeans 30% off their regular price of $40. Find the cheaper price.

1/4 = .25 so .25(36) = $9.00 off $36 - 9 = $27 sale price

30% = .30 so .30(40) = $12 off $40 - 12 = $28 sale price

The price at J.C Nickels is actually lower.

The **unit rate** for purchasing an item is its price divided by the number of pounds/ ounces, etc. in the item. The item with the lower unit rate is the lower price.

Example: Find the item with the best unit price:

$1.79 for 10 ounces
$1.89 for 12 ounces
$5.49 for 32 ounces

$\dfrac{1.79}{10} = .179$ per ounce $\dfrac{1.89}{12} = .1575$ per ounce $\dfrac{5.49}{32} = .172$ per ounce

$1.89 for 12 ounces is the best price.

A second way to find the better buy is to make a proportion with the price over the number of ounces, etc. Cross multiply the proportion, writing the products above the numerator that is used. The better price will have the smaller product.

Example: Find the better buy:

$8.19 for 40 pounds or $4.89 for 22 pounds

Find the unit price.

$$\frac{40}{8.19} = \frac{1}{x} \qquad \frac{22}{4.89} = \frac{1}{x}$$
$$40x = 8.19 \qquad 22x = 4.89$$
$$x = .20475 \qquad x = .222\overline{27}$$

Since $.20475 < .222\overline{27}$, $8.19 is less and is a better buy.

To find the amount of **sales tax** on an item, change the percent of sales tax into an equivalent decimal number. Then multiply the decimal number times the price of the object to find the sales tax. The total cost of an item will be the price of the item plus the sales tax.

Example: A guitar costs $120 plus 7% sales tax. How much are the sales tax and the total bill?

7% = .07 as a decimal   (.07)(120) = $8.40 sales tax
$120 + $8.40 = $128.40 ← total price

Example: A suit costs $450 plus 6½% sales tax. How much are the sales tax and the total bill?

6½% = .065 as a decimal
(.065)(450) = $29.25 sales tax
$450 + $29.25 = $479.25 ← total price

Multiplication can be shown using arrays.

3×4 may be expressed as 3 rows of 4 each

Addition and subtractions can be demonstrated with symbols.
ψ ψ ψ ξ ξ ξ ξ
3 + 4 = 7
7 - 3 = 4

MATHEMATICS (Secondary) 30

Fractions can be clarified using pattern blocks, fraction bars, or paper folding.

Estimation and approximation may be used to check the reasonableness of answers.

Example: Estimate the answer.

$$\frac{58 \times 810}{1989}$$

58 becomes 60, 810 becomes 800 and 1989 becomes 2000.

$$\frac{60 \times 800}{2000} = 24$$

Word problems: An estimate may sometimes be all that is needed to solve a problem.

Example: Janet goes into a store to purchase a CD on sale for $13.95. While shopping, she sees two pairs of shoes, prices $19.95 and $14.50. She only has $50. Can she purchase everything?

Solve by rounding:

$19.95 → $20.00
$14.50 → $15.00
$13.95 → $14.00
$49.00   Yes, she can purchase the CD and the shoes.

Integer algorithms

Addition –
Three common algorithms for addition of integers are the partial sums method, column addition method and fast method. The partial sums method is a two-stage process. First, we sum the columns from left to right. To complete the operation we add the column values.

```
   125
 +  89
 + 376     Step 1 – column addition
   400
 + 170
 +  20     Step 2 – final sum
   590
```

The column addition method is also a two-stage process. First, we add the digits in each column. To complete the operation we perform the place carries from right to left.

```
  1|  2|  5
+  |  8|  9         Stage 1 – column addition
+ 3|  7|  6
  4| 17| 20
  4| 19|  0    ◄─── First carry
  5|  9|  0 = 590  ◄─── Second carry = final answer
```

The fast method of addition is the traditional method of right to left addition. We sum the columns from left to right, performing carries mentally or writing them down.

```
    12    ◄─── Carries
   125
 +  89
 + 376
   590
```

All of the integer addition algorithms rely on the commutative and associative properties of addition, allowing re-grouping and re-ordering of numbers.

Subtraction –

Three common algorithms of integer subtraction are left to right subtraction, partial differences and the same change rule. In left to right subtraction, we decompose the second number into smaller values and perform the individual subtractions. For example, to solve 335 – 78, we break 78 down into 70 + 8.

```
   335
 -  70
   265
 -   8
   257
```

The partial differences method is a two-stage process. First, we operate on each column individually, being careful to record the sign of each result. Then, we sum the results to yield the final answer.

```
   335
 -  78
  +300
 -  40
 -   3
   257
```

The same change rule takes advantage of the knowledge that subtraction is easier if the smaller number ends in zero. Thus, we change each number by the same amount to produce a smaller number ending in zero.

$$
\begin{array}{r} 335 \\ -\ 78 \end{array} \rightarrow \begin{array}{r} 333 \\ -\ 80 \\ \hline 257 \end{array}
$$

Like the addition algorithms, the subtraction algorithms rely on the commutative and associative properties of addition (because subtraction is addition of a negative number).

Multiplication –

Two common multiplication algorithms are the partial products method and the short method. In the partial products method, we decompose each term into base-ten forms and multiply each pair of terms.

$$
\begin{array}{r} 84 \\ \times\ 26 \end{array}
$$

$$
\begin{array}{rl} 80 \times 20 \rightarrow & 1600 \\ 80 \times 6 \rightarrow & 480 \\ 20 \times 4 \rightarrow & 80 \\ 6 \times 4 \rightarrow & \underline{\ \ 24} \\ & 2184 \end{array}
$$

The short method is a traditional multiplication algorithm. In the short method, we only decompose the second term.

$$
\begin{array}{r} 84 \\ \times\ 26 \end{array}
$$

$$
\begin{array}{rl} 84 \times 20 \rightarrow & 1680 \\ 84 \times 6 \rightarrow & \underline{\ 504} \\ & 2184 \end{array}
$$

The multiplication algorithms rely on the associative and commutative properties of multiplication and the distribution of multiplication over addition.

MATHEMATICS (Secondary)

Division –
A common division algorithm is the partial quotients method. In this method, we make note of two, simple products and estimate our way toward a final answer. For example, to find the quotient of 1440 divided by 18 we first make note that 5 x 18 = 90 and 2 x 18 = 32.

```
18)   1440 |
    -  900 | 50
       540 |
    -  360 | 20
       180 |
    -   90 | 5
        90 |
    -   90 | 5
         0   80   ⟶ final quotient = 80 with no remainder
```

Rational and real number algorithms –
Operations involving rational numbers represented as fractions require unique algorithms. For example, when adding or subtracting fractions we use the distributive property of multiplication over division to find common denominators.

When completing operations involving real numbers in decimal form we use similar algorithms to those used with integers. We use the associative, commutative and distributive properties of numbers to generate algorithms.

Concrete and visual representations can help demonstrate the logic behind operational algorithms. Blocks or other objects modeled on the base ten system are useful concrete tools. Base ten blocks represent ones, tens and hundreds. For example, modeling the partial sums algorithm with base ten blocks helps clarify the thought process. Consider the sum of 242 and 193. We represent 242 with two one hundred blocks, four ten blocks and 2 one blocks. We represent 193 with one one hundred block, nine ten blocks and 3 one blocks. In the partial sums algorithm, we manipulate each place value separately and total the results. Thus, we group the hundred blocks, ten blocks and one blocks and derive a total for each place value. We combine the place values to complete the sum.

An example of a visual representation of an operational algorithm is the modeling of a two-term multiplication as the area of a rectangle. For example, consider the product of 24 and 39. We can represent the product in geometric form. Note that the four sections of the rectangle equate to the four products of the partial products method.

	30	9
20	A = 600	A = 180
4	A = 120	A = 36

Thus, the final product is the sum of the areas or 600 + 180 + 120 + 36 = 936.

Apply the order of operations

For standardization purposes, there is an accepted order in which operations are performed in any given algebraic expression. The following pneumonic is often used for the order in which operations are performed.

Please	Parentheses	
Excuse	Exponents	
My	Multiply	Multiply or Divide depending on which
Dear	Divide	operation is encountered first from left to right.
Aunt	Add	Add or Subtract depending on which
Sally	Subtract	operation is encountered first from left to right.

Apply inverse operations

Subtraction is the inverse of Addition, and vice-versa.
Division is the inverse of Multiplication, and vice-versa.
Taking a square root is the inverse of squaring, and vice-versa.

These inverse operations are used when solving equations.

The **exponent form** is a shortcut method to write repeated multiplication.

The **base** is the factor. The **exponent** tells how many times that number is multiplied by itself.

The following are basic rules for exponents:

$a^1 = a$ for all values of a; thus $17^1 = 17$
$b^0 = 1$ for all values of b; thus $24^0 = 1$
$10^n = 1$ with n zeros; thus $10^6 = 1,000,000$

Coefficients are the numbers in front of the variables in a term.

Addition/Subtraction with integral exponents.

-**Like terms** have the same variables raised to the same powers. Like terms can be combined by adding or subtracting their coefficients and by keeping the variables and their exponents the same. Unlike terms cannot be combined.

$$5x^4 + 3x^4 - 2x^4 = 6x^4$$
$$3ab^2 + 5ab + ab^2 = 4ab^2 + 5ab$$

Multiplication with integral exponents.
-When multiplying terms together, multiply their coefficients and add the exponents of the same variables. When a term is raised to a power, raise the term's coefficient to the power outside the parentheses. Then multiply the outside exponent times each of the inside exponents.

$$(3a^7b^5)(^-4a^2b^9c^4) = {}^-12a^9b^{14}c^4$$
$$(^-2x^3yz^7)^5 = {}^-32x^{15}y^5z^{35}$$

Division with integral exponents.
-When dividing any number of terms by a single term, divide or reduce their coefficients. Then subtract the exponent of a variable on the bottom from the exponent of the same variable on the top.

$$\frac{24a^8b^7 + 16a^7b^5 - 8a^6}{8a^6} = 3a^2b^7 + 2ab^5 - 1$$

MATHEMATICS (Secondary)

Negative exponents are usually changed into positive exponents by moving those variables from numerator to denominator (or vice versa) to make the exponents become positive.

$$\frac{^-60a^8b^{^-7}c^{^-6}d^5e^{^-12}}{12a^{^-2}b^3c^{^-9}d^5e^{^-4}} = {^-}5a^{10}b^{^-10}c^3e^{^-8} = \frac{^-5a^{10}c^3}{b^{10}e^8}$$

$$(6x^{^-9}y^3)(^-2x^5y^{^-1}) = {^-}12x^{^-4}y^2 = \frac{^-12y^2}{x^4}$$

Practice:

1. $(4x^4y^2)(^-3xy^{^-3}z^5)$
2. $(100a^6 + 60a^4 - 28a^2b^3) \div (4a^2)$
3. $(3x^5y^2)^4 + 8x^9y^6 + 19x^{20}y^8$

Complex numbers are of the form $a + b\mathbf{i}$, where a and b are real numbers and $i = \sqrt{^-1}$. When **i** appears in an answer, it is acceptable unless it is in a denominator. When **i²** appears in a problem, it is always replaced by –1. Remember, **i² = –1**.

To add or subtract complex numbers, add or subtract the real parts. Then add or subtract the imaginary parts and keep the **i** (just like combining like terms).

Examples: Add $(2 + 3i) + (^-7 - 4i)$.

$2 + {^-}7 = {^-}5 \qquad 3i + {^-}4i = {^-}i$ so,

$(2 + 3i) + (^-7 - 4i) = {^-}5 - i$

Subtract $(8 - 5i) - (^-3 + 7i)$

$8 - 5i + 3 - 7i = 11 - 12i$

To multiply 2 complex numbers, F.O.I.L. the 2 numbers together. Replace **i²** with **–1** and finish combining like terms. Answers should have the form $a + b\mathbf{i}$.

Example: Multiply $(8 + 3i)(6 - 2i)$ F.O.I.L. this.

$48 - 16i + 18i - 6i^2$ Let $i^2 = {^-}1$.

$48 - 16i + 18i - 6(^-1)$

$48 - 16i + 18i + 6$

$54 + 2i$ This is the answer.

Example: Multiply $(5+8i)^2$ ← Write this out twice.
$(5+8i)(5+8i)$ F.O.I.L. this
$25 + 40i + 40i + 64i^2$ Let $i^2 = {}^-1$.
$25 + 40i + 40i + 64({}^-1)$
$25 + 40i + 40i - 64$
${}^-39 + 80i$ This is the answer.

When dividing 2 complex numbers, you must eliminate the complex number in the denominator. If the complex number in the denominator is of the form $b\ \mathbf{i}$, multiply both the numerator and denominator by $\mathbf{i}$. Remember to replace $\mathbf{i}^2$ with **−1** and then continue simplifying the fraction.

Example:

$$\frac{2+3i}{5i} \quad \text{Multiply this by } \frac{i}{i}$$

$$\frac{2+3i}{5i} \times \frac{i}{i} = \frac{(2+3i)\,i}{5i \cdot i} = \frac{2i+3i^2}{5i^2} = \frac{2i+3({}^-1)}{{}^-5} = \frac{{}^-3+2i}{{}^-5} = \frac{3-2i}{5}$$

If the complex number in the denominator is of the form $a + b\ \mathbf{i}$, multiply both the numerator and denominator by **the conjugate of the denominator**. **The conjugate of the denominator** is the same 2 terms with the opposite sign between the 2 terms (the real term does not change signs). The conjugate of $2 - 3i$ is $2 + 3i$. The conjugate of $-6 + 11i$ is $-6 - 11i$. Multiply together the factors on the top and bottom of the fraction. Remember to replace $\mathbf{i}^2$ with **−1**, combine like terms, and then continue simplifying the fraction.

Example:

$$\frac{4+7i}{6-5i} \quad \text{Multiply by } \frac{6+5i}{6+5i}\text{, the conjugate.}$$

$$\frac{(4+7i)}{(6-5i)} \times \frac{(6+5i)}{(6+5i)} = \frac{24+20i+42i+35i^2}{36+30i-30-25i^2} = \frac{24+62i+35(-1)}{36-25(-1)} = \frac{-11+62i}{61}$$

Example:

$$\frac{24}{-3-5i} \qquad \text{Multiply by } \frac{-3+5i}{-3+5i}, \text{ the conjugate.}$$

$$\frac{24}{-3-5i} \times \frac{-3+5i}{-3+5i} = \frac{-72+120i}{9-25i^2} = \frac{-72+120i}{9+25} = \frac{-72+120i}{34} = \frac{-36+60i}{17}$$

Divided everything by 2.

One way to graph points is in the rectangular coordinate system. In this system, the point (a, b) describes the point whose distance along the x-axis is "a" and whose distance along the y-axis is "b." The other method used to locate points is the **polar plane coordinate system**. This system consists of a fixed point called the pole or origin (labeled O) and a ray with O as the initial point called the polar axis. The ordered pair of a point P in the polar coordinate system is (r, θ), where $|r|$ is the distance from the pole and θ is the angle measure from the polar axis to the ray formed by the pole and point P. The coordinates of the pole are $(0, \theta)$, where θ is arbitrary. Angle θ can be measured in either degrees or in radians.

Sample problem:
1. Graph the point P with polar coordinates $(-2, -45 \text{ degrees})$.

Draw $\theta = -45$ degrees in standard position. Since r is negative, locate the point $|-2|$ units from the pole on the ray opposite the terminal side of the angle. Note that P can be represented by $(-2, -45 \text{ degrees} + 180 \text{ degrees}) = (2, 135 \text{ degrees})$ or by $(-2, -45 \text{ degrees} - 180 \text{ degrees}) = (2, -225 \text{ degrees})$.

2. Graph the point $P = \left(3, \dfrac{\pi}{4}\right)$ and show another graph that also represents the same point P.

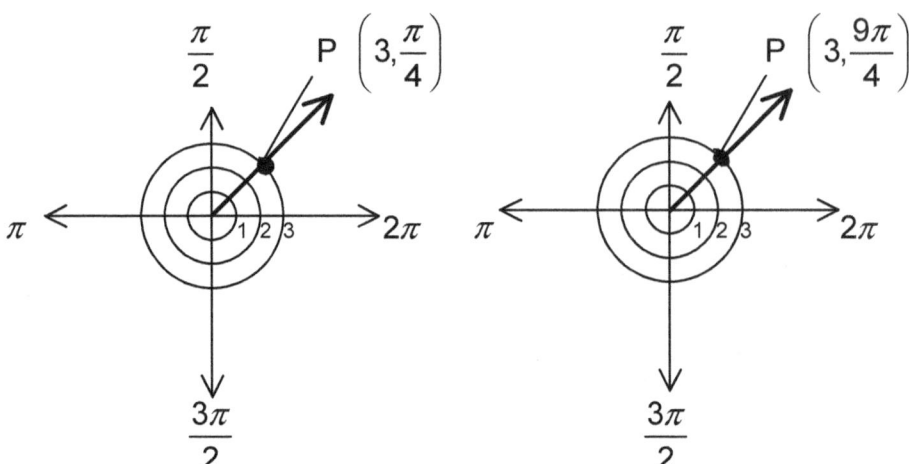

In the second graph, the angle 2π is added to $\dfrac{\pi}{4}$ to give the point $\left(3, \dfrac{9\pi}{4}\right)$.

It is possible that r be allowed to be negative. Now instead of measuring $|r|$ units along the terminal side of the angle, we would locate the point $|^-3|$ units from the pole on the ray opposite the terminal side. This would give the points $\left(^-3, \dfrac{5\pi}{4}\right)$ and $\left(^-3, \dfrac{^-3\pi}{4}\right)$.

TEACHER CERTIFICATION STUDY GUIDE

A **matrix** is a square array of numbers called its entries or elements. The dimensions of a matrix are written as the number of rows (r) by the number of columns (r × c).

$\begin{pmatrix} 1 & 2 & 3 \\ 4 & 5 & 6 \end{pmatrix}$ is a 2 × 3 matrix (2 rows by 3 columns)

$\begin{pmatrix} 1 & 2 \\ 3 & 4 \\ 5 & 6 \end{pmatrix}$ is a 3 × 2 matrix (3 rows by 2 columns)

Associated with every square matrix is a number called the determinant.
Use these formulas to calculate determinants.

2 × 2 $\begin{pmatrix} a & b \\ c & d \end{pmatrix} = ad - bc$

3 × 3
$\begin{pmatrix} a_1 & b_1 & c_1 \\ a_2 & b_2 & c_2 \\ a_3 & b_3 & c_3 \end{pmatrix} = (a_1 b_2 c_3 + b_1 c_2 a_3 + c_1 a_2 b_3) - (a_3 b_2 c_1 + b_3 c_2 a_1 + c_3 a_2 b_1)$

This is found by repeating the first two columns and then using the diagonal lines to find the value of each expression as shown below:

$\begin{pmatrix} a_1^* & b_1^\circ & c_1^\bullet \\ a_2 & b_2^* & c_2^\circ \\ a_3 & b_3 & c_3^* \end{pmatrix} \begin{matrix} a_1 & b_1 \\ a_2^\bullet & b_2 \\ a_3^\circ & b_3^\bullet \end{matrix} = (a_1 b_2 c_3 + b_1 c_2 a_3 + c_1 a_2 b_3) - (a_3 b_2 c_1 + b_3 c_2 a_1 + c_3 a_2 b_1)$

Sample Problem:

1. Find the value of the determinant:

$\begin{pmatrix} 4 & ^-8 \\ 7 & 3 \end{pmatrix} = (4)(3) - (7)(^-8)$ Cross multiply and subtract.

$12 - (^-56) = 68$ Then simplify.

MATHEMATICS (Secondary)

Addition of matrices is accomplished by adding the corresponding elements of the two matrices. Subtraction is defined as the inverse of addition. In other words, change the sign on all the elements in the second matrix and add the two matrices.

Sample problems:

Find the sum or difference.

1. $\begin{pmatrix} 2 & 3 \\ {}^-4 & 7 \\ 8 & {}^-1 \end{pmatrix} + \begin{pmatrix} 8 & {}^-1 \\ 2 & {}^-1 \\ 3 & {}^-2 \end{pmatrix} =$

$\begin{pmatrix} 2+8 & 3+({}^-1) \\ {}^-4+2 & 7+({}^-1) \\ 8+3 & {}^-1+({}^-2) \end{pmatrix}$ Add corresponding elements.

$\begin{pmatrix} 10 & 2 \\ {}^-2 & 6 \\ 11 & {}^-3 \end{pmatrix}$ Simplify.

2. $\begin{pmatrix} 8 & {}^-1 \\ 7 & 4 \end{pmatrix} - \begin{pmatrix} 3 & 6 \\ {}^-5 & 1 \end{pmatrix} =$

$\begin{pmatrix} 8 & {}^-1 \\ 7 & 4 \end{pmatrix} + \begin{pmatrix} {}^-3 & {}^-6 \\ 5 & {}^-1 \end{pmatrix} =$ Change all of the signs in the second matrix and then add the two matrices.

$\begin{pmatrix} 8+({}^-3) & {}^-1+({}^-6) \\ 7+5 & 4+({}^-1) \end{pmatrix} =$ Simplify.

$\begin{pmatrix} 5 & {}^-7 \\ 12 & 3 \end{pmatrix}$

Practice problems:

1. $\begin{pmatrix} 8 & {}^-1 \\ 5 & 3 \end{pmatrix} + \begin{pmatrix} 3 & 8 \\ 6 & {}^-2 \end{pmatrix} =$

2. $\begin{pmatrix} 3 & 7 \\ {}^-4 & 12 \\ 0 & {}^-5 \end{pmatrix} - \begin{pmatrix} 3 & 4 \\ 6 & {}^-1 \\ {}^-5 & {}^-5 \end{pmatrix} =$

Scalar multiplication is the product of the scalar (the outside number) and each element inside the matrix.

Sample problem:

Given: $A = \begin{pmatrix} 4 & 0 \\ 3 & -1 \end{pmatrix}$ Find 2A.

$2A = 2 \begin{pmatrix} 4 & 0 \\ 3 & -1 \end{pmatrix}$

$\begin{pmatrix} 2 \times 4 & 2 \times 0 \\ 2 \times 3 & 2 \times -1 \end{pmatrix}$ Multiply each element in the matrix by the scalar.

$\begin{pmatrix} 8 & 0 \\ 6 & -2 \end{pmatrix}$ Simplify.

Practice problems:

1. $-2 \begin{pmatrix} 2 & 0 & 1 \\ -1 & -2 & 4 \end{pmatrix}$

2. $3 \begin{pmatrix} 6 \\ 2 \\ 8 \end{pmatrix} + 4 \begin{pmatrix} 0 \\ 7 \\ 2 \end{pmatrix}$

3. $2 \begin{pmatrix} -6 & 8 \\ -2 & -1 \\ 0 & 3 \end{pmatrix}$

The variable in a **matrix equation** represents a matrix. When solving for the answer use the adding, subtracting and scalar multiplication properties.

Sample problem:

Solve the matrix equation for the variable X.

$$2x + \begin{pmatrix} 4 & 8 & 2 \\ 7 & 3 & 4 \end{pmatrix} = 2\begin{pmatrix} 1 & {}^-2 & 0 \\ 3 & {}^-5 & 7 \end{pmatrix}$$

$$2x = 2\begin{pmatrix} 1 & {}^-2 & 0 \\ 3 & {}^-5 & 7 \end{pmatrix} - \begin{pmatrix} 4 & 8 & 2 \\ 7 & 3 & 4 \end{pmatrix} \qquad \text{Subtract } \begin{pmatrix} 4 & 8 & 2 \\ 7 & 3 & 4 \end{pmatrix} \text{ from both sides.}$$

$$2x = \begin{pmatrix} 2 & {}^-4 & 0 \\ 6 & {}^-10 & 14 \end{pmatrix} + \begin{pmatrix} {}^-4 & {}^-8 & {}^-2 \\ {}^-7 & {}^-3 & {}^-4 \end{pmatrix} \qquad \text{Scalar multiplication and matrix subtraction.}$$

$$2x = \begin{pmatrix} {}^-2 & {}^-12 & {}^-2 \\ {}^-1 & {}^-13 & 10 \end{pmatrix} \qquad \text{Matrix addition.}$$

$$x = \begin{pmatrix} {}^-1 & {}^-6 & {}^-1 \\ -\frac{1}{2} & -\frac{13}{2} & 5 \end{pmatrix} \qquad \text{Multiply both sides by } \frac{1}{2}.$$

Solve for the unknown values of the elements in the matrix.

$$\begin{pmatrix} x+3 & y-2 \\ z+3 & w-4 \end{pmatrix} + \begin{pmatrix} {}^-2 & 4 \\ 2 & 5 \end{pmatrix} = \begin{pmatrix} 4 & 8 \\ 6 & 1 \end{pmatrix}$$

$$\begin{pmatrix} x+1 & y+2 \\ z+5 & w+1 \end{pmatrix} = \begin{pmatrix} 4 & 8 \\ 6 & 1 \end{pmatrix} \qquad \text{Matrix addition.}$$

$$\begin{array}{llll} x+1=4 & y+2=8 & z+5=6 & w+1=1 \\ x=3 & y=6 & z=1 & w=0 \end{array} \qquad \text{Definition of equal matrices.}$$

Practice problems:

1. $x + \begin{pmatrix} 7 & 8 \\ 3 & {}^-1 \\ 2 & {}^-3 \end{pmatrix} = \begin{pmatrix} 0 & 8 \\ {}^-9 & {}^-4 \\ 8 & 2 \end{pmatrix}$

2. $4x - 2\begin{pmatrix} 0 & 10 \\ 6 & {}^-4 \end{pmatrix} = 3\begin{pmatrix} 4 & 9 \\ 0 & 12 \end{pmatrix}$

3. $\begin{pmatrix} 7 & 3 \\ 2 & 4 \\ 3 & 7 \end{pmatrix} + \begin{pmatrix} a+2 & b+4 \\ c-3 & d+1 \\ e & f+3 \end{pmatrix} = \begin{pmatrix} 4 & 6 \\ {}^-1 & 1 \\ 3 & 0 \end{pmatrix}$

The **product of two matrices** can only be found if the number of columns in the first matrix is equal to the number of rows in the second matrix. Matrix multiplication is not necessarily commutative.

Sample problems:

1. Find the product AB if:

$A = \begin{pmatrix} 2 & 3 & 0 \\ 1 & {}^-4 & {}^-2 \\ 0 & 1 & 1 \end{pmatrix}$ $\qquad B = \begin{pmatrix} {}^-2 & 3 \\ 6 & {}^-1 \\ 0 & 2 \end{pmatrix}$

$\qquad 3 \times 3 \qquad\qquad\qquad 3 \times 2$

Note: Since the number of columns in the first matrix (3 × <u>3</u>) matches the number of rows (<u>3</u> ×2) this product is defined and can be found. The dimensions of the product will be equal to the number of rows in the first matrix (<u>3</u> ×3) by the number of columns in the second matrix (3 × <u>2</u>). The answer will be a 3 × 2 matrix.

$AB = \begin{pmatrix} 2 & 3 & 0 \\ 1 & {}^-4 & {}^-2 \\ 0 & 1 & 1 \end{pmatrix} \times \begin{pmatrix} {}^-2 & 3 \\ 6 & {}^-1 \\ 0 & 2 \end{pmatrix}$

$$\begin{pmatrix} 2(-2)+3(6)+0(0) \end{pmatrix}$$ Multiply 1st row of A by 1st column of B.

$$\begin{pmatrix} 14 & 2(3)+3(^-1)+0(2) \end{pmatrix}$$ Multiply 1st row of A by 2nd column of B.

$$\begin{pmatrix} 14 & 3 \\ 1(^-2)-4(6)-2(0) & \end{pmatrix}$$ Multiply 2nd row of A by 1st column of B.

$$\begin{pmatrix} 14 & 3 \\ ^-26 & 1(3)-4(^-1)-2(2) \end{pmatrix}$$ Multiply 2nd row of A by 2nd column of B.

$$\begin{pmatrix} 14 & 3 \\ ^-26 & 3 \\ 0(^-2)+1(6)+1(0) & \end{pmatrix}$$ Multiply 3rd row of A by 1st column of B.

$$\begin{pmatrix} 14 & 3 \\ ^-26 & 3 \\ 6 & 0(3)+1(^-1)+1(2) \end{pmatrix}$$ Multiply 3rd row of A by 2nd column of B.

$$\begin{pmatrix} 14 & 3 \\ ^-26 & 3 \\ 6 & 1 \end{pmatrix}$$

The product of BA is not defined since the number of columns in B is not equal to the number of rows in A.

Practice problems:

1. $\begin{pmatrix} 3 & 4 \\ ^-2 & 1 \end{pmatrix} \begin{pmatrix} ^-1 & 7 \\ ^-3 & 1 \end{pmatrix}$

2. $\begin{pmatrix} 1 & ^-2 \\ 3 & 4 \\ 2 & 5 \\ -1 & 6 \end{pmatrix} \begin{pmatrix} 3 & ^-1 & ^-4 \\ ^-1 & 2 & 3 \end{pmatrix}$

Vector Resolution

Occasionally, it is important to reverse the addition or subtraction process and express the single vector as the sum or difference of two other vectors. It may be critically important for a pilot to understand not only the air velocity but also the ground speed and the climbing speed.

Sample problem:

A pilot is traveling at an air speed of 300 mph and a direction of 20 degrees. Find the horizontal vector (ground speed) and the vertical vector (climbing speed).

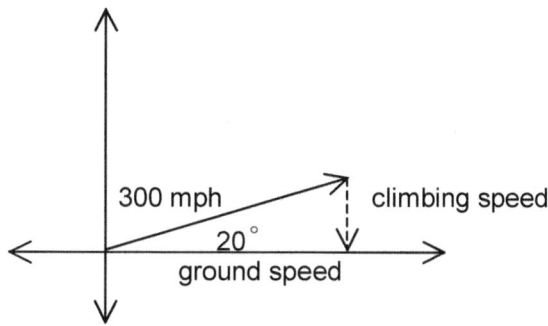

1. Draw sketch.
2. Use appropriate trigonometric ratio to calculate the component vectors.

To find the vertical vector:

$$\sin x = \frac{\text{opposite}}{\text{hypotenuse}}$$

$$\sin(20) = \frac{c}{300}$$
$$c = (.3420)(300)$$
$$c = 102.606$$

To find the horizontal vector:

$$\cos x = \frac{\text{adjacent}}{\text{hypotenuse}}$$

$$\cos(20) = \frac{g}{300}$$
$$g = (.9397)(300)$$
$$g = 281.908$$

Vectors are used to measure displacement of an object or force.

Addition of vectors:

$$(a,b)+(c,d)=(a+c,b+d)$$

Addition Properties of vectors:

$$a+b=b+a$$
$$a+(b+c)=(a+b)+c$$
$$a+0=a$$
$$a+(^-a)=0$$

Subtraction of vectors:

$$a-b=a+(^-b) \text{ therefore,}$$
$$a-b=(a_1,a_2)+(^-b_1,^-b_2) \text{ or}$$
$$a-b=(a_1-b_1,a_2-b_2)$$

Sample problem:

If $a=(4,^-1)$ and $b=(^-3,6)$, find $a+b$ and $a-b$.

Using the rule for addition of vectors:

$$(4,^-1)+(^-3,6)=(4+(^-3),^-1+6)$$
$$=(1,5)$$

Using the rule for subtraction of vectors:

$$(4,^-1)-(^-3,6)=(4-(^-3),^-1-6)$$
$$=(7,^-7)$$

The dot product $a \cdot b$:

$$a = (a_1, a_2) = a_1 i + a_2 j \quad \text{and} \quad b = (b_1, b_2) = b_1 i + b_2 j$$

$$a \cdot b = a_1 b_1 + a_2 b_2$$

$a \cdot b$ is read "a dot b". Dot products are also called scalar or inner products. When discussing dot products, it is important to remember that "a dot b" is not a vector, but a real number.

Properties of the dot product:

$$a \cdot a = |a|^2$$
$$a \cdot b = b \cdot a$$
$$a \cdot (b + c) = a \cdot b + a \cdot c$$
$$(ca) \cdot b = c(a \cdot b) = a \cdot (cb)$$
$$0 \cdot a = 0$$

Sample problems:

Find the dot product.

1. $a = (5, 2), b = (^-3, 6)$
   $a \cdot b = (5)(^-3) + (2)(6)$
   $\quad = ^-15 + 12$
   $\quad = ^-3$

2. $a = (5i + 3j), b = (4i - 5j)$
   $a \cdot b = (5)(4) + (3)(^-5)$
   $\quad = 20 - 15$
   $\quad = 5$

3. The magnitude and direction of a constant force are given by $a = 4i + 5j$. Find the amount of work done if the point of application of the force moves from the origin to the point $P(7, 2)$.

The work W done by a constant force a as its point of application moves along a vector b is $W = a \cdot b$.

Sketch the constant force vector a and the vector b.

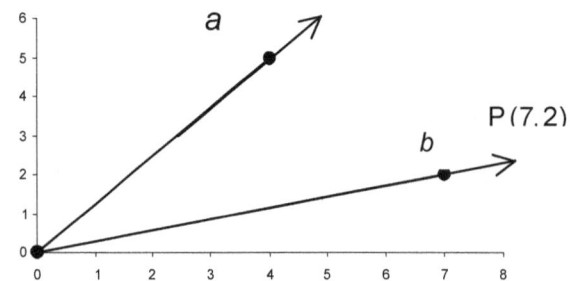

$b = (7,2) = 7i + 2j$

Use the definition of work done to solve.

$$W = a \cdot b$$
$$= (4i + 5j)(7i + 2j)$$
$$= (4)(7) + (5)(2)$$
$$= (28) + (10)$$
$$= 38$$

Vectors are used often in **navigation of ships and aircraft** as well as in force and work problems.

Sample problem:

1. An airplane is flying with a heading of 60 degrees east of north at 450 mph. A wind is blowing at 37 mph from the north. Find the plane's ground speed to the nearest mph and direction to the nearest degree.

Draw a sketch.

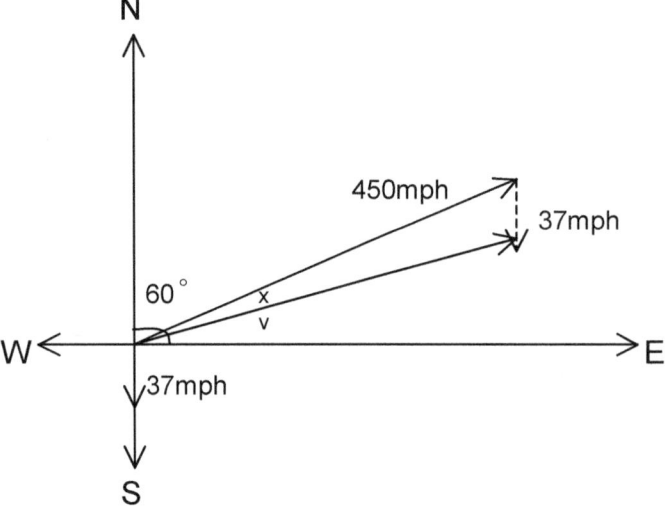

Use the law of cosines to find the ground speed.

$$a^2 = b^2 + c^2 - 2bc \cos A$$
$$|v|^2 = 450^2 + 37^2 - 2(450)(37)\cos 60$$
$$|v|^2 = 187,219$$
$$|v| = 432.688$$
$$|v| \approx 433 \text{ mph}$$

Use the law of sines to find the measure of x.

$$\frac{\sin A}{a} = \frac{\sin C}{c}$$
$$\frac{\sin 60}{433} = \frac{\sin x}{37}$$
$$\sin x = \frac{37(\sin 60)}{433}$$
$$x = 4.24$$
$$x \approx 4 \text{ degrees}$$

The plane's actual course is $60 + 4 = 64$ degrees east of north and the ground speed is approximately 433 miles per hour.

TEACHER CERTIFICATION STUDY GUIDE

SUBAREA II. PATTERNS, ALGEBRAIC RELATIONSHIPS, AND FUNCTIONS

Competency 5   Describe, analyze, and generalize mathematical patterns.

Example: Find the recursive formula for the sequence 1, 3, 9, 27, 81...

We see that any term other than the first term is obtained by multiplying the preceding term by 3. Then, we may express the formula in symbolic notation as

$$a_n = 3a_{n-1}, \ a_1 = 1,$$

where a represents a term, the subscript n denotes the place of the term in the sequence and the subscript $n-1$ represents the preceding term.

Example: Conjecture about pattern presented in tabular form.

Kepler discovered a relationship between the average distance of a planet from the sun and the time it takes the planet to orbit the sun.

The following table shows the data for the six planets closest to the sun:

	Mercury	Venus	Earth	Mars	Jupiter	Saturn
Average distance, x	0.387	0.723	1	1.523	5.203	9.541
x^3	0.058	.378	1	3.533	140.852	868.524
Time, y	0.241	0.615	1	1.881	11.861	29.457
y^2	0.058	0.378	1	3.538	140.683	867.715

Looking at the data in the table, we see that $x^3 \square y^2$. We can conjecture the following function for Kepler's relationship: $y = \sqrt{x^3}$.

A **Tessellation** is an arrangement of closed shapes that completely covers the plane without overlapping or leaving gaps. Unlike **tilings**, tessellations do not require the use of regular polygons. In art the term is used to refer to pictures or tiles mostly in the form of animals and other life forms, which cover the surface of a plane in a symmetrical way without overlapping or leaving gaps.

MATHEMATICS (Secondary)

M. C. Escher is known as the "Father" of modern tessellations. Tessellations are used for tiling, mosaics, quilts and art.

If you look at a completed tessellation, you will see the original motif repeats in a pattern. There are 17 possible ways that a pattern can be used to tile a flat surface or "wallpaper."

A **fractal** is an endlessly repeating pattern that varies according to a set formula, a mixture of art and geometry. A fractal is any pattern that reveals greater complexity as it is enlarged. An example of a fractal is an ice crystal freezing on a glass window.

Fractals are **self-similar** and have **fractional (fractal) dimension**. Self-similar means that a fractal looks the same over all ranges of scale.

Example:

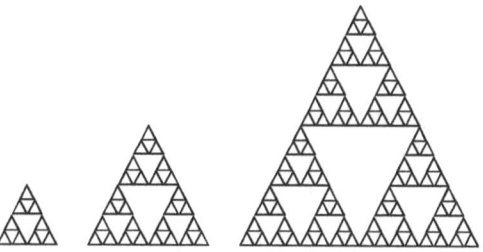

Fractional, or fractal dimension, means that the dimension of the figure is a non-integer, or fraction.

Example,

In the above figure, notice that the second triangle is composed of three miniature triangles exactly like the original. The length of any side of one of the miniature triangles could be multiplied by two to produce the entire triangle (S=2). The resulting figure consists of three separate identical miniature pieces (N=3). The formula to find the dimension of a strictly self-similar fractal is

$$D = \frac{\log N}{\log S}$$

For the above figure,

$$D = \frac{\log 3}{\log 2}$$

$$D = 1.585$$

Arithmetic Sequences

When given a set of numbers where the common difference between the terms is constant, use the following formula:

$$a_n = a_1 + (n-1)d$$

where a_1 = the first term
n = the nth term (general term)
d = the common difference

Sample problem:

1. Find the 8th term of the arithmetic sequence 5, 8, 11, 14, ...

   $a_n = a_1 + (n-1)d$
   $a_1 = 5$ Identify 1st term.
   $d = 3$ Find d.
   $a_8 = 5 + (8-1)3$ Substitute.
   $a_8 = 26$

2. Given two terms of an arithmetic sequence find a and d.

   $a_4 = 21$ $a_6 = 32$
   $a_n = a_1 + (n-1)d$
   $21 = a_1 + (4-1)d$
   $32 = a_1 + (6-1)d$

   $21 = a_1 + 3d$ Solve the system of equations.
   $32 = a_1 + 5d$

   $21 = a_1 + 3d$
   $-32 = {}^-a_1 - 5d$ Multiply by $^-1$ and add the equations.

   $^-11 = {}^-2d$
   $5.5 = d$
   $21 = a_1 + 3(5.5)$ Substitute $d = 5.5$ into one of the equations.
   $21 = a_1 + 16.5$
   $a_1 = 4.5$

The sequence begins with 4.5 and has a common difference of 5.5 between numbers.

When using **geometric sequences** consecutive numbers are compared to find the common ratio.

$$r = \frac{a_{n+1}}{a_n}$$

$r =$ the common ratio
$a_n =$ the nth term

The ratio is then used in the geometric sequence formula:

$$a_n = a_1 r^{n-1}$$

Sample problems:

1. Find the 8th term of the geometric sequence 2, 8, 32, 128 ...

$r = \dfrac{a_{n+1}}{a_n}$ Use the common ratio formula to find ratio.

$r = \dfrac{8}{2}$ Substitute $a_n = 2$ $a_{n+1} = 8$

$r = 4$

$a_n = a_1 \times r^{n-1}$ Use $r = 4$ to solve for the 8th term.
$a_8 = 2 \times 4^{8-1}$
$a_8 = 32768$

The **sums of terms in a progression** is simply found by determining if it is an arithmetic or geometric sequence and then using the appropriate formula.

Sum of first n terms of an arithmetic sequence.

$$S_n = \frac{n}{2}(a_1 + a_n)$$

or

$$S_n = \frac{n}{2}\left[2a_1 + (n-1)d\right]$$

Sum of first n terms of a geometric sequence.

$$S_n = \frac{a_1(r^n - 1)}{r - 1}, r \neq 1$$

Sample Problems:

1. $\sum_{i=1}^{10}(2i + 2)$

   This means find the sum of the terms beginning with the first term and ending with the 10th term of the sequence $a = 2i + 2$.

   $a_1 = 2(1) + 2 = 4$
   $a_{10} = 2(10) + 2 = 22$
   $S_n = \frac{n}{2}(a_1 + a_n)$
   $S_n = \frac{10}{2}(4 + 22)$
   $S_n = 130$

2. Find the sum of the first 6 terms in an arithmetic sequence if the first term is 2 and the common difference d, is $^-3$.

   $n = 6 \quad a_1 = 2 \quad d = {}^-3$

   $S_n = \frac{n}{2}\left[2a_1 + (n-1)d\right]$

   $S_6 = \frac{6}{2}\left[2 \times 2 + (6-1)^-3\right]$ Substitute known values.

   $S_6 = 3\left[4 + (^-15)\right]$ Solve.

   $S_6 = 3(-11) = -33$

TEACHER CERTIFICATION STUDY GUIDE

3. Find $\sum_{i=1}^{5} 4 \times 2^i$

This means the sum of the first 5 terms where $a_i = a \times b^i$ and $r = b$.

$a_1 = 4 \times 2^1 = 8$ Identify a_1, r, n
$r = 2 \qquad n = 5$

$S_n = \dfrac{a_1(r^n - 1)}{r - 1}$ Substitute a, r, n

$S_5 = \dfrac{8(2^5 - 1)}{2 - 1}$ Solve.

$S_5 = \dfrac{8(31)}{1} = 248$

Practice problems:

1. Find the sum of the first five terms of the sequence if $a = 7$ and $d = 4$.

2. $\sum_{i=1}^{7} (2i - 4)$

3. $\sum_{i=1}^{6} {}^-3\left(\dfrac{2}{5}\right)^i$

A **recurrence relation** is an equation that defines a sequence recursively; in other words, each term of the sequence is defined as a function of the preceding terms.

A real-life application would be using a recurrence relation to determine how much your savings would be in an account at the end of a certain period of time. For example:

You deposit $5,000 in your savings account. Your bank pays 5% interest compounded annually. How much will your account be worth at the end of 10 years?

Let V represent the amount of money in the account and V_n represent the amount of money after n years.

MATHEMATICS (Secondary)

The amount in the account after *n* years equals the amount in the account after *n* – 1 years plus the interest for the *n*th year. This can be expressed as the recurrence relation V_0 where your initial deposit is represented by $V_0 = 5,000$.

$$V_0 = V_0$$
$$V_1 = 1.05 V_0$$
$$V_2 = 1.05 V_1 = (1.05)^2 V_0$$
$$V_3 = 1.05 V_2 = (1.05)^3 V_0$$
$$......$$
$$V_n = (1.05) V_{n-1} = (1.05)^n V_0$$

Inserting the values into the equation, you get $V_{10} = (1.05)^{10}(5,000) = 8,144$.

You determine that after investing $5,000 in an account earning 5% interest, compounded annually for 10 years, you would have $8,144.

Competency 6 Use symbolic expressions to describe and analyze patterns of change and functional relationships.

A **linear function** is a function defined by the equation $f(x) = mx + b$.

Example: A model for the distance traveled by a migrating monarch butterfly looks like $f(t) = 80t$, where t represents time in days. We interpret this to mean that the average speed of the butterfly is 80 miles per day and distance traveled may be computed by substituting the number of days traveled for t. In a linear function, there is a **constant** rate of change.

The standard form of a **quadratic function** is $f(x) = ax^2 + bx + c$.

Example: What patterns appear in a table for $y = x^2 - 5x + 6$?

x	y
0	6
1	2
2	0
3	0
4	2
5	6

We see that the values for y are **symmetrically** arranged.

An **exponential function** is a function defined by the equation $y = ab^x$, where a is the starting value, b is the growth factor, and x tells how many times to multiply by the growth factor.

Example: $y = 100(1.5)^x$

x	y
0	100
1	150
2	225
3	337.5
4	506.25

This is an **exponential** or multiplicative pattern of growth.

A rational function is given in the form $f(x) = p(x)/q(x)$. In the equation, $p(x)$ and $q(x)$ both represent polynomial functions where $q(x)$ does not equal zero. The branches of rational functions approach asymptotes. Setting the denominator equal to zero and solving will give the value(s) of the vertical asymptotes(s) since the function will be undefined at this point. If the value of $f(x)$ approaches b as the $|x|$ increases, the equation $y = b$ is a horizontal asymptote. To find the horizontal asymptote it is necessary to make a table of values for x that are to the right and left of the vertical asymptotes. The pattern for the horizontal asymptotes will become apparent as the $|x|$ increases.

If there are more than one vertical asymptotes, remember to choose numbers to the right and left of each one in order to find the horizontal asymptotes and have sufficient points to graph the function.

Sample problem:

1. Graph $f(x) = \dfrac{3x + 1}{x - 2}$.

$x - 2 = 0$
$x = 2$

1. Set denominator $= 0$ to find the vertical asymptote.

x	f(x)
3	10
10	3.875
100	3.07
1000	3.007
1	⁻4
⁻10	2.417
⁻100	2.93
⁻1000	2.99

2. Make table choosing numbers to the right and left of the vertical asymptote.

3. The pattern shows that as the $|x|$ increases $f(x)$ approaches the value 3, therefore a horizontal asymptote exists at $y = 3$

Sketch the graph.

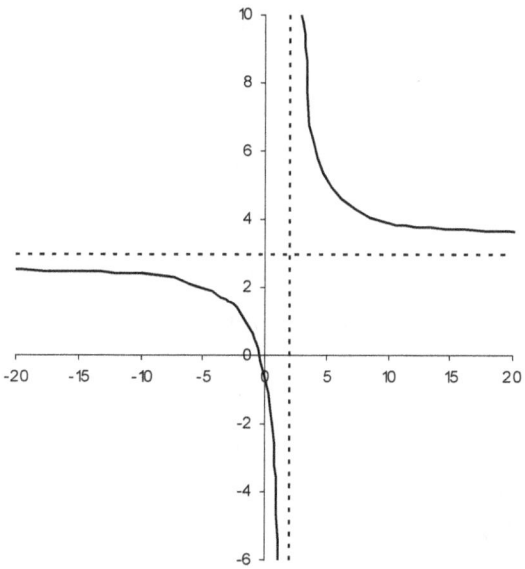

- A **relation** is any set of ordered pairs.

- The **domain** of a relation is the set made of all the first coordinates of the ordered pairs.

- The **range** of a relation is the set made of all the second coordinates of the ordered pairs.

- A **function** is a relation in which different ordered pairs have different first coordinates. (No x values are repeated.)

- A **mapping** is a diagram with arrows drawn from each element of the domain to the corresponding elements of the range. If 2 arrows are drawn from the same element of the domain, then it is not a function.

- On a graph, use the **vertical line test** to look for a function. If any vertical line intersects the graph of a relation in more than one point, then the relation is not a function.

1. Determine the domain and range of this mapping.

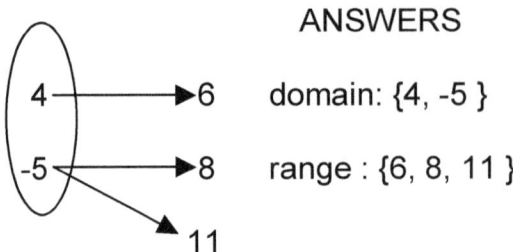

ANSWERS

domain: {4, -5 }

range : {6, 8, 11 }

2. Determine which of these are functions:

   a. $\{(1,^-4),(27,1)(94,5)(2,^-4)\}$
   b. $f(x) = 2x - 3$
   c. $A = \{(x,y) \mid xy = 24\}$
   d. $y = 3$
   e. $x = {}^-9$
   f. $\{(3,2),(7,7),(0,5),(2,^-4),(8,^-6),(1,0),(5,9),(6,^-4)\}$

- A **relation** is any set of ordered pairs.
- The **domain** of the relation is the set of all first co-ordinates of the ordered pairs. (These are the x coordinates.)
- The **range** of the relation is the set of all second co-ordinates of the ordered pairs. (These are the y coordinates.)

3. If $A = \{(x,y) \mid y = x^2 - 6\}$, find the domain and range.

4. Give the domain and range of set B if:

   $B = \{(1,^-2),(4,^-2),(7,^-2),(6,^-2)\}$

5. Determine the domain of this function:

   $$f(x) = \frac{5x+7}{x^2 - 4}$$

6. Determine the domain and range of these graphs.

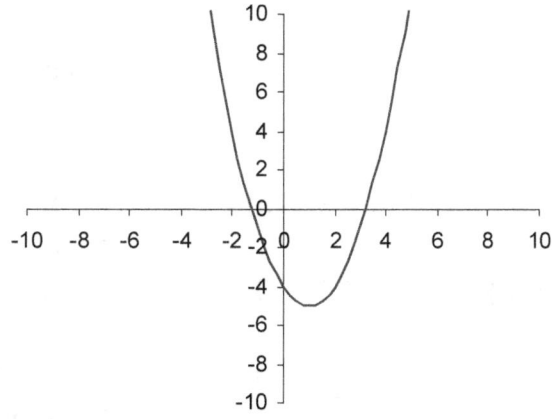

7. If $E = \{(x, y) \mid y = 5\}$, find the domain and range.

8. Determine the ordered pairs in the relation shown in this mapping.

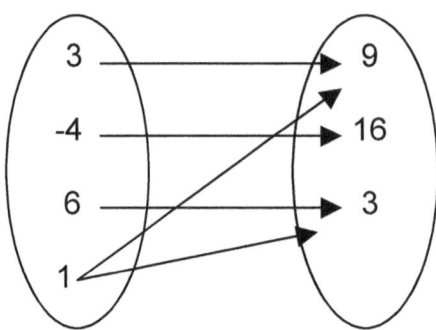

Function Operations

If $f(x)$ is a function and the value of 3 is in the domain, the corresponding element in the range would be f(3). It is found by evaluating the function for $x = 3$. The same holds true for adding, subtracting, and multiplying in function form.

The symbol f^{-1} is read "the inverse of f". The $^-1$ is not an exponent. The inverse of a function can be found by reversing the order of coordinates in each ordered pair that satisfies the function. Finding the inverse functions means switching the place of x and y and then solving for y.

Sample problem:

1. Find $p(a+1) + 3\{p(4a)\}$ if $p(x) = 2x^2 + x + 1$.

Find $p(a+1)$.

$p(a+1) = 2(a+1)^2 + (a+1) + 1$ Substitute $(a+1)$ for x.
$p(a+1) = 2a^2 + 5a + 4$ Solve.

Find $3\{p(4a)\}$.

$3\{p(4a)\} = 3[2(4a)^2 + (4a) + 1]$ Substitute $(4a)$ for x, multiply by 3.
$3\{p(4a)\} = 96a^2 + 12a + 3$ Solve.

$p(a+1) + 3\{p(4a)\} = 2a^2 + 5a + 4 + 96a^2 + 12a + 3$
 Combine like terms.

$p(a+1) + 3\{p(4a)\} = 98a^2 + 17a + 7$

Inverses

How to write the equation of the inverse of a function.

1. To find the inverse of an equation using x and y, replace each letter with the other letter. Then solve the new equation for y, when possible. Given an equation like $y = 3x - 4$, replace each letter with the other:
2.
$x = 3y - 4$. Now solve this for y:
$x + 4 = 3y$
$1/3\, x + 4/3 = y$ This is the inverse.

Sometimes the function is named by a letter:
$f(x) = 5x + 10$

Temporarily replace f(x) with y.
$y = 5x + 10$

Now replace each letter with the other: $x = 5y + 10$

Solve for the new y: $x - 10 = 5y$
$1/5\, x - 2 = y$

The inverse of f(x) is denoted as $f^{-1}(x)$, so the answer is $f^{-1}(x) = 1/5\, X - 2$.

Functions defined by two or more formulas are **piecewise functions**. The formula used to evaluate piecewise functions varies depending on the value of x. The graphs of piecewise functions consist of two or more pieces, or intervals, and are often discontinuous.

Example 1:

$$f(x) = \begin{array}{ll} x + 1 & \text{if } x > 2 \\ x - 2 & \text{if } x \leq 2 \end{array}$$

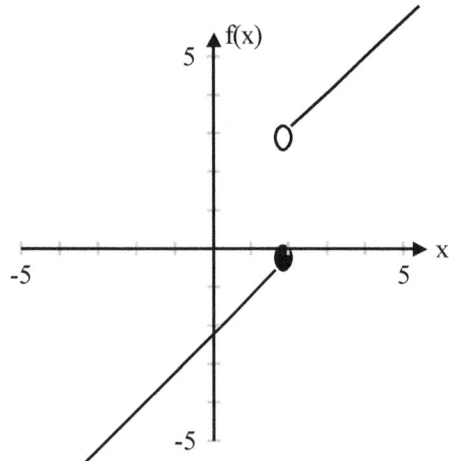

Example 2:

$$f(x) = \begin{array}{ll} x & \text{if } x \geq 1 \\ x^2 & \text{if } x < 1 \end{array}$$

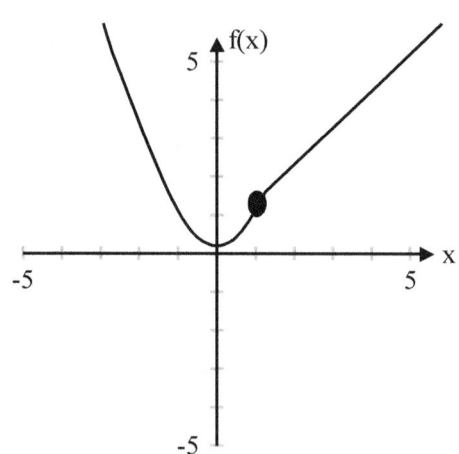

When graphing or interpreting the graph of piecewise functions it is important to note the points at the beginning and end of each interval because the graph must clearly indicate what happens at the end of each interval. Note that in the graph of Example 1, point (2, 3) is not part of the graph and is represented by an empty circle. On the other hand, point (2, 0) is part of the graph and is represented as a solid circle. Note also that the graph of Example 2 is continuous despite representing a piecewise function.

Practice: Graph the following piecewise equations.

1. $f(x) = x^2$ if $x > 0$
   $\quad\quad = x + 4$ if $x \leq 0$

2. $f(x) = x^2 - 1$ if $x > 2$
   $\quad\quad = x^2 + 2$ if $x \leq 2$

Different types of function transformations affect the graph and characteristics of a function in predictable ways. The basic types of transformation are horizontal and vertical shift, horizontal and vertical scaling, and reflection. As an example of the types of transformations, we will consider transformations of the functions $f(x) = x^2$.

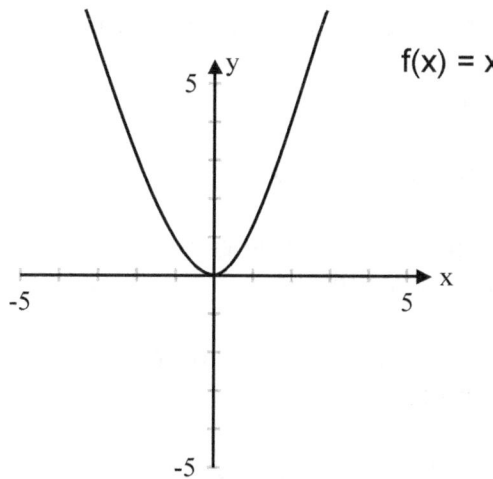

Horizontal shifts take the form $g(x) = f(x \pm c)$. For example, we obtain the graph of the function $g(x) = (x + 2)^2$ by shifting the graph of $f(x) = x^2$ two units to the left. The graph of the function $h(x) = (x - 2)^2$ is the graph of $f(x) = x^2$ shifted two units to the right.

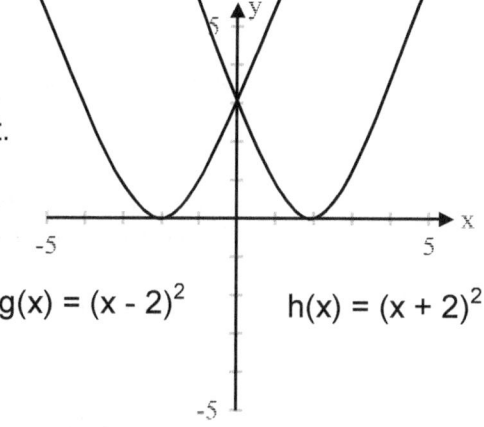

Vertical scaling takes the form $g(x) = cf(x)$. For example, we obtain the graph of $g(x) = 1/2(x^2)$ by compressing the graph of $f(x) = x^2$ in the y-direction by a factor of 1/2. If $c > 1$ the graph is stretched in the y-direction while if $1 > c > 0$ the graph is compressed in the y-direction.

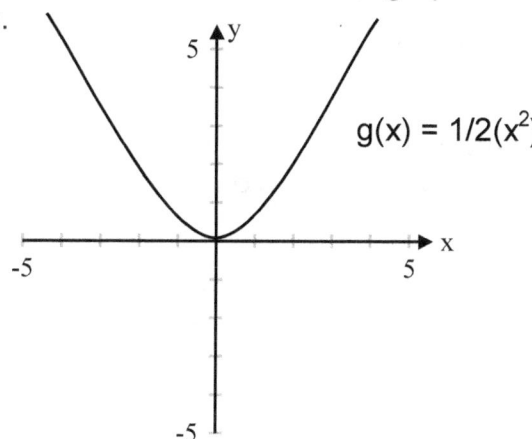

Competency 7 Understand properties and applications of linear and quadratic functions, and solve related equations and inequalities.

Graph of the linear equation
The graph of the linear equation represents a straight line. It has two points to define a unique straight line.

Procedure for graphing:

1) Choose only 3 values of x.

2) Substitute each chosen value of x in the equation to find the corresponding y value.

3) Plot the 3 points on the coordinate system and join the points with a straight line.

Note: It is typically helpful to choose the x-intercept and y-intercept as the two key points (when possible).

Recall:

1) The x-intercept is the point where the line intersects the x axis. To find this point, we substitute 0 for y and solve for x.

2) The y-intercept is the point where the line intersects the y axis. To find this point, we substitute 0 for x and solve for y.

Example: Sketch the graph of the line represented by $2x + 3y = 6$.

Let $x = 0 \rightarrow 2(0) + 3y = 6$
$\rightarrow 3y = 6$
$\rightarrow y = 2$
$\rightarrow (0,2)$ is the y intercept.

Let $y = 0 \rightarrow 2x + 3(0) = 6$
$\rightarrow 2x = 6$
$\rightarrow x = 3$
$\rightarrow (3,0)$ is the x intercept.

Let $x = 1 \rightarrow 2(1) + 3y = 6$
$\rightarrow 2 + 3y = 6$
$\rightarrow 3y = 4$
$\rightarrow y = \dfrac{4}{3}$
$\rightarrow \left(1, \dfrac{4}{3}\right)$ is the third point.

Plotting the three points on the coordinate system, we get the following:

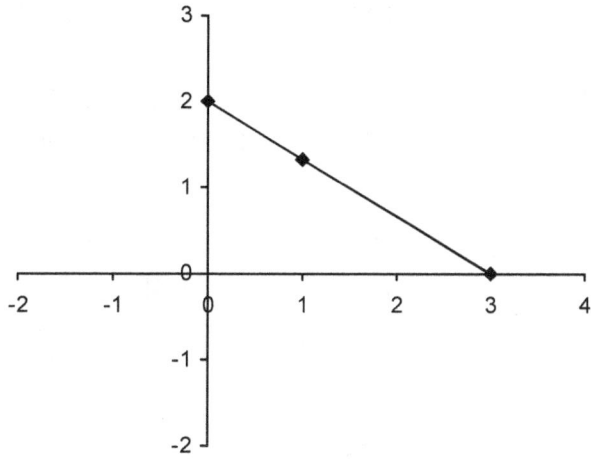

To solve an **equation or inequality**, follow these steps:

STEP 1. If there are parentheses, use the distributive property to eliminate them.

STEP 2. If there are fractions, determine their LCD (least common denominator). Multiply every term of the equation by the LCD. This will cancel out all of the fractions while solving the equation or inequality.

STEP 3. If there are decimals, find the largest decimal. Multiply each term by a power of 10(10, 100, 1000,etc.) with the same number of zeros as the length of the decimal. This will eliminate all decimals while solving the equation or inequality.

STEP 4. Combine like terms on each side of the equation or inequality.

STEP 5. If there are variables on both sides of the equation, add or subtract one of those variable terms to move it to the other side. Combine like terms.

STEP 6. If there are constants on both sides, add or subtract one of those constants to move it to the other side. Combine like terms.

STEP 7. If there is a coefficient in front of the variable, divide both sides by this number. This is the answer to an equation. However, remember:

Dividing or multiplying an inequality by a negative number will reverse the direction of the inequality sign.

STEP 8. The solution of a linear equation solves to one single number. The solution of an inequality is always stated including the inequality sign.

Example: Solve: $3(2x+5)-4x=5(x+9)$
$6x+15-4x=5x+45$ ref. step 1
$2x+15=5x+45$ ref. step 4
$^-3x+15=45$ ref. step 5
$^-3x=30$ ref. step 6
$x=^-10$ ref. step 7

Example: Solve: $1/2(5x+34)=1/4(3x-5)$
$5/2x+17=3/4x-5/4$ ref. step 1
LCD of 5/2, 3/4, and 5/4 is 4.
Multiply by the LCD of 4.
$4(5/2x+17)=(3/4x-5/4)4$ ref. step 2
$10x+68=3x-5$
$7x+68=^-5$ ref. step 5
$7x=^-73$ ref. step 6
$x=^-73/7$ or $^-10\ 3/7$ ref. step 7

MATHEMATICS (Secondary)

Check:

$$\frac{1}{2}\left[5\frac{-13}{7}+34\right]=\frac{1}{4}\left[3\left(\frac{-13}{7}\right)-\frac{5}{4}\right]$$

$$\frac{1}{2}\left[\frac{-13(5)}{7}+34\right]=\frac{1}{4}\left[3\left(\frac{-13}{7}\right)-\frac{5}{4}\right]$$

$$\frac{-13(5)}{7}+17=\frac{3(-13)}{28}-\frac{5}{4}$$

$$\frac{-13(5)+17(14)}{14}=\frac{3(-13)}{28}-\frac{5}{4}$$

$$\left[-13(5)+17(14)\right]2=\frac{3(-13)-35}{28}$$

$$\frac{-130+476}{28}=\frac{-219-35}{28}$$

$$\frac{-254}{28}=\frac{-254}{28}$$

Example: Solve: $6x+21<8x+31$

$^{-}2x+21<31 $ ref. step 5

$^{-}2x<10 $ ref. step 6

$x>{}^{-}5 $ ref. step 7

Note that the inequality sign has changed.

To solve an **absolute value equation**, follow these steps:

1. Get the absolute value expression alone on one side of the equation.

2. Split the absolute value equation into 2 separate equations without absolute value bars. Write the expression inside the absolute value bars (without the bars) equal to the expression on the other side of the equation. Now write the expression inside the absolute value bars equal to the opposite of the expression on the other side of the equation.

3. Now solve each of these equations.

4. **Check each answer by substituting it into the original equation** (with the absolute value symbol). There will be answers that do not check in the original equation. These answers are discarded as they are **extraneous solutions**. If all answers are discarded as incorrect, then the answer to the equation is $\varnothing$, which means the empty set or the null set. (0, 1, or 2 solutions could be correct.)

To solve an absolute value inequality, follow these steps:

1. Get the absolute value expression alone on one side of the inequality. Remember:

    Dividing or multiplying by a negative number will reverse the direction of the inequality sign.

2. Remember what the inequality sign is at this point.

3. Split the absolute value inequality into 2 separate inequalities without absolute value bars. First rewrite the inequality without the absolute bars and solve it. Next write the expression inside the absolute value bar followed by the opposite inequality sign and then by the opposite of the expression on the other side of the inequality. Now solve it.

4. If the sign in the inequality on step 2 is $<$ or $\leq$, the answer is those 2 inequalities connected by the word **and**. The solution set consists of the points between the 2 numbers on the number line. If the sign in the inequality on step 2 is $>$ or $\geq$, the answer is those 2 inequalities connected by the word **or**. The solution set consists of the points outside the 2 numbers on the number line.

If an expression inside an absolute value bar is compared to a negative number, the answer can also be either all real numbers or the empty set ($\varnothing$). For instance,

$$|x+3| < {}^-6$$

would have the empty set as the answer, since an absolute value is always positive and will never be less than $^-6$. However,

$$|x+3| > {}^-6$$

would have all real numbers as the answer, since an absolute value is always positive or at least zero, and will never be less than -6. In similar fashion,

$$|x+3| = {}^-6$$

would never check because an absolute value will never give a negative value.

Example: Solve and check:

$$|2x-5|+1=12$$
$$|2x-5|=11 \quad \text{Get absolute value alone.}$$

Rewrite as 2 equations and solve separately.

	same equation without absolute value		same equation without absolute value but right side is opposite
	$2x-5=11$		$2x-5={}^-11$
	$2x=16$	and	$2x={}^-6$
	$x=8$		$x={}^-3$
Checks:	$\|2x-5\|+1=12$		$\|2x-5\|+1=12$
	$\|2(8)-5\|+1=12$		$\|2({}^-3)-5\|+1=12$
	$\|11\|+1=12$		$\|{}^-11\|+1=12$
	$12=12$		$12=12$

This time both 8 and $^-3$ check.

Example: Solve and check:

$$2|x-7|-13 \geq 11$$

$$2|x-7| \geq 24 \quad \text{Get absolute value alone.}$$

$$|x-7| \geq 12$$

Rewrite as 2 inequalities and solve separately.

same inequality without absolute value		same inequality without absolute value but right side and inequality sign are both the opposite
$x - 7 \geq 12$	or	$x - 7 \leq {}^-12$
$x \geq 19$	or	$x \leq {}^-5$

Equations and inequalities can be used to **solve various types of word problems**. Examples follow.

Example: The YMCA wants to sell raffle tickets to raise at least $32,000. If they must pay $7,250 in expenses and prizes out of the money collected from the tickets, how many tickets worth $25 each must they sell?

Solution: Since they want to raise **at least $32,000**, that means they would be happy to get 32,000 **or more**. This requires an inequality.

    Let $x =$ number of tickets sold
    Then $25x =$ total money collected for x tickets

Total money minus expenses is greater than $32,000.

$$25x - 7250 \geq 32000$$
$$25x \geq 39250$$
$$x \geq 1570$$

If they sell **1,570 tickets or more**, they will raise AT LEAST $32,000.

MATHEMATICS (Secondary)

Example: The Simpsons went out for dinner. All 4 of them ordered the aardvark steak dinner. Bert paid for the 4 meals and included a tip of $12 for a total of $84.60. How much was an aardvark steak dinner?

Let $x =$ the price of one aardvark dinner
So $4x =$ the price of 4 aardavark dinners
$4x = 84.60 - 12$
$4x = 72.60$
$x = \dfrac{72.60}{4} = \$18.15$ The price of one aardvark dinner.

Some word problems can be solved using a system of equations or inequalities. Watch for words like greater than, less than, at least, or no more than which indicate the need for inequalities.

Example: Farmer Greenjeans bought 4 cows and 6 sheep for $1700. Mr. Ziffel bought 3 cows and 12 sheep for $2400. If all the cows were the same price and all the sheep were another price, find the price charged for a cow or for a sheep.

Let $x =$ price of a cow
Let $y =$ price of a sheep

Then Farmer Greenjeans' equation would be: $4x + 6y = 1700$
Mr. Ziffel's equation would be: $3x + 12y = 2400$

To solve by **addition-subtraction**:

Multiply the first equation by $^-2$: $^-2(4x + 6y = 1700)$
Keep the other equation the same : $(3x + 12y = 2400)$
By doing this, the equations can be added to each other to eliminate one variable and solve for the other variable.

$^-8x - 12y = {}^-3400$
$3x + 12y = 2400$ Add these equations.
$^-5x = {}^-1000$

$x = 200 \leftarrow$ the price of a cow was $200.
Solving for y, $y = 150 \leftarrow$ the price of a sheep, $150.

(This problem can also solved by substitution or determinants.)

MATHEMATICS (Secondary)

Example: John has 9 coins, which are either dimes or nickels, that are worth $.65. Determine how many of each coin he has.

Let d = number of dimes.
Let n = number of nickels.
The number of coins total 9.
The value of the coins equals 65.

Then: $n + d = 9$
$5n + 10d = 65$

Multiplying the first equation by −5, it becomes:

$$-5n - 5d = -45$$
$$\underline{5n + 10d = 65}$$
$$5d = 20$$

$d = 4$ There are 4 dimes, so there are $(9 - 4)$ or 5 nickels.

Example: Sharon's Bike Shoppe can assemble a 3 speed bike in 30 minutes or a 10 speed bike in 60 minutes. The profit on each bike sold is $60 for a 3 speed or $75 for a 10 speed bike. How many of each type of bike should they assemble during an 8 hour day (480 minutes) to make the maximum profit? Total daily profit must be at least $300.

Let x = number of 3 speed bikes.
y = number of 10 speed bikes.

Since there are only 480 minutes to use each day,

$30x + 60y \leq 480$ is the first inequality.
$30x + 60y \leq 480$ solves to $y \leq 8 - 1/2 x$
$60y \leq -30x + 480$
$$y \leq -\frac{1}{2}x + 8$$

Since the total daily profit must be at least $300,

$60x + 75y \geq 300$ is the second inequality.
$60x + 75y \geq 300$ solves to $y \geq 4 - 4/5 x$
$75y + 60x \geq 300$
$75y \geq -60x + 300$
$$y \geq -\frac{4}{5}x + 4$$

This problem can be solved by graphing these 2 inequalities:

$$y \leq 8 - 1/2\, x$$
$$y \geq 4 - 4/5\, x$$

Realize that $x \geq 0$ and $y \geq 0$, since the number of bikes assembled can not be a negative number. Graph these as additional constraints on the problem. The number of bikes assembled must always be an integer value, so points within the shaded area of the graph must have integer values. The maximum profit will occur at or near a corner of the shaded portion of this graph. Those points occur at (0,4), (0,8), (16,0), or (5,0).

Since profits are $60/3-speed or $75/10-speed, the profit would be:

(0,4) $60(0) + 75(4) = 300$
(0,8) $60(0) + 75(8) = 600$
(16,0) $60(16) + 75(0) = 960$ ← Maximum profit
(5,0) $60(5) + 75(0) = 300$

The maximum profit would occur if 16 3-speed bikes are made daily.

- A first degree equation has an equation of the form $ax + by = c$. To graph this equation, find either one point and the slope of the line or find two points. To find a point and slope, solve the equation for y. This gets the equation in **slope intercept form**, $y = mx + b$. The point (0,b) is the y-intercept and m is the line's slope. To find any 2 points, substitute any 2 numbers for x and solve for y. To find the intercepts, substitute 0 for x and then 0 for y.

- Remember that graphs will go up as they go to the right when the slope is positive. Negative slopes make the lines go down as they go to the right.

- If the equation solves to **x = any number**, then the graph is a **vertical line**.

- If the equation solves to **y = any number**, then the graph is a **horizontal line**.

- When graphing a linear inequality, the line will be dotted if the inequality sign is < or >. If the inequality signs are either ≥ or ≤, the line on the graph will be a solid line. Shade above the line when the inequality sign is ≥ or >. Shade below the line when the inequality sign is < or ≤. Inequalities of the form $x >, x \leq, x <,$ or $x \geq$ number, draw a vertical line (solid or dotted). Shade to the right for > or ≥. Shade to the left for < or ≤. Remember: **Dividing or multiplying by a negative number will reverse the direction of the inequality sign.**

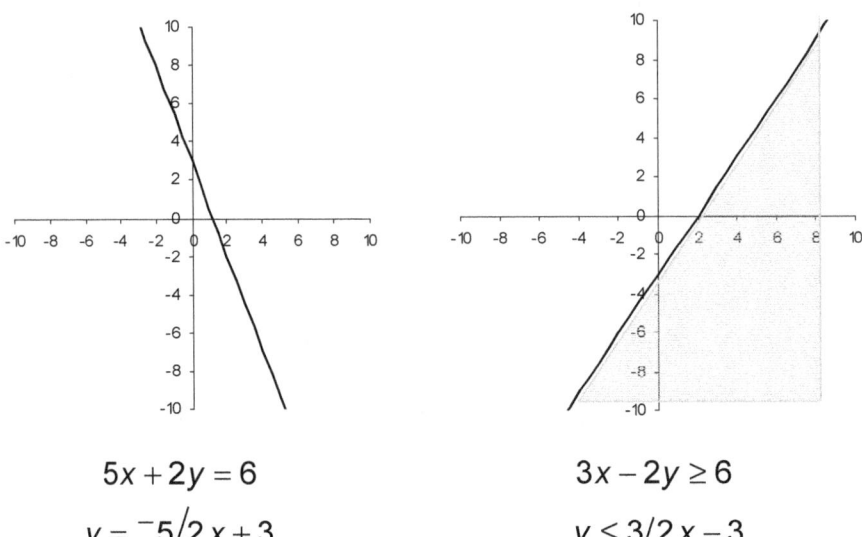

$5x + 2y = 6$

$y = {-5}/2\,x + 3$

$3x - 2y \geq 6$

$y \leq 3/2\,x - 3$

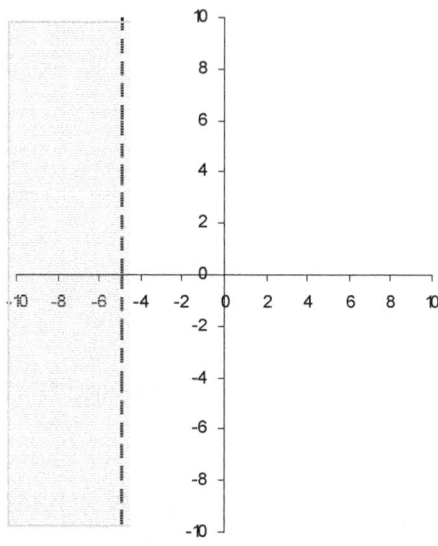

$$3x + 12 < -3$$
$$x < {}^-5$$

Graph the following:

1. $2x - y = {}^-4$
2. $x + 3y > 6$
3. $3x + 2y \le 2y - 6$

- A first degree equation has an equation of the form $ax + by = c$. To find the slope of a line, solve the equation for y. This gets the equation into **slope intercept form**, $y = mx + b$. m is the line's slope.

- To find the y intercept, substitute 0 for x and solve for y. This is the y intercept. The y intercept is also the value of b in $y = mx + b$.

- To find the x intercept, substitute 0 for y and solve for x. This is the x intercept.

- If the equation solves to **x = any number**, then the graph is a **vertical line**. It only has an x intercept. Its slope is **undefined**.

- If the equation solves to **y = any number**, then the graph is a **horizontal line**. It only has a y intercept. Its slope is 0 (zero).

Find the slope and intercepts of $3x + 2y = 14$.

$$3x + 2y = 14$$
$$2y = {}^-3x + 14$$
$$y = {}^-3/2\ x + 7$$

The slope of the line is $^-3/2$, the value of m.
The y intercept of the line is 7.

The intercepts can also be found by substituting 0 in place of the other variable in the equation.

To find the y intercept:
let $x = 0$; $3(0) + 2y = 14$
$0 + 2y = 14$
$2y = 14$
$y = 7$
$(0,7)$ is the y intercept.

To find the x intercept:
let $y = 0$; $3x + 2(0) = 14$
$3x + 0 = 14$
$3x = 14$
$x = 14/3$
$(14/3, 0)$ is the x intercept.

Find the slope and the intercepts (if they exist) for these equations:

1. $5x + 7y = {}^-70$
2. $x - 2y = 14$
3. $5x + 3y = 3(5 + y)$
4. $2x + 5y = 15$

- The equation of a graph can be found by finding its slope and its y intercept. To find the slope, find 2 points on the graph where co-ordinates are integer values. Using points:

$$(x_1, y_1) \text{ and } (x_2, y_2).$$

$$\text{slope} = \frac{y_2 - y_1}{x_2 - x_1}$$

The y intercept is the y coordinate of the point where a line crosses the y axis. The equation can be written in slope-intercept form, which is $y = mx + b$, where m is the slope and b is the y intercept. To rewrite the equation into some other form, multiply each term by the common denominator of all the fractions. Then rearrange terms as necessary.

- If the graph is a **vertical line**, then the equation solves to **x = the x co-ordinate of any point on the line**.

- If the graph is a **horizontal line**, then the equation solves to **y = the y coordinate of any point on the line**.

- Given two points on a line, the first thing to do is to find the slope of the line. If 2 points on the graph are (x_1, y_1) and (x_2, y_2), then the slope is found using the formula:

$$\text{slope} = \frac{y_2 - y_1}{x_2 - x_1}$$

The slope will now be denoted by the letter **m**. To write the equation of a line, choose either point. Substitute them into the formula:

$$Y - y_a = m(X - x_a)$$

Remember (x_a, y_a) can be (x_1, y_1) or (x_2, y_2) If **m**, the value of the slope, is distributed through the parentheses, the equation can be rewritten into other forms of the equation of a line.

Find the equation of a line through $(9, {}^-6)$ and $({}^-1, 2)$.

$$\text{slope} = \frac{y_2 - y_1}{x_2 - x_1} = \frac{2 - {}^-6}{{}^-1 - 9} = \frac{8}{{}^-10} = \frac{{}^-4}{5}$$

$Y - y_a = m(X - x_a) \rightarrow Y - 2 = {}^-4/5(X - {}^-1) \rightarrow$
$Y - 2 = {}^-4/5(X + 1) \rightarrow Y - 2 = {}^-4/5 X - 4/5 \rightarrow$
$Y = {}^-4/5 \, X + 6/5$ This is the slope-intercept form.

Multiplying by 5 to eliminate fractions, it is:
$5Y = {}^-4X + 6 \rightarrow 4X + 5Y = 6$ Standard form.

Write the equation of a line through these two points:
1. $(5, 8)$ and $({}^-3, 2)$
2. $(11, 10)$ and $(11, {}^-3)$
3. $({}^-4, 6)$ and $(6, 12)$
4. $(7, 5)$ and $({}^-3, 5)$

Word problems can sometimes be solved by using a system of two equations in 2 unknowns. This system can then be solved using substitution, the addition-subtraction method, determinants, or graphing.

Example: Mrs. Winters bought 4 dresses and 6 pairs of shoes for $340. Mrs. Summers went to the same store and bought 3 dresses and 8 pairs of shoes for $360. If all the dresses were the same price and all the shoes were the same price, find the price charged for a dress and for a pair of shoes.

Let x = price of a dress
Let y = price of a pair of shoes

Then Mrs. Winters' equation would be: $4x + 6y = 340$
Mrs. Summers' equation would be: $3x + 8y = 360$

To solve by addition-subtraction:

Multiply the first equation by 4: $4(4x + 6y = 340)$

Multiply the other equation by $^-3$: $^-3(3x + 8y = 360)$

By doing this, the equations can be added to each other to eliminate one variable and solve for the other variable.

$$16x + 24y = 1360$$
$$\underline{-9x - 24y = {}^-1080}$$
$$7x = 280$$
$$x = 40 \leftarrow \text{the price of a dress was \$40}$$

solving for y, $y = 30$ ← the price of a pair of shoes, $30

Example: Aardvark Taxi charges $4 initially plus $1 for every mile traveled. Baboon Taxi charges $6 initially plus $.75 for every mile traveled. Determine when it is cheaper to ride with Aardvark Taxi or to ride with Baboon Taxi.

Aardvark Taxi's equation: $y = 1x + 4$
Baboon Taxi's equation: $y = .75x + 6$
Using substitution: $.75x + 6 = x + 4$
Multiplying by 4: $3x + 24 = 4x + 16$
Solving for x: $8 = x$

This tells you that at 8 miles the total charge for the 2 companies is the same. If you compare the charge for 1 mile, Aardvark charges $5 and Baboon charges $6.75. Clearly Aardvark is cheaper for distances up to 8 miles, but Baboon Taxi is cheaper for distances greater than 8 miles.

This problem can also be solved by graphing the 2 equations.
$y = 1x + 4$ $y = .75x + 6$

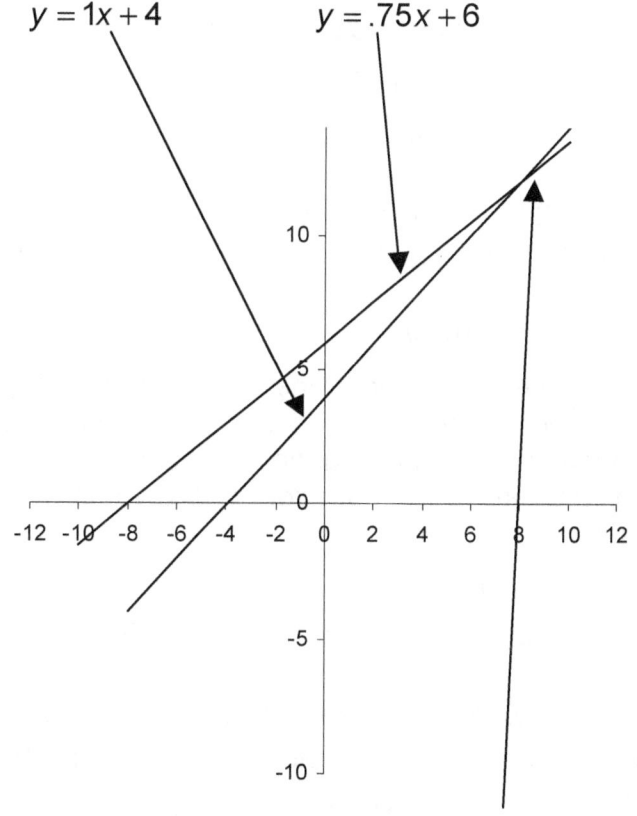

The lines intersect at (8, 12), therefore at 8 miles both companies charge $12. At values less than 8 miles, Aardvark Taxi charges less (the graph is below Baboon). Greater than 8 miles, Aardvark charges more (the graph is above Baboon).

Example: Farmer Greenjeans bought 4 cows and 6 sheep for $1700. Mr. Ziffel bought 3 cows and 12 sheep for $2400. If all the cows were the same price and all the sheep were another price, find the price charged for a cow or for a sheep.

Let x = price of a cow
Let y = price of a sheep

Then Farmer Greenjeans' equation would be: $4x + 6y = 1700$

Mr. Ziffel's equation would be: $3x + 12y = 2400$

To solve by **addition-subtraction**:

Multiply the first equation by $^-2$: $^-2(4x + 6y = 1700)$
Keep the other equation the same: $(3x + 12y = 2400)$
By doing this, the equations can be added to each other to eliminate one variable and solve for the other variable.

$$^-8x - 12y = ^-3400$$
$$3x + 12y = 2400 \quad \text{Add these equations.}$$
$$^-5x = ^-1000$$

$x = 200 \leftarrow$ the price of a cow was $200.
Solving for y, $y = 150 \leftarrow$ the price of a sheep, $150.

To solve by **substitution**:

Solve one of the equations for a variable. (Try to make an equation without fractions if possible.) Substitute this expression into the equation that you have not yet used. Solve the resulting equation for the value of the remaining variable.

$$4x + 6y = 1700$$
$$3x + 12y = 2400 \leftarrow \text{Solve this equation for } x.$$

It becomes $x = 800 - 4y$. Now substitute $800 - 4y$ in place of x in the OTHER equation. $4x + 6y = 1700$ now becomes:

$$4(800 - 4y) + 6y = 1700$$
$$3200 - 16y + 6y = 1700$$
$$3200 - 10y = 1700$$
$$^-10y = ^-1500$$
$$y = 150, \text{ or } \$150 \text{ for a sheep.}$$

Substituting 150 back into an equation for y, find x.

$$4x + 6(150) = 1700$$
$$4x + 900 = 1700$$
$$4x = 800 \text{ so } x = 200 \text{ for a cow.}$$

To solve by **determinants**:

Let x = price of a cow
Let y = price of a sheep

Then Farmer Greenjeans' equation would be:

$$4x + 6y = 1700$$
Mr. Ziffel's equation would be: $\quad 3x + 12y = 2400$

To solve this system using determinants, make one 2 by 2 determinant divided by another 2 by 2 determinant. The bottom determinant is filled with the x and y term coefficients. The top determinant is almost the same as this bottom determinant. The only difference is that when you are solving for x, the x coefficients are replaced with the constants. Likewise, when you are solving for y, the y coefficients are replaced with the constants. To find the value of a 2 by 2 determinant, $\begin{pmatrix} a & b \\ c & d \end{pmatrix}$, is found by $ad - bc$.

$$x = \frac{\begin{pmatrix} 1700 & 6 \\ 2400 & 12 \end{pmatrix}}{\begin{pmatrix} 4 & 6 \\ 3 & 12 \end{pmatrix}} = \frac{1700(12) - 6(2400)}{4(12) - 6(3)} = \frac{20400 - 14400}{48 - 18} = \frac{6000}{30} = 200$$

$$y = \frac{\begin{pmatrix} 4 & 1700 \\ 3 & 2400 \end{pmatrix}}{\begin{pmatrix} 4 & 6 \\ 3 & 12 \end{pmatrix}} = \frac{2400(4) - 3(1700)}{4(12) - 6(3)} = \frac{9600 - 5100}{48 - 18} = \frac{4500}{30} = 150$$

NOTE: The bottom determinant is always the same value for each letter.

Word problems can sometimes be solved by using a system of three equations in 3 unknowns. This system can then be solved using **substitution**, the **addition-subtraction method**, or **determinants**.

To solve by **substitution**:

Example: Mrs. Allison bought 1 pound of potato chips, a 2 pound beef roast, and 3 pounds of apples for a total of $ 8.19. Mr. Bromberg bought a 3 pound beef roast and 2 pounds of bananas for $ 9.05. Kathleen Kaufman bought 2 pounds of potato chips, a 3 pound beef roast, and 5 pounds of apples for $ 13.25. Find the per pound price of each item.

Let x = price of a pound of potato chips
Let y = price of a pound of roast beef
Let z = price of a pound of bananas

Mrs. Allison's equation would be: $1x + 2y + 3z = 8.19$
Mr. Bromberg's equation would be: $3y + 2z = 9.05$
K. Kaufman's equation would be: $2x + 3y + 5z = 13.25$

Take the first equation and solve it for x. (This was chosen because x is the easiest variable to get alone in this set of equations.) This equation would become:

$$x = 8.19 - 2y - 3z$$

Substitute this expression into the other equations in place of the letter x:

$3y + 2z = 9.05 \leftarrow$ equation 2
$2(8.19 - 2y - 3z) + 3y + 5z = 13.25 \leftarrow$ equation 3

Simplify the equation by combining like terms:

$3y + 2z = 9.05 \leftarrow$ equation 2
* $^{-}1y - 1z = ^{-}3.13 \leftarrow$ equation 3

Solve equation 3 for either y or z:

$y = 3.13 - z$ Substitute this into equation 2 for y:

$$3(3.13 - z) + 2z = 9.05 \leftarrow \text{equation 2}$$
$$^-1y - 1z = {}^-3.13 \leftarrow \text{equation 3}$$

Combine like terms in equation 2:

$$9.39 - 3z + 2z = 9.05$$
$$z = .34 \quad \text{per pound price of bananas}$$

Substitute .34 for z in the starred equation above to solve for y:

$y = 3.13 - z$ becomes $y = 3.13 - .34$, so
$y = 2.79 =$ per pound price of roast beef

Substituting .34 for z and 2.79 for y in one of the original equations, solve for x:

$1x + 2y + 3z = 8.19$
$1x + 2(2.79) + 3(.34) = 8.19$
$x + 5.58 + 1.02 = 8.19$
$x + 6.60 = 8.19$
$x = 1.59$ per pound of potato chips

$$(x, y, z) = (1.59, 2.79, .34)$$

To solve by **addition-subtraction**:

Choose a letter to eliminate. Since the second equation is already missing an x, let's eliminate x from equations 1 and 3.

1) $1x + 2y + 3x = 8.19 \leftarrow$ Multiply by $^-2$ below.
2) $3y + 2z = 9.05$
3) $2x + 3y + 5z = 13.25$

$^-2(1x + 2y + 3z = 8.19)$ $=$ $^-2x - 4y - 6z = {}^-16.38$
Keep equation 3 the same : $2x + 3y + 5z = 13.25$
$\overline{}$
$^-y - z = {}^-3.13 \leftarrow$ equation 4

By doing this, the equations can be added to each other to eliminate one variable.

The equations left to solve are equations 2 and 4:
$$^-y - z = {}^-3.13 \leftarrow \text{equation 4}$$
$$3y + 2z = 9.05 \leftarrow \text{equation 2}$$

Multiply equation 4 by 3: $3(^-y - z = {}^-3.13)$
Keep equation 2 the same: $3y + 2z = 9.05$

$$^-3y - 3z = {}^-9.39$$
$$\underline{3y + 2z = 9.05} \qquad \text{Add these equations.}$$
$$^-1z = {}^-.34$$

$z = .34 \leftarrow$ the per pound price of bananas
solving for y, $y = 2.79 \leftarrow$ the per pound roast beef price
solving for x, $x = 1.59 \leftarrow$ potato chips, per pound price

To solve by **substitution**:

Solve one of the 3 equations for a variable. (Try to make an equation without fractions if possible.) Substitute this expression into the other 2 equations that you have not yet used.

1) $1x + 2y + 3z = 8.19 \leftarrow$ Solve for x.
2) $\quad 3y + 2z = 9.05$
3) $\quad 2x + 3y + 5z = 13.25$

Equation 1 becomes $x = 8.19 - 2y - 3z$.

Substituting this into equations 2 and 3, they become:

2) $\quad 3y + 2z = 9.05$
3) $\quad 2(8.19 - 2y - 3z) + 3y + 5z = 13.25$
$\quad\quad 16.38 - 4y - 6z + 3y + 5z = 13.25$
$\quad\quad {}^-y - z = {}^-3.13$

The equations left to solve are :

$\quad 3y + 2z = 9.05$
$\quad {}^-y - z = {}^-3.13 \leftarrow$ Solve for either y or z.

It becomes $y = 3.13 - z$.

Now substitute $3.13 - z$ in place of y in the OTHER equation.

$3y + 2z = 9.05$ now becomes:

$$3(3.13 - z) + 2z = 9.05$$
$$9.39 - 3z + 2z = 9.05$$
$$9.39 - z = 9.05$$
$$-z = -.34$$
$$z = .34, \text{ or } \$.34/\text{lb of bananas}$$

Substituting .34 back into an equation for z, find y.
$$3y + 2z = 9.05$$
$$3y + 2(.34) = 9.05$$
$$3y + .68 = 9.05 \text{ so } y = 2.79/\text{lb of roast beef}$$

Substituting .34 for z and 2.79 for y into one of the original equations, it becomes:

$$2x + 3y + 5z = 13.25$$
$$2x + 3(2.79) + 5(.34) = 13.25$$
$$2x + 8.37 + 1.70 = 13.25$$
$$2x + 10.07 = 13.25, \text{ so } x = 1.59/\text{lb of potato chips}$$

To solve by **determinants**:

Let x = price of a pound of potato chips
Let y = price of a pound of roast beef
Let z = price of a pound of apples

1) $\quad 1x + 2y + 3z = 8.19$
2) $\quad\quad\quad 3y + 2z = 9.05$
3) $\quad 2x + 3y + 5z = 13.25$

To solve this system using determinants, make one 3 by 3 determinant divided by another 3 by 3 determinant. The bottom determinant is filled with the x, y, and z term coefficients. The top determinant is almost the same as this bottom determinant. The only difference is that when you are solving for x, the x coefficients are replaced with the constants. When you are solving for y, the y coefficients are replaced with the constants. Likewise, when you are solving for z, the z coefficients are replaced with the constants. To find the value of a 3 by 3 determinant,

$$\begin{pmatrix} a & b & c \\ d & e & f \\ g & h & i \end{pmatrix}$$ is found by the following steps:

Copy the first two columns to the right of the determinant:
$$\begin{pmatrix} a & b & c \\ d & e & f \\ g & h & i \end{pmatrix} \begin{matrix} a & b \\ d & e \\ g & h \end{matrix}$$

Multiply the diagonals from top left to bottom right, and add these diagonals together.

$$\begin{pmatrix} a^* & b^\circ & c^\bullet \\ d & e^* & f^\circ \\ g & h & i^* \end{pmatrix} \begin{matrix} a & b \\ d^\bullet & e \\ g^\circ & h^\bullet \end{matrix} = a^*e^*i^* + b^\circ f^\circ g^\circ + c^\bullet d^\bullet h^\bullet$$

Then multiply the diagonals from bottom left to top right, and add these diagonals together.

$$\begin{pmatrix} a & b & c^* \\ d & e^* & f^\circ \\ g^* & h^\circ & i^\bullet \end{pmatrix} \begin{matrix} a^\circ & b^\bullet \\ d^\bullet & e \\ g & h \end{matrix} = g^*e^*c^* + h^\circ f^\circ a^\circ + i^\bullet d^\bullet b^\bullet$$

Subtract the first diagonal total minus the second diagonal total:

$$(= a^*e^*i^* + b^\circ f^\circ g^\circ + c^\bullet d^\bullet h^\bullet) - (= g^*e^*c^* + h^\circ f^\circ a^\circ + i^\bullet d^\bullet b^\bullet)$$

This gives the value of the determinant. To find the value of a variable, divide the value of the top determinant by the value of the bottom determinant.

1) $1x + 2y + 3z = 8.19$
2) $3y + 2z = 9.05$
3) $2x + 3y + 5z = 13.25$

$$x = \dfrac{\begin{pmatrix} 8.19 & 2 & 3 \\ 9.05 & 3 & 2 \\ 13.25 & 3 & 5 \end{pmatrix}}{\begin{pmatrix} 1 & 2 & 3 \\ 0 & 3 & 2 \\ 2 & 3 & 5 \end{pmatrix}}$$ solve each determinant using the method shown below

Multiply the diagonals from top left to bottom right, and add these diagonals together.

$$\begin{pmatrix} 8.19^* & 2^\circ & 3^\bullet \\ 9.05 & 3^* & 2^\circ \\ 13.25 & 3 & 5^* \end{pmatrix} \begin{matrix} 8.19 & 2 \\ 9.05^\bullet & 3 \\ 13.25^\circ & 3^\bullet \end{matrix} = (8.19^*)(3^*)(5^*) + (2^\circ)(2^\circ)(13.25^\circ) + (3^\bullet)(9.05^\bullet)(3^\bullet)$$

Then multiply the diagonals from bottom left to top right, and add these diagonals together.

$$\begin{pmatrix} 8.19 & 2 & 3^* \\ 9.05 & 3^* & 2^\circ \\ 13.25^* & 3^\circ & 5^\bullet \end{pmatrix} \begin{matrix} 8.19^\circ & 2^\bullet \\ 9.05^\bullet & 3 \\ 13.25 & 3 \end{matrix}$$

$$= (13.25^*)(3^*)(3^*) + (3^\circ)(2^\circ)(8.19^\circ) + (5^\bullet)(9.05^\bullet)(2^\bullet)$$

Subtract the first diagonal total minus the second diagonal total:

$$\begin{aligned} & (8.19^*)(3^*)(5^*) + (2^\circ)(2^\circ)(13.25^\circ) + (3^\bullet)(9.05^\bullet)(3^\bullet) = 257.30 \\ - & (13.25^*)(3^*)(3^*) + (3^\circ)(2^\circ)(8.19^\circ) + (5^\bullet)(9.05^\bullet)(2^\bullet) = {}^-258.89 \\ \hline & \phantom{(13.25^*)(3^*)(3^*) + (3^\circ)(2^\circ)(8.19^\circ) + (5^\bullet)(9.05^\bullet)(2^\bullet) = {}}{}^-1.59 \end{aligned}$$

Do same multiplying and subtraction procedure for the bottom determinant to get $^-1$ as an answer. Now divide:

$$\frac{^-1.59}{^-1} = \$1.59/\text{lb of potato chips}$$

$$y = \frac{\begin{pmatrix} 1 & 8.19 & 3 \\ 0 & 9.05 & 2 \\ 2 & 13.25 & 5 \end{pmatrix}}{\begin{pmatrix} 1 & 2 & 3 \\ 0 & 3 & 2 \\ 2 & 3 & 5 \end{pmatrix}} = \frac{^-2.79}{^-1} = \$2.79/\text{lb of roast beef}$$

NOTE: The bottom determinant is always the same value for each letter.

$$z = \frac{\begin{pmatrix} 1 & 2 & 8.19 \\ 0 & 3 & 9.05 \\ 2 & 3 & 13.25 \end{pmatrix}}{\begin{pmatrix} 1 & 2 & 3 \\ 0 & 3 & 2 \\ 2 & 3 & 5 \end{pmatrix}} = \frac{^-.34}{^-1} = \$.34/\text{lb of bananas}$$

When given the following system of equations:

$$ax + by = e$$
$$cx + dy = f$$

the matrix equation is written in the form:

$$\begin{pmatrix} a & b \\ c & d \end{pmatrix} \begin{pmatrix} x \\ y \end{pmatrix} = \begin{pmatrix} e \\ f \end{pmatrix}$$

The solution is found using the inverse of the matrix of coefficients. Inverse of matrices can be written as follows:

$$A^{-1} = \frac{1}{\text{determinant of } A} \begin{pmatrix} d & -b \\ -c & a \end{pmatrix}$$

Sample Problem:
1. Write the matrix equation of the system.

$$3x - 4y = 2$$
$$2x + y = 5$$

$\begin{pmatrix} 3 & -4 \\ 2 & 1 \end{pmatrix} \begin{pmatrix} x \\ y \end{pmatrix} = \begin{pmatrix} 2 \\ 5 \end{pmatrix}$ Definition of matrix equation.

$\begin{pmatrix} x \\ y \end{pmatrix} = \frac{1}{11} \begin{pmatrix} 1 & 4 \\ -2 & 3 \end{pmatrix} \begin{pmatrix} 2 \\ 5 \end{pmatrix}$ Multiply by the inverse of the coefficient matrix.

$\begin{pmatrix} x \\ y \end{pmatrix} = \frac{1}{11} \begin{pmatrix} 22 \\ 11 \end{pmatrix}$ Matrix multiplication.

$\begin{pmatrix} x \\ y \end{pmatrix} = \begin{pmatrix} 2 \\ 1 \end{pmatrix}$ Scalar multiplication.

The solution is (2,1).

Practice problems:

1. $\begin{aligned} x + 2y &= 5 \\ 3x + 5y &= 14 \end{aligned}$

2. $\begin{aligned} -3x + 4y - z &= 3 \\ x + 2y - 3z &= 9 \\ y - 5z &= -1 \end{aligned}$

To graph an inequality, solve the inequality for y. This gets the inequality in **slope intercept form**, (for example : $y < mx + b$). The point (0,b) is the y-intercept and m is the line's slope.

- If the inequality solves to $x \geq$ **any number**, then the graph includes a **vertical line**.

- If the inequality solves to $y \leq$ **any number**, then the graph includes a **horizontal line**.

- When graphing a linear inequality, the line will be dotted if the inequality sign is $<$ or $>$. If the inequality signs are either $\geq$ or $\leq$, the line on the graph will be a solid line. Shade above the line when the inequality sign is $\geq$ or $>$. Shade below the line when the inequality sign is $<$ or $\leq$. For inequalities of the forms $x >$ number, $x \leq$ number, $x <$ number, or $x \geq$ number, draw a vertical line (solid or dotted). Shade to the right for $>$ or $\geq$. Shade to the left for $<$ or $\leq$.

> Remember: **Dividing or multiplying by a negative number will reverse the direction of the inequality sign.**

Use these rules to graph and shade each inequality. The solution to a system of linear inequalities consists of the part of the graph that is shaded for each inequality. For instance, if the graph of one inequality was shaded with red, and the graph of another inequality was shaded with blue, then the overlapping area would be shaded purple. The purple area would be the points in the solution set of this system.

Example: Solve by graphing:

$$x + y \leq 6$$
$$x - 2y \leq 6$$

Solving the inequalities for y, they become:

$y \leq {}^-x + 6$ (y intercept of 6 and slope = $^-1$)
$y \geq 1/2 x - 3$ (y intercept of $^-3$ and slope = $1/2$)

A graph with shading is shown below:

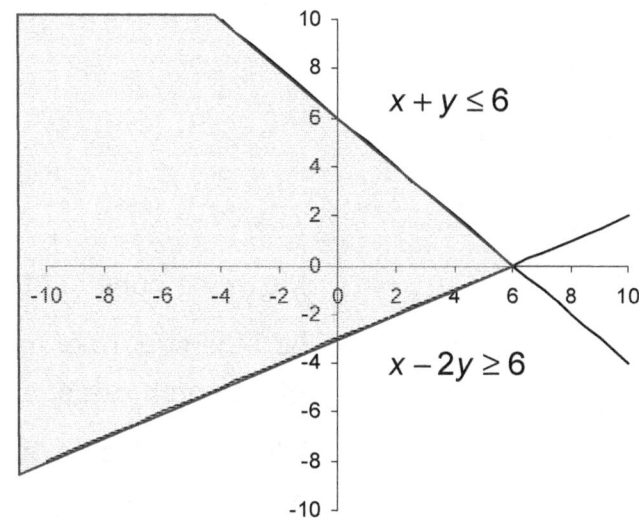

A **quadratic equation** is written in the form $ax^2 + bx + c = 0$. To solve a quadratic equation by factoring, at least one of the factors must equal zero.

Example:
Solve the equation.

$x^2 + 10x - 24 = 0$
$(x + 12)(x - 2) = 0$ Factor.
$x + 12 = 0$ or $x - 2 = 0$ Set each factor equal to 0.
$x = {}^-12$ $x = 2$ Solve.

Check:
$x^2 + 10x - 24 = 0$
$({}^-12)^2 + 10({}^-12) - 24 = 0$ $(2)^2 + 10(2) - 24 = 0$
$144 - 120 - 24 = 0$ $4 + 20 - 24 = 0$
$0 = 0$ $0 = 0$

A quadratic equation that cannot be solved by factoring can be solved by **completing the square**.

Example:

Solve the equation.

$x^2 - 6x + 8 = 0$	
$x^2 - 6x = {}^-8$	Move the constant to the right side.
$x^2 - 6x + 9 = {}^-8 + 9$	Add the square of half the coefficient of x to both sides.
$(x - 3)^2 = 1$	Write the left side as a perfect square.
$x - 3 = \pm\sqrt{1}$	Take the square root of both sides.
$x - 3 = 1 \quad x - 3 = {}^-1$	Solve.
$x = 4 \quad\quad x = 2$	

Check:

$x^2 - 6x + 8 = 0$

$4^2 - 6(4) + 8 = 0 \quad\quad 2^2 - 6(2) + 8 = 0$

$16 - 24 + 8 = 0 \quad\quad 4 - 12 + 8 = 0$

$0 = 0 \quad\quad\quad\quad\quad 0 = 0$

The general technique for graphing quadratics is the same as for graphing linear equations. Graphing quadratic equations, however, results in a parabola instead of a straight line.

Example:

Graph $y = 3x^2 + x - 2$.

MATHEMATICS (Secondary)

x	$y = 3x^2 + x - 2$
−2	8
−1	0
0	−2
1	2
2	12

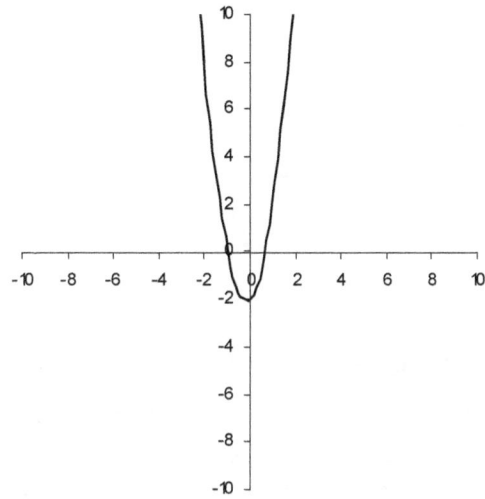

To solve a quadratic equation using the quadratic formula, be sure that your equation is in the form $ax^2 + bx + c = 0$. Substitute these values into the formula:

$$x = \frac{-b \pm \sqrt{b^2 - 4ac}}{2a}$$

(Remember, there could be 2 real answers, one real answer, or 2 complex answers that include "i").

Example:

Solve the equation.

$$3x^2 = 7 + 2x \rightarrow 3x^2 - 2x - 7 = 0$$

$$a = 3 \quad b = {}^-2 \quad c = {}^-7$$

$$x = \frac{-({}^-2) \pm \sqrt{({}^-2)^2 - 4(3)({}^-7)}}{2(3)}$$

$$x = \frac{2 \pm \sqrt{4 + 84}}{6}$$

$$x = \frac{2 \pm \sqrt{88}}{6}$$

$$x = \frac{2 \pm 2\sqrt{22}}{6}$$

$$x = \frac{1 \pm \sqrt{22}}{3}$$

To solve a quadratic inequality (with x^2), solve for y. The axis of symmetry is located at $x = {}^-b/2a$. Find coordinates of points to each side of the axis of symmetry. Graph the parabola as a dotted line if the inequality sign is either $<$ or $>$. Graph the parabola as a solid line if the inequality sign is either $\leq$ or $\geq$. Shade above the parabola if the sign is $\geq$ or $>$. Shade below the parabola if the sign is $\leq$ or $<$.

Example: Solve: $8x^2 - 10x - 3 = 0$

In this equation $a = 8$, $b = {}^-10$, and $c = {}^-3$.
Substituting these into the quadratic equation, it becomes:

$$x = \frac{{}^-({}^-10) \pm \sqrt{({}^-10)^2 - 4(8)({}^-3)}}{2(8)} = \frac{10 \pm \sqrt{100 + 96}}{16}$$

$$x = \frac{10 \pm \sqrt{196}}{16} = \frac{10 \pm 14}{16} = 24/16 = 3/2 \text{ or } {}^-4/16 = {}^-1/4$$

Check:

$$x = -\frac{1}{4}$$

$$\frac{1}{2} + \frac{10}{4} - 3 = 0 \qquad \text{Both Check}$$

$$3 - 3 = 0$$

Example: Solve and graph: $y > x^2 + 4x - 5$.

The axis of symmetry is located at $x = {}^-b/2a$. Substituting 4 for b, and 1 for a, this formula becomes:

$$x = {}^-(4)/2(1) = {}^-4/2 = {}^-2$$

Find coordinates of points to each side of $x = {}^-2$.

x	y
$^-5$	0
$^-4$	$^-5$
$^-3$	$^-8$
$^-2$	$^-9$
$^-1$	$^-8$
0	$^-5$
1	0

Graph these points to form a parabola. Draw it as a dotted line. Since a greater than sign is used, shade above and inside the parabola.

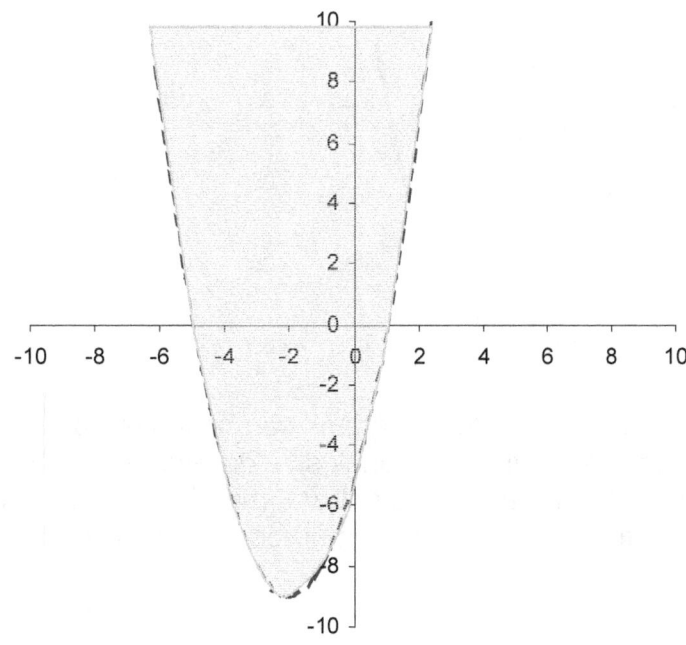

To graph an inequality, graph the quadratic as if it was an equation; however, if the inequality has just a > or < sign, then make the curve itself dotted. Shade above the curve for > or ≥. Shade below the curve for < or ≤.

Examples:

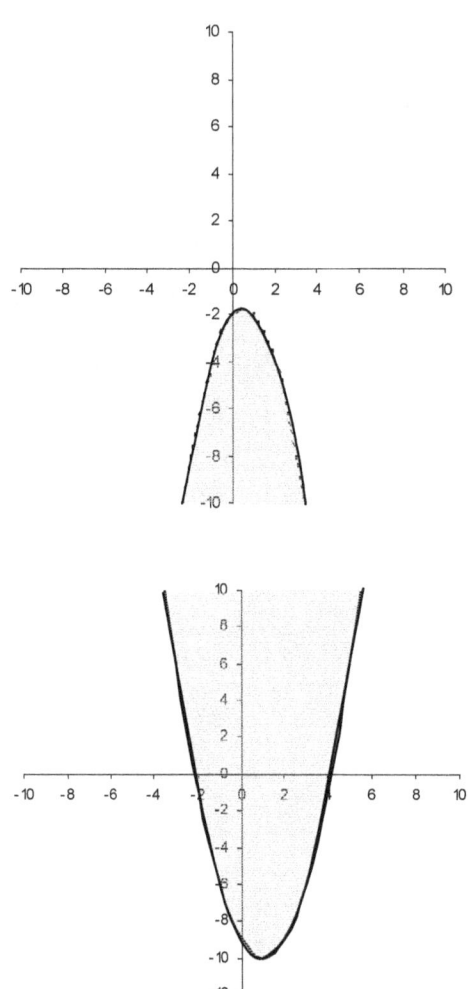

Systems of quadratic equations can be solved by graphing but this method is sometimes inconclusive depending on the accuracy of the graphs and can also be cumbersome. It is recommended that either a substitution or elimination method be considered.

Sample problems:

Find the solution to the system of equations.

1. $y^2 - x^2 = {}^-9$
   $2y = x - 3$

   1. Use substitution method solving the second equation for x.

   $2y = x - 3$
   $x = 2y + 3$

   2. Substitute this into the first equation in place of (x).

   $y^2 - (2y + 3)^2 = {}^-9$
   $y^2 - (4y^2 + 12y + 9) = {}^-9$
   $y^2 - 4y^2 - 12y - 9 = {}^-9$
   ${}^-3y^2 - 12y - 9 = {}^-9$
   ${}^-3y^2 - 12y = 0$

   3. Solve.

   4. Factor.

   ${}^-3y(y + 4) = 0$

   ${}^-3y = 0 \qquad y + 4 = 0$
   $y = 0 \qquad\quad y = {}^-4$

   5. Set each factor equal to zero.
   6. Use these values for y to solve for x.

   $2y = x - 3 \qquad 2y = x - 3$
   $2(0) = x - 3 \qquad 2({}^-4) = x - 3$
   $0 = x - 3 \qquad\quad {}^-8 = x - 3$
   $x = 3 \qquad\qquad x = {}^-5$

   7. Choose an equation.
   8. Substitute.
   9. Write ordered pairs.

   (3,0) and (${}^-5, {}^-4$) satisfy the system of equations given.

2. ${}^-9x^2 + y^2 = 16$
   $5x^2 + y^2 = 30$

   Use elimination to solve.

   ${}^-9x^2 + y^2 = 16$
   ${}^-5x^2 - y^2 = {}^-30$
   _____
   ${}^-14x^2 = {}^-14$
   $x^2 = 1$
   $x = \pm 1$

   1. Multiply second row by ${}^-1$.
   2. Add.
   3. Divide by ${}^-14$.
   4. Take the square root of both sides

MATHEMATICS (Secondary)

$-9(1)+y^2=16$	$-9(-1)+y^2=16$	5. Substitute both values of x into the equation.
$^-9+y^2=16$	$^-9+y^2=16$	
$y^2=25$	$y^2=25$	6. Take the square root of both sides.
$y=\pm 5$	$y=\pm 5$	
$(1,\pm 5)$	$(^-1,\pm 5)$	7. Write the ordered pairs.

$(1,\pm 5)$ and $(-1,\pm 5)$ Satisfy the system of equations

Quadratic equations can be used to model different real life situations. The graphs of these quadratics can be used to determine information about this real life situation.

Example:
The height of a projectile fired upward at a velocity of v meters per second from an original height of h meters is $y = h + vx - 4.9x^2$. If a rocket is fired from an original height of 250 meters with an original velocity of 4800 meters per second, find the approximate time the rocket would drop to sea level (a height of 0).

Solution:

The equation for this problem is: $y = 250 + 4800x - 4.9x^2$. If the height at sea level is zero, then $y = 0$ so $0 = 250 + 4800x - 4.9x^2$. Solving this for x could be done by using the quadratic formula. In addition, the approximate time in x seconds until the rocket would be at sea level could be estimated by looking at the graph. When the y value of the graph goes from positive to negative then there is a root (also called the solution or x intercept) in that interval.

$$x = \frac{^-4800 \pm \sqrt{4800^2 - 4(^-4.9)(250)}}{2(^-4.9)} \approx 980 \text{ or } ^-0.05 \text{ seconds}$$

Since the time has to be positive, it will be about 980 seconds until the rocket is at sea level.

Some word problems will give a quadratic equation to be solved. When the quadratic equation is found, set it equal to zero and solve the equation by factoring or the quadratic formula. Examples of this type of problem follow.

Example:
Alberta (A) is a certain distance north of Boston (B). The distance from Boston east to Carlisle (C) is 5 miles more than the distance from Alberta to Boston. The distance from Alberta to Carlisle is 10 miles more than the distance from Alberta to Boston. How far is Alberta from Carlisle?

Solution:
Since north and east form a right angle, these distances are the lengths of the legs of a right triangle. If the distance from Alberta to Boston is x, then from Boston to Carlisle is $x+5$, and the distance from Alberta to Carlisle is $x+10$.

The equation is: $AB^2 + BC^2 = AC^2$
$x^2 + (x+5)^2 = (x+10)^2$
$x^2 + x^2 + 10x + 25 = x^2 + 20x + 100$
$2x^2 + 10x + 25 = x^2 + 20x + 100$
$x^2 - 10x - 75 = 0$
$(x-15)(x+5) = 0$ Distance cannot be negative.
$x = 15$ Distance from Alberta to Boston.
$x + 5 = 20$ Distance from Boston to Carlisle.
$x + 10 = 25$ Distance from Alberta to Carlisle.

Example:
The square of a number is equal to 6 more than the original number. Find the original number.

Solution: If $x =$ original number, then the equation is:
$x^2 = 6 + x$ Set this equal to zero.
$x^2 - x - 6 = 0$ Now factor.
$(x-3)(x+2) = 0$
$x = 3$ or $x = {}^-2$ There are 2 solutions, 3 or $^-2$.

Try these:

1. One side of a right triangle is 1 less than twice the shortest side, while the third side of the triangle is 1 more than twice the shortest side. Find all 3 sides.

2. Twice the square of a number equals 2 less than 5 times the number. Find the number(s).

Example:

A family wants to enclose 3 sides of a rectangular garden with 200 feet of fence. In order to have a garden with an area of **at least** 4800 square feet, find the dimensions of the garden. Assume that the fourth side of the garden is already bordered by a wall or a fence.

Solution:
Let x = distance from the wall

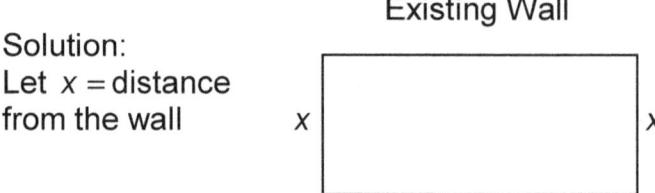

Then $2x$ feet of fence is used for these 2 sides. The remaining side of the garden would use the rest of the 200 feet of fence, that is, $200-2x$ feet of fence. Therefore the width of the garden is x feet and the length is $200-2x$ ft.

The area, $200x - 2x^2$, needs to be greater than or equal to 4800 sq. ft. So, this problem uses the inequality $4800 \leq 200x - 2x^2$. This becomes $2x^2 - 200x + 4800 \leq 0$. Solving this, we get:

$$200x - 2x^2 \geq 4800$$
$$-2x^2 + 200x - 4800 \geq 0$$
$$2(-x^2 + 100x - 2400) \geq 0$$
$$-x^2 + 100x - 2400 \geq 0$$
$$(-x + 60)(x - 40) \geq 0$$
$$-x + 60 \geq 0$$
$$-x \geq -60$$
$$x \leq 60$$
$$x - 40 \geq 0$$
$$x \geq 40$$

So the area will be at least 4800 square feet if the width of the garden is from 40 up to 60 feet.

Competency 8   Understand properties and applications of polynomial, rational, radical, exponential, logarithmic, and trigonometric functions, and solve related equations and inequalities.

There are 2 easy ways to find the values of a function. First to find the value of a function when $x = 3$, substitute 3 in place of every letter x. Then simplify the expression following the order of operations. For example, if $f(x) = x^3 - 6x + 4$, then to find f(3), substitute 3 for x.

The equation becomes $f(3) = 3^3 - 6(3) + 4 = 27 - 18 + 4 = 13$.
So (3, 13) is a point on the graph of f(x).

A second way to find the value of a function is to use synthetic division. To find the value of a function when $x = 3$, divide 3 into the coefficients of the function. (Remember that coefficients of missing terms, like x^2, must be included). The remainder is the value of the function.

If $f(x) = x^3 - 6x + 4$, then to find f(3) using synthetic division:

Note the 0 for the missing x^2 term.

$$
\begin{array}{r|rrrr}
3 & 1 & 0 & ^-6 & 4 \\
  &   & 3 & 9 & 9 \\
\hline
  & 1 & 3 & 3 & 13
\end{array}
$$
← this is the value of the function.

Therefore, (3, 13) is a point on the graph of $f(x) = x^3 - 6x + 4$.

<u>Example</u>: Find values of the function at integer values from $x = -3$ to $x = 3$ if $f(x) = x^3 - 6x + 4$.

If $x = {^-}3$:

$$f(^-3) = (^-3)^3 - 6(^-3) + 4$$
$$= (^-27) - 6(^-3) + 4$$
$$= {^-}27 + 18 + 4 = {^-}5$$

synthetic division:

$$\begin{array}{r|rrrr} -3 & 1 & 0 & -6 & 4 \\ & & -3 & 9 & -9 \\ \hline & 1 & -3 & 3 & -5 \end{array}$$ ← this is the value of the function if $x = -3$.

Therefore, $(-3, -5)$ is a point on the graph.

If $x = -2$:

$$f(-2) = (-2)^3 - 6(-2) + 4$$
$$= (-8) - 6(-2) + 4$$
$$= -8 + 12 + 4 = 8$$ ← this is the value of the function if $x = -2$.

Therefore, $(-2, 8)$ is a point on the graph.

If $x = -1$:

$$f(-1) = (-1)^3 - 6(-1) + 4$$
$$= (-1) - 6(-1) + 4$$
$$= -1 + 6 + 4 = 9$$

synthetic division:

$$\begin{array}{r|rrrr} -1 & 1 & 0 & -6 & 4 \\ & & -1 & 1 & 5 \\ \hline & 1 & -1 & -5 & 9 \end{array}$$ ← this is the value if the function if $x = -1$.

Therefore, $(-1, 9)$ is a point on the graph.

If $x = 0$:

$$f(0) = (0)^3 - 6(0) + 4$$
$$= 0 - 6(0) + 4$$
$$= 0 - 0 + 4 = 4$$ ← this is the value of the function if $x = 0$.

Therefore, $(0, 4)$ is a point on the graph.

If $x = 1$:

$$f(1) = (1)^3 - 6(1) + 4$$
$$= (1) - 6(1) + 4$$
$$= 1 - 6 + 4 = -1$$

synthetic division:

$$\begin{array}{r|rrr} 1 & 1 & 0 & ^-6 & 4 \\ & & 1 & 1 & ^-5 \\ \hline & 1 & 1 & ^-5 & ^-1 \end{array}$$ ← this is the value if the function of $x = 1$.
Therefore, $(1, ^-1)$ is a point on the graph.

If $x = 2$:

$$f(2) = (2)^3 - 6(2) + 4$$
$$= 8 - 6(2) + 4$$
$$= 8 - 12 + 4 = 0$$

synthetic division:

$$\begin{array}{r|rrr} 2 & 1 & 0 & ^-6 & 4 \\ & & 2 & 4 & ^-4 \\ \hline & 1 & 2 & ^-2 & 0 \end{array}$$ ← this is the value of the function if $x = 2$.
Therefore, $(2, 0)$ is a point on the graph.

If $x = 3$:

$$f(3) = (3)^3 - 6(3) + 4$$
$$= 27 - 6(3) + 4$$
$$= 27 - 18 + 4 = 13$$

synthetic division:

$$\begin{array}{r|rrr} 3 & 1 & 0 & ^-6 & 4 \\ & & 3 & 9 & 9 \\ \hline & 1 & 3 & 3 & 13 \end{array}$$ ← this is the value of the function if $x = 3$.
Therefore, $(3, 13)$ is a point on the graph.

The following points are points on the graph:

X	Y
⁻3	⁻5
⁻2	8
⁻1	9
0	4
1	⁻1
2	0
3	13

Note the change in sign of the y value between $x = {}^-3$ and $x = {}^-2$. This indicates there is a zero between $x = {}^-3$ and $x = {}^-2$. Since there is another change in sign of the y value between $x = 0$ and $x = {}^-1$, there is a second root there. When $x = 2$, $y = 0$ so $x = 2$ is an exact root of this polynomial.

Rational expressions can be changed into other equivalent fractions by either reducing them or by changing them to have a common denominator. When dividing any number of terms by a single term, divide or reduce their coefficients. Then subtract the exponent of a variable on the bottom from the exponent of the same variable from the numerator.

To reduce a rational expression with more than one term in the denominator, the expression must be factored first. Factors that are exactly the same will cancel and each become a 1. Factors that have exactly the opposite signs of each other, such as $(a-b)$ and $(b-a)$, will cancel and one factor becomes a 1 and the other becomes a ⁻1.

To make a fraction have a common denominator, factor the fraction. Determine what factors are missing from that particular denominator, and multiply both the numerator and the denominator by those missing factors. This gives a new fraction which now has the common denominator.

Examples:

1. $\dfrac{24x^3y^6z^3}{8x^2y^2z} = 3xy^4z^2$

2. $\dfrac{3x^2 - 14xy - 5y^2}{x^2 - 25y^2} = \dfrac{(3x+y)(x-5y)}{(x+5y)(x-5y)} = \dfrac{3x+y}{x+5y}$

3. Re-write this fraction with a denominator of $(x+3)(x-5)(x+4)$.

$\dfrac{x+2}{x^2+7x+12} = \dfrac{x+2}{(x+3)(x+4)} = \dfrac{(x+2)(x-5)}{(x+3)(x+4)(x-5)}$

Try these:

1. $\dfrac{72x^4y^9z^{10}}{8x^3y^9z^5}$

2. $\dfrac{3x^2 - 13xy - 10y^2}{x^3 - 125y^3}$

3. Re-write this fraction with a denominator of $(x+2)(x+3)(x-7)$.
$$\dfrac{x+5}{x^2-5x-14}$$

An expression with a **radical sign** can be rewritten using a rational exponent. The radicand becomes the base which will have the rational exponent. The index number on the front of the radical sign becomes the denominator of the rational exponent. The numerator of the rational exponent is the exponent which was originally inside the radical sign on the original base. Note: If no index number appears on the front of the radical, then it is a 2. If no exponent appears inside the radical, then use a 1 as the numerator of the rational exponent.

$$\sqrt[5]{b^3} = b^{3/5}$$
$$\sqrt[4]{ab^3} = a^{1/4}b^{3/4}$$

When an expression has a rational exponent, it can be rewritten using a radical sign. The denominator of the rational exponent becomes the index number on the front of the radical sign. The base of the original expression goes inside the radical sign. The numerator of the rational exponent is an exponent which can be placed either inside the radical sign on the original base or outside the radical as an exponent on the radical expression.

$$a^{2/9}b^{4/9}c^{8/9} = \sqrt[9]{a^2b^4c^8}$$
$$3^{1/5} = \sqrt[5]{3}$$

If an expression contains rational expressions with different denominators, rewrite the exponents with a common denominator and then change the problem into a radical.

$$a^{2/3}b^{1/2}c^{3/5} = a^{20/30}b^{15/30}c^{18/30} = \sqrt[30]{a^{20}b^{15}c^{18}}$$

Trigonometric Functions

It is easiest to graph trigonometric functions when using a calculator by making a table of values.

DEGREES

	0	30	45	60	90	120	135	150	180	210	225	240	270	300	315	330	360
sin	0	.5	.71	.87	1	.87	.71	.5	0	-.5	-.71	-.87	-1	-.87	-.71	-.5	0
cos	1	.87	.71	.5	0	-.5	-.71	-.87	-1	-.87	-.71	-.5	0	.5	.71	.87	1
tan	0	.58	1	1.7	--	-1.7	-1	-.58	0	.58	1	1.7	--	-1.7	-1	-.58	0
	0	$\frac{\pi}{6}$	$\frac{\pi}{4}$	$\frac{\pi}{3}$	$\frac{\pi}{2}$	$\frac{2\pi}{3}$	$\frac{3\pi}{4}$	$\frac{5\pi}{6}$	π	$\frac{7\pi}{6}$	$\frac{5\pi}{4}$	$\frac{4\pi}{3}$	$\frac{3\pi}{2}$	$\frac{5\pi}{3}$	$\frac{7\pi}{4}$	$\frac{11\pi}{6}$	2π

RADIANS

Remember the graph always ranges from +1 to ⁻1 for sine and cosine functions unless noted as the coefficient of the function in the equation. For example, $y = 3\cos x$ has an amplitude of 3 units from the center line (0). Its maximum and minimum points would be at +3 and ⁻3.

Tangent is not defined at the values 90 and 270 degrees or $\frac{\pi}{2}$ and $\frac{3\pi}{2}$. Therefore, vertical asymptotes are drawn at those values.

The inverse functions can be graphed in the same manner using a calculator to create a table of values.

Rational Functions

- Some problems can be solved using equations with rational expressions. First write the equation. To solve it, multiply each term by the LCD of all fractions. This will cancel out all of the denominators and give an equivalent algebraic equation that can be solved.

1. The denominator of a fraction is two less than three times the numerator. If 3 is added to both the numerator and denominator, the new fraction equals 1/2.

original fraction: $\dfrac{x}{3x-2}$ revised fraction: $\dfrac{x+3}{3x+1}$

$$\dfrac{x+3}{3x+1} = \dfrac{1}{2}$$

$$2x + 6 = 3x + 1$$

$$x = 5$$

original fraction: $\dfrac{5}{13}$

2. Elly Mae can feed the animals in 15 minutes. Jethro can feed them in 10 minutes. How long will it take them if they work together?

Solution: If Elly Mae can feed the animals in 15 minutes, then she could feed 1/15 of them in 1 minute, 2/15 of them in 2 minutes, $x/15$ of them in x minutes. In the same fashion Jethro could feed $x/10$ of them in x minutes. Together they complete 1 job. The equation is:

$$\dfrac{x}{15} + \dfrac{x}{10} = 1$$

Multiply each term by the LCD of 30:

$$2x + 3x = 30$$
$$x = 6 \text{ minutes}$$

3. A salesman drove 480 miles from Pittsburgh to Hartford. The next day he returned the same distance to Pittsburgh in half an hour less time than his original trip took, because he increased his average speed by 4 mph. Find his original speed.

Since distance = rate x time then time = $\frac{distance}{rate}$

original time – 1/2 hour = shorter return time

$$\frac{480}{x} - \frac{1}{2} = \frac{480}{x+4}$$

Multiplying by the LCD of $2x(x+4)$, the equation becomes:

$$480[2(x+4)] - 1[x(x+4)] = 480(2x)$$
$$960x + 3840 - x^2 - 4x = 960x$$
$$x^2 + 4x - 3840 = 0$$
$$(x+64)(x-60) = 0 \quad \text{Either (x-60=0) or (x+64=0) or both=0}$$
$$x = 60 \quad\quad\quad\quad\quad 60 \text{ mph is the original speed.}$$

This is the solution since the time cannot be negative. Check your answer

$$x + 4 = 64$$
$$\frac{480}{60} - \frac{1}{2} = \frac{480}{64}$$
$$8 - \frac{1}{2} = 7\frac{1}{2}$$
$$7\frac{1}{2} = 7\frac{1}{2}$$

Try these:

1. Working together, Larry, Moe, and Curly can paint an elephant in 3 minutes. Working alone, it would take Larry 10 minutes or Moe 6 minutes to paint the elephant. How long would it take Curly to paint the elephant if he worked alone?

2. The denominator of a fraction is 5 more than twice the numerator. If the numerator is doubled, and the denominator is increased by 5, the new fraction is equal to 1/2. Find the original number.

3. A trip from Augusta, Maine to Galveston, Texas is 2108 miles. If one car drove 6 mph faster than a truck and got to Galveston 3 hours before the truck, find the speeds of the car and truck.

Polynomials - Factoring

- To factor the sum or the difference of perfect cubes, follow this procedure:

a. Factor out any greatest common factor (GCF).

b. Make a parentheses for a binomial (2 terms) followed by a trinomial (3 terms).

c. The sign in the first parentheses is the same as the sign in the problem. The difference of cubes will have a "-" sign in the first parentheses. The sum of cubes will use a "+".

d. The first sign in the second parentheses is the opposite of the sign in the first parentheses. The second sign in the other parentheses is always a "+".

e. Determine what would be cubed to equal each term of the problem. Put those expressions in the first parentheses.

f. To make the 3 terms of the trinomial, think square - product - square. Looking at the binomial, square the first term. This is the trinomial's first term. Looking at the binomial, find the product of the two terms, ignoring the signs. This is the trinomial's second term. Looking at the binomial, square the third term. This is the trinomial's third term. Except in rare instances, the trinomial does not factor again.

Example Problems:

1.

$16x^3 + 54y^3$

$2(8x^3 + 27y^3)$ ← GCF

$2(\ +\ )(\ -\ +\ )$ ← signs

$2(2x+3y)(\ -\ +\ )$ ← what is cubed to equal $8x^3$ or $27y^3$

$2(2x+3y)(4x^2 - 6xy + 9y^2)$ ← square-product-square

2.

$64a^3 - 125b^3$

$(\ -\ )(\ +\ +\ )$ ← signs

$(4a-5b)(\ +\ +\ )$ ← what is cubed to equal $64a^3$ or $125b^3$

$(4a-5b)(16a^2 + 20ab + 25b^2)$ ← square-product-square

3.

$27x^{27} + 343y^{12} = (3x^9 + 7y^4)(9x^{18} - 21x^9y^4 + 49y^8)$

Note: The coefficient 27 is different from the exponent 27.

Try These:

1. $216x^3 - 125y^3$
2. $4a^3 - 32b^3$
3. $40x^{29} + 135x^2y^3$

- To factor a polynomial, follow these steps:

a. **Factor out any GCF** (greatest common factor)

b. For a binomial (2 terms), check to see if the problem is the **difference of perfect squares**. If both factors are perfect squares, then it factors this way:

$$a^2 - b^2 = (a-b)(a+b)$$

If the problem is not the difference of perfect squares, then check to see if the problem is either the sum or difference of perfect cubes.

$$x^3 - 8y^3 = (x-2y)(x^2 + 2xy + 4y^2) \quad \leftarrow \text{difference}$$

$$64a^3 + 27b^3 = (4a+3b)(16a^2 - 12ab + 9b^2) \quad \leftarrow \text{sum}$$

** The sum of perfect squares does NOT factor.

c. Trinomials could be perfect squares. Trinomials can be factored into 2 binomials (un-FOILing). Be sure the terms of the trinomial are in descending order. If last sign of the trinomial is a "+", then the signs in the parentheses will be the same as the sign in front of the second term of the trinomial. If the last sign of the trinomial is a "-", then there will be one "+" and one "-" in the two parentheses. The first term of the trinomial can be factored to equal the first terms of the two factors. The last term of the trinomial can be factored to equal the last terms of the two factors. Work backwards to determine the correct factors to multiply together to get the correct center term.

Examples:

1. $4x^2 - 25y^2$
2. $6b^2 - 2b - 8$
3. Find a factor of $6x^2 - 5x - 4$
   a. $(3x+2)$ b. $(3x-2)$ c. $(6x-1)$ d. $(2x+1)$

Answers:

1. No GCF; this is the difference of perfect squares.

$$4x^2 - 25y^2 = (2x - 5y)(2x + 5y)$$

1. GCF of 2; Try to factor into 2 binomials:

$$6b^2 - 2b - 8 = 2(3b^2 - b - 4)$$

Signs are one "+", one "−". $3b^2$ factors into $3b$ and b. Find factors of 4: 1 & 4; 2 & 2.

$$6b^2 - 2b - 8 = 2(3b^2 - b - 4) = 2(3b - 4)(b + 1)$$

3. If an answer choice is correct, find the other factor:

a. $(3x+2)(2x-2) = 6x^2 - 2x - 4$
b. $(3x-2)(2x+2) = 6x^2 + 2x - 4$
c. $(6x-1)(x+4) = 6x^2 + 23x - 4$
d. $(2x+1)(3x-4) = 6x^2 - 5x - 4$ ← correct factors

MATHEMATICS (Secondary)

- In order to add or subtract **rational expressions**, they must have a common denominator. If they don't have a common denominator, then factor the denominators to determine what factors are missing from each denominator to make the LCD. Multiply both numerator and denominator by the missing factor(s). Once the fractions have a common denominator, add or subtract their numerators, but keep the common denominator the same. Factor the numerator if possible and reduce if there are any factors that can be cancelled.

1. Find the least common denominator for $6a^3b^2$ and $4ab^3$.

These factor into $2 \cdot 3 \cdot a^3 \cdot b^2$ and $2 \cdot 2 \cdot a \cdot b^3$.
The first expression needs to be multiplied by another 2 and b.
The other expression needs to be multiplied by 3 and a^2.
Then both expressions would be $2 \cdot 2 \cdot 3 \cdot a^3 \cdot b^3 = 12a^3b^3 = $ LCD.

2. Find the LCD for $x^2 - 4$, $x^2 + 5x + 6$, and $x^2 + x - 6$.

$x^2 - 4$ factors into $(x-2)(x+2)$
$x^2 + 5x + 6$ factors into $(x+3)(x+2)$
$x^2 + x - 6$ factors into $(x+3)(x-2)$

To make these lists of factors the same, they must all be $(x+3)(x+2)(x-2)$. This is the LCD.

3.
$$\frac{5}{6a^3b^2} + \frac{1}{4ab^3} = \frac{5(2a)}{6a^3b^2(2a)} + \frac{1(3b^2)}{4ab^3(3b^2)} = \frac{10b}{12a^3b^3} + \frac{3a^2}{12a^3b^3} = \frac{10b + 3a^2}{12a^3b^3}$$

This will not reduce as all 3 terms are not divisible by anything.

4.

$$\frac{2}{x^2-4} - \frac{3}{x^2+5x+6} + \frac{7}{x^2+x-6} =$$

$$\frac{2}{(x-2)(x+2)} - \frac{3}{(x+3)(x+2)} + \frac{7}{(x+3)(x-2)} =$$

$$\frac{2(x+3)}{(x-2)(x+2)(x+3)} - \frac{3(x-2)}{(x+3)(x+2)(x-2)} + \frac{7(x+2)}{(x+3)(x-2)(x+2)} =$$

$$\frac{2x+6}{(x-2)(x+2)(x+3)} - \frac{3x-6}{(x+3)(x+2)(x-2)} + \frac{7x+14}{(x+3)(x-2)(x+2)} =$$

$$\frac{2x+6-(3x-6)+7x+14}{(x+3)(x-2)(x+2)} = \frac{6x+26}{(x+3)(x-2)(x+2)}$$

This will not reduce.

Try These:

1. $\dfrac{6}{x-3} + \dfrac{2}{x+7}$

2. $\dfrac{5}{4a^2b^5} + \dfrac{3}{5a^4b^3}$

3. $\dfrac{x+3}{x^2-25} + \dfrac{x-6}{x^2-2x-15}$

To solve an equation with rational expressions, find the least common denominator of all the fractions. Multiply each term by the LCD of all fractions. This will cancel out all of the denominators and give an equivalent algebraic equation that can be solved. Solve the resulting equation. Once you have found the answer(s), substitute them back into the original equation to check them. Sometimes there are solutions that do not check in the original equation. These are extraneous solutions, which are not correct and must be eliminated. f a problem has more than one potential solution, each solution must be checked separately.

NOTE: What this really means is that you can substitute the answers from any multiple choice test back into the question to determine which answer choice is correct.

Solve and **check**:

1. $\dfrac{72}{x+3} = \dfrac{32}{x+3} + 5$ LCD $= x + 3$, so multiply by this.

   $(x+3) \times \dfrac{72}{x+3} = (x+3) \times \dfrac{32}{x+3} + 5(x+3)$

   $72 = 32 + 5(x+3) \rightarrow 72 = 32 + 5x + 15$

   $72 = 47 + 5x \quad \rightarrow 25 = 5x$

   $5 = x$ (This checks too).

2. $\dfrac{12}{2x^2 - 4x} + \dfrac{13}{5} = \dfrac{9}{x-2}$ Factor $2x^2 - 4x = 2x(x-2)$.

   LCD $= 5 \times 2x(x-2)$ or $10x(x-2)$

   $10x(x-2) \times \dfrac{12}{2x(x-2)} + 10x(x-2) \times \dfrac{13}{5} = \dfrac{9}{x-2} \times 10x(x-2)$

   $60 + 2x(x-2)(13) = 90x$

   $26x^2 - 142x + 60 = 0$

   $2(13x^2 - 71x + 30) = 0$

   $2(x-5)(13x-6)$ so $x = 5$ or $x = 6/13$ ← both check

Try these:

1. $\dfrac{x+5}{3x-5} + \dfrac{x-3}{2x+2} = 1$

2. $\dfrac{2x-7}{2x+5} = \dfrac{x-6}{x+8}$

MATHEMATICS (Secondary)

The conjugate of a binomial is the same expression as the original binomial with the sign between the 2 terms changed.

$$\text{The conjugate of } 3+2\sqrt{5} \text{ is } 3-2\sqrt{5}.$$
$$\text{The conjugate of } \sqrt{5}-\sqrt{7} \text{ is } \sqrt{5}+\sqrt{7}.$$
$$\text{The conjugate of } {}^-6-\sqrt{11} \text{ is } {}^-6+\sqrt{11}.$$

To multiply binomials including radicals, "FOIL" the binomials together. (that is, distribute each term of the first binomial times each term of the second binomial). Multiply what is in front of the radicals together. Multiply what is inside of the two radicals together. Check to see if any of the radicals can be simplified. Combine like terms, if possible.

When one binomial is divided by another binomial, multiply both the numerator and denominator by the conjugate of the denominator. "FOIL" or distribute one binomial through the other binomial. Simplify the radicals, if possible, and combine like terms. Reduce the resulting fraction if every term is divisible outside the radical signs by the same number.

1. $(5+\sqrt{10})(4-3\sqrt{2}) = 20 - 15\sqrt{2} + 4\sqrt{10} - 3\sqrt{20} =$
   $20 - 15\sqrt{2} + 4\sqrt{10} - 6\sqrt{5}$

2. $(\sqrt{6}+5\sqrt{2})(3\sqrt{6}-8\sqrt{2}) = 3\sqrt{36} - 8\sqrt{12} + 15\sqrt{12} - 40\sqrt{4} =$
   $3 \cdot 6 - 8 \cdot 2\sqrt{3} + 15 \cdot 2\sqrt{3} - 40 \cdot 2 = 18 - 16\sqrt{3} + 30\sqrt{3} - 80 = {}^-62 + 14\sqrt{3}$

3. $\dfrac{1-\sqrt{2}}{3+5\sqrt{2}} = \dfrac{1-\sqrt{2}}{3+5\sqrt{2}} \cdot \dfrac{3-5\sqrt{2}}{3-5\sqrt{2}} = \dfrac{3-5\sqrt{2}-3\sqrt{2}+5\sqrt{4}}{9-25\sqrt{4}} = \dfrac{3-5\sqrt{2}-3\sqrt{2}+10}{9-50} =$

   $\dfrac{13-8\sqrt{2}}{{}^-41}$ or $-\dfrac{13-8\sqrt{2}}{41}$ or $\dfrac{{}^-13+8\sqrt{2}}{41}$

Try These:
1. $(3+2\sqrt{6})(4-\sqrt{6})$
2. $(\sqrt{5}+2\sqrt{15})(\sqrt{3}-\sqrt{15})$
3. $\dfrac{6+2\sqrt{3}}{4-\sqrt{6}}$

Before you can add or subtract square roots, the numbers or expressions inside the radicals must be the same. First, simplify the radicals, if possible. If the numbers or expressions inside the radicals are the same, add or subtract the numbers (or like expressions) in front of the radicals. Keep the expression inside the radical the same. Be sure that the radicals are as simplified as possible.

Note: If the expressions inside the radicals are not the same, and can not be simplified to become the same, then they can not be combined by addition or subtraction.

To multiply 2 square roots together, follow these steps:

1. Multiply what is outside the radicals together.
2. Multiply what is inside the radicals together.
3. Simplify the radical if possible. Multiply whatever is in front of the radical times the expression that is coming out of the radical.

To divide one square root by another, follow these steps:

1. Work separately on what is inside or outside the square root sign.

2. Divide or reduce the coefficients outside the radical.

3. Divide any like variables outside the radical.

4. Divide or reduce the coefficients inside the radical.

5. Divide any like variables inside the radical.

6. If there is still a radical in the denominator, multiply both the numerator and denominator by the radical in the denominator. Simplify both resulting radicals and reduce again outside the radical (if possible).

Examples:

1. $6\sqrt{7} + 2\sqrt{5} + 3\sqrt{7} = 9\sqrt{7} + 2\sqrt{5}$ These cannot be combined further.

2. $5\sqrt{12} + \sqrt{48} - 2\sqrt{75} = 5\sqrt{2 \cdot 2 \cdot 3} + \sqrt{2 \cdot 2 \cdot 2 \cdot 2 \cdot 3} - 2\sqrt{3 \cdot 5 \cdot 5} =$
$5 \cdot 2\sqrt{3} + 2 \cdot 2\sqrt{3} - 2 \cdot 5\sqrt{3} = 10\sqrt{3} + 4\sqrt{3} - 10\sqrt{3} \qquad = 4\sqrt{3}$

3. $(6\sqrt{15x})(7\sqrt{10x}) = 42\sqrt{150x^2} = 42\sqrt{2 \cdot 3 \cdot 5 \cdot 5 \cdot x^2} = 42 \cdot 5x\sqrt{2 \cdot 3} = 210x\sqrt{6}$

4. $\dfrac{105x^8 \sqrt{18x^5y^6}}{30x^2 \sqrt{27x^2y^4}} = \dfrac{7x^6(x^2)(y^3)\sqrt{2x}}{2(x)(y^2)\sqrt{3}} = \dfrac{7x^7y\sqrt{2x}}{2\sqrt{3}}$

$= \dfrac{7x^7y\sqrt{2x}}{2\sqrt{3}} \cdot \dfrac{\sqrt{3}}{\sqrt{3}} = \dfrac{7x^7y\sqrt{6x}}{6}$

Try these:

1. $6\sqrt{24} + 3\sqrt{54} - \sqrt{96}$
2. $(2x^2y\sqrt{18x})(7xy^7\sqrt{4x})$
3. $\dfrac{125a^5 \sqrt{56a^4b^7}}{40a^2 \sqrt{40a^2b^8}}$
4. $2\sqrt{3} + 4\sqrt{5} + 6\sqrt{25} - 7\sqrt{9} + 2\sqrt{5} - 8\sqrt{20} - 6\sqrt{16} - 7\sqrt{3}$

To solve a **radical equation**, follow these steps:

1. Get a radical alone on one side of the equation.
2. Raise both **sides** of the equation to the power equal to the index number. **Do not raise them to that power term by term, but raise the entire side to that power**. Combine any like terms.
3. If there is another radical still in the equation, repeat steps one and two (i.e. get that radical alone on one side of the equation and raise both sides to a power equal to the index). Repeat as necessary until the radicals are all gone.
4. Solve the resulting equation.
5. Once you have found the answer(s), substitute them back into the original equation to check them. Sometimes there are solutions that do not check in the original equation. These are extraneous solutions, which are not correct and must be eliminated. If a problem has more than one potential solution, each solution must be checked separately.

> **NOTE: What this really means is that you can substitute the answers from any multiple choice test back into the question to determine which answer choice is correct.**

Solve and **check**.

1. $\sqrt{2x+1} + 7 = x$

   $\sqrt{2x+1} = x - 7$

   $\left(\sqrt{2x+1}\right)^2 = (x-7)^2$ ← BOTH sides are squared.

   $2x + 1 = x^2 - 14x + 49$

   $0 = x^2 - 16x + 48$

   $0 = (x-12)(x-4)$

   $x = 12, \ x = 4$

When you check these answers in the original equation, 12 checks; however, **4 does not check in the original equation**. Therefore, the only answer is $x = 12$.

2. $\sqrt{3x+4} = 2\sqrt{x-4}$

   $\left(\sqrt{3x+4}\right)^2 = \left(2\sqrt{x-4}\right)^2$

   $3x + 4 = 4(x - 4)$

   $3x + 4 = 4x - 16$

   $20 = x$ ← This checks in the original equaion.

3. $\sqrt[4]{7x-3} = 3$

   $\left(\sqrt[4]{7x-3}\right)^4 = 3^4$

   $7x - 3 = 81$

   $7x = 84$

   $x = 12$ ← This checks out with the original equation.

3. $\sqrt{x} = {}^-3$

   $\left(\sqrt{x}\right)^2 = \left({}^-3\right)^2$

   $x = 9$ ← This does NOT check in the original equation. Since there is no other answer to check, the correct answer is the empty set or the null set or $\varnothing$.

Try these:

Solve and check.

1. $\sqrt{8x-24} + 14 = 2x$
2. $\sqrt{6x-17} = 3\sqrt{x+2} - 4$

   Hint: Remember to square both sides, not term by term!
3. $\sqrt{6x-2} = 5\sqrt{x-13}$

To solve **logarithms or exponential functions** it is necessary to use several properties.

Multiplication Property $\quad\quad\quad \log_b mn = \log_b m + \log_b n$

Quotient Property $\quad\quad\quad\quad\; \log_b \dfrac{m}{n} = \log_b m - \log_b n$

Powers Property $\quad\quad\quad\quad\;\; \log_b n^r = r \log_b n$

Equality Property $\quad\quad\quad\quad \log_b n = \log_b m \quad$ if and only if $n = m$.

Change of Base Formula $\quad\quad \log_b n = \dfrac{\log n}{\log b}$

$$\log_b b^x = x \text{ and } b^{\log_b x} = x$$

Sample problem.

Solve for x.
1. $\log_6 (x-5) + \log_6 x = 2$

   $\log_6 x(x-5) = 2$ $\quad\quad\quad\quad$ Use product property.

   $\log_6 x^2 - 5x = 2$ $\quad\quad\quad\quad$ Distribute.

   $x^2 - 5x = 6^2$ $\quad\quad\quad\quad\quad\;$ Write in exponential form.

   $x^2 - 5x - 36 = 0$ $\quad\quad\quad\quad$ Solve quadratic equation.

   $(x+4)(x-9) = 0$

   $x = {}^-4 \quad x = 9$

***Be sure to check results. Remember x must be greater than zero in $\log x = y$.

Check: $\quad \log_6 (x-5) + \log_6 x = 2$

$\quad\quad\quad \log_6({}^-4-5) + \log_6({}^-4) = 2 \quad$ Substitute the first answer ${}^-4$.

$\quad\quad\quad \log_6({}^-9) + \log_6({}^-4) = 2 \quad\quad$ This is undefined, x is less than zero.

$\quad\quad\quad \log_6(9-5) + \log_6 9 = 2 \quad\quad\;$ Substitute the second answer 9.

$\quad\quad\quad \log_6 4 + \log_6 9 = 2$

$\quad\quad\quad \log_6(4)(9) = 2 \quad\quad\quad\quad\quad\quad$ Multiplication property.

$\quad\quad\quad \log_6 36 = 2$

$\quad\quad\quad 6^2 = 36 \quad\quad\quad\quad\quad\quad\quad\quad\;\;$ Write in exponential form.

$\quad\quad\quad 36 = 36$

Practice problems:
1. $\log_4 x = 2\log_4 3$
2. $2\log_3 x = 2 + \log_3(x-2)$
3. Use change of base formula to find $(\log_3 4)(\log_4 3)$.

Unlike **trigonometric identities** that are true for all values of the defined variable, trigonometric equations are true for some, but not all, of the values of the variable. Most often trigonometric equations are solved for values between 0 and 360 degrees or 0 and 2π radians.

Some algebraic operation, such as squaring both sides of an equation, will give you extraneous answers. You must remember to check all solutions to be sure that they work.

Sample problems:

1. Solve: $\cos x = 1 - \sin x$ if $0 \leq x < 360$ degrees.

$\cos^2 x = (1 - \sin x)^2$	1. square both sides
$1 - \sin^2 x = 1 - 2\sin x + \sin^2 x$	2. substitute
$0 = {}^-2\sin x + 2\sin^2 x$	3. set = to 0
$0 = 2\sin x({}^-1 + \sin x)$	4. factor
$2\sin x = 0 \qquad {}^-1 + \sin x = 0$	5. set each factor = 0
$\sin x = 0 \qquad \sin x = 1$	6. solve for $\sin x$
$x = 0$ or $180 \qquad x = 90$	7. find value of sin at x

   The solutions appear to be 0, 90 and 180. Remember to check each solution and you will find that 180 does not give you a true equation. Therefore, the only solutions are 0 and 90 degrees.

2. Solve: $\cos^2 x = \sin^2 x$ if $0 \leq x < 2\pi$

$\cos^2 x = 1 - \cos^2 x$	1. substitute
$2\cos^2 x = 1$	2. simplify
$\cos^2 x = \dfrac{1}{2}$	3. divide by 2
$\sqrt{\cos^2 x} = \pm\sqrt{\dfrac{1}{2}}$	4. take square root
$\cos x = \dfrac{\pm\sqrt{2}}{2}$	5. rationalize denominator
$x = \dfrac{\pi}{4}, \dfrac{3\pi}{4}, \dfrac{5\pi}{4}, \dfrac{7\pi}{4}$	

In order to **solve a right triangle** using trigonometric functions it is helpful to identify the given parts and label them. Usually more than one trigonometric function may be appropriately applied.

Some items to know about right triangles:

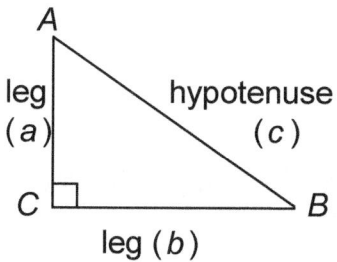

Given angle A, the side labeled leg (a) Is adjacent angle A. And the side labeled leg (b) is opposite to angle A.

Sample problem:

1. Find the missing side.

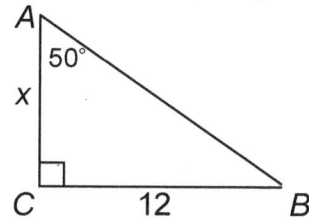

1. Identify the known values. Angle $A = 50$ degrees and the side opposite the given angle is 12. The missing side is the adjacent leg.

2. The information suggests the use of the tangent function

$\tan A = \dfrac{\text{opposite}}{\text{adjacent}}$ 3. Write the function.

$\tan 50 = \dfrac{12}{x}$ 4. Substitute.

$1.192 = \dfrac{12}{x}$ 5. Solve.

$x(1.192) = 12$

$x = 10.069$

Remember that since angle A and angle B are complimentary, then angle $B = 90 - 50$ or 40 degrees.

Using this information we could have solved for the same side only this time it is the leg opposite from angle B.

$\tan B = \dfrac{\text{opposite}}{\text{adjacent}}$ 1. Write the formula.

$\tan 40 = \dfrac{x}{12}$ 2. Substitute.

$12(.839) = x$ 3. Solve.

$10.069 \approx x$

Now that the two sides of the triangle are known, the third side can be found using the Pythagorean Theorem.

MATHEMATICS (Secondary)

Definition: For any triangle ABC, when given two sides and the included angle, the other side can be found using one of the formulas below:

$$a^2 = b^2 + c^2 - (2bc)\cos A$$
$$b^2 = a^2 + c^2 - (2ac)\cos B$$
$$c^2 = a^2 + b^2 - (2ab)\cos C$$

Similarly, when given three sides of a triangle, the included angles can be found using the derivation:

$$\cos A = \frac{b^2 + c^2 - a^2}{2bc}$$
$$\cos B = \frac{a^2 + c^2 - b^2}{2ac}$$
$$\cos C = \frac{a^2 + b^2 - c^2}{2ab}$$

Sample problem:

1. Solve triangle ABC, if angle $B = 87.5°$, $a = 12.3$, and $c = 23.2$. (Compute to the nearest tenth).

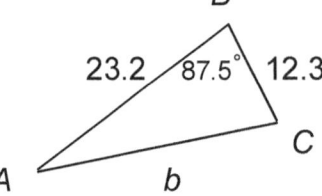

1. Draw and label a sketch.

Find side b.

$b^2 = a^2 + c^2 - (2ac)\cos B$ 2. Write the formula.

$b^2 = (12.3)^2 + (23.2)^2 - 2(12.3)(23.2)(\cos 87.5)$ 3. Substitute.

$b^2 = 664.636$

$b = 25.8$ (rounded)

4. Solve.

Use the law of sines to find angle A.

$\dfrac{\sin A}{a} = \dfrac{\sin B}{b}$ 1. Write formula.

$\dfrac{\sin A}{12.3} = \dfrac{\sin 87.5}{25.8} = \dfrac{12.29}{25.8}$ 2. Substitute.

$\sin A = 0.47629$ 3. Solve.

Angle $A = 28.4$

Therefore, angle $C = 180 - (87.5 + 28.4)$

2. Solve triangle ABC if $a = 15$, $b = 21$, and $c = 18$. (Round to the nearest tenth).

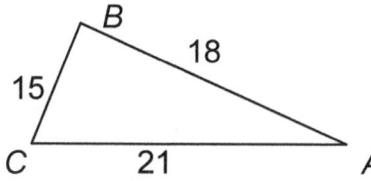

1. Draw and label a sketch.

Find angle A.

$\cos A = \dfrac{b^2 + c^2 - a^2}{2bc}$ 2. Write formula.

$\cos A = \dfrac{21^2 + 18^2 - 15^2}{2(21)(18)}$ 3. Substitute.

$\cos A = 0.714$ 4. Solve.

Angle $A = 44.4$

Find angle B.

$\cos B = \dfrac{a^2 + c^2 - b^2}{2ac}$ 5. Write formula.

$\cos B = \dfrac{15^2 + 18^2 - 21^2}{2(15)(18)}$ 6. Substitute.

$\cos B = 0.2$ 7. Solve.

Angle $B = 78.5$

Therefore, angle $C = 180 - (44.4 + 78.5)$
$= 57.1$

Definition: For any triangle ABC, where a, b, and c are the lengths of the sides opposite angles A, B, and C respectively.

$$\frac{\sin A}{a} = \frac{\sin B}{b} = \frac{\sin C}{c}$$

Sample problem:

1. An inlet is 140 feet wide. The lines of sight from each bank to an approaching ship are 79 degrees and 58 degrees. What are the distances from each bank to the ship?

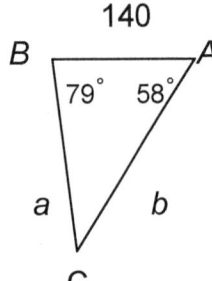

1. Draw and label a sketch.

2. The missing angle is $180 - (79 + 58) = 43$ degrees.

$$\frac{\sin A}{a} = \frac{\sin B}{b} = \frac{\sin C}{c}$$

3. Write formula.

Side opposite 79 degree angle:

$$\frac{\sin 79}{b} = \frac{\sin 43}{140}$$

4. Substitute.

$$b = \frac{140(.9816)}{.6820}$$

5. Solve.

$b \approx 201.501$ feet

Side opposite 58 degree angle:

$$\frac{\sin 58}{a} = \frac{\sin 43}{140}$$

6. Substitute.

$$a = \frac{140(.848)}{.6820}$$

7. Solve.

$a \approx 174.076$ feet

When changing common logarithms to exponential form,

$$y = \log_b x \quad \text{if and only if} \quad x = b^y$$

Natural logarithms can be changed to exponential form by using,

$$\log_e x = \ln x \quad \text{or} \quad \ln x = y \text{ can be written as } e^y = x$$

Practice Problems:

Express in exponential form.

1. $\log_3 81 = 4$
   $x = 81 \quad b = 3 \quad y = 4$ Identify values.
   $81 = 3^4$ Rewrite in exponential form.

Solve by writing in exponential form.

2. $\log_x 125 = 3$

   $x^3 = 125$ Write in exponential form.
   $x^3 = 5^3$ Write 125 in exponential form.
   $x = 5$ Bases must be equal if exponents are equal.

Use a scientific calculator to solve.

3. Find $\ln 72$.
   $\ln 72 = 4.2767$ Use the $\ln x$ key to find natural logs.
4. Find $\ln x = 4.2767$ Write in exponential form.
   $e^{4.2767} = x$ Use the key (or 2nd $\ln x$) to find x.
   $x = 72.002439$ The small difference is due to rounding.

Unlike trigonometric identities that are true for all values of the defined variable, trigonometric equations are true for some, but not all, of the values of the variable. Most often trigonometric equations are solved for values between 0 and 360 degrees or 0 and 2π radians.

Some algebraic operation, such as squaring both sides of an equation, will give you extraneous answers. You must remember to check all solutions to be sure that they work.

Sample problems:

1. Solve: $\cos x = 1 - \sin x$ if $0 \leq x < 360$ degrees.

$\cos^2 x = (1 - \sin x)^2$	1. square both sides
$1 - \sin^2 x = 1 - 2\sin x + \sin^2 x$	2. substitute
$0 = {}^-2\sin x + 2\sin^2 x$	3. set = to 0
$0 = 2\sin x({}^-1 + \sin x)$	4. factor
$2\sin x = 0 \quad\quad {}^-1 + \sin x = 0$	5. set each factor = 0
$\sin x = 0 \quad\quad\quad \sin x = 1$	6. solve for $\sin x$
$x = 0$ or $180 \quad\quad x = 90$	7. find value of sin at x

The solutions appear to be 0, 90 and 180. Remember to check each solution and you will find that 180 does not give you a true equation. Therefore, the only solutions are 0 and 90 degrees.

2. Solve: $\cos^2 x = \sin^2 x$ if $0 \leq x < 2\pi$

$\cos^2 x = 1 - \cos^2 x$	1. substitute
$2\cos^2 x = 1$	2. simplify
$\cos^2 x = \dfrac{1}{2}$	3. divide by 2
$\sqrt{\cos^2 x} = \pm\sqrt{\dfrac{1}{2}}$	4. take square root
$\cos x = \dfrac{\pm\sqrt{2}}{2}$	5. rationalize denominator
$x = \dfrac{\pi}{4}, \dfrac{3\pi}{4}, \dfrac{5\pi}{4}, \dfrac{7\pi}{4}$	

The **unit circle** is a circle with a radius of one centered at (0,0) on the coordinate plane. Thus, any ray from the origin to a point on the circle forms an angle, t, with the positive x-axis. In addition, the ray from the origin to a point on the circle in the first quadrant forms a right triangle with a hypotenuse measuring one unit. Applying the Pythagorean theorem, $x^2 + y^2 = 1$. Because the reflections of the triangle about both the x- and y-axis are on the unit circle and $x^2 = (-x)^2$ for all x values, the formula holds for all points on the unit circle.

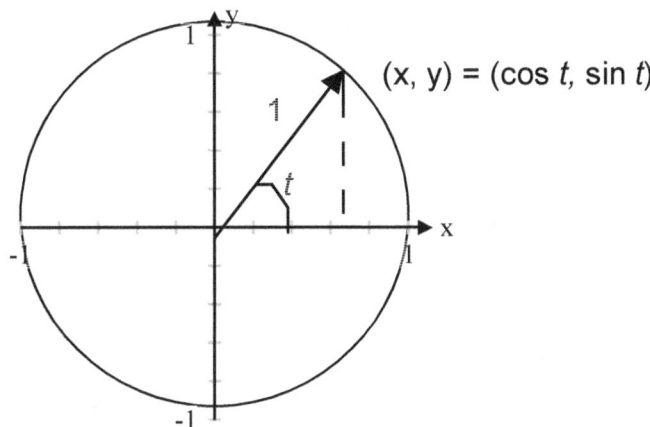

Note that because the length of the hypotenuse of the right triangles formed in the unit circle is one, the point on the unit circle that forms the triangle is (cos t, sin t). In other words, for any point on the unit circle, the x value represents the cosine of t, the y value represents the sine of t, and the ratio of the y-coordinate to the x-coordinate is the tangent of t.

The unit circle illustrates several properties of trigonometric functions. For example, applying the Pythagorean theorem to the unit circle yields the equation $\cos^2(t) + \sin^2(t) = 1$. In addition, the unit circle reveals the periodic nature of trigonometric functions. When we increase the angle t beyond 2π radians or 360 degrees, the values of x and y coordinates on the unit circle remain the same. Thus, the sine and cosine values repeat with each revolution. The unit circle also reveals the range of the sine and cosine functions. The values of sine and cosine are always between one and negative one. Finally, the unit circle shows that when the x coordinate of a point on the circle is zero, the tangent function is undefined. Thus, tangent is undefined at the angles $\frac{\pi}{2}, \frac{3\pi}{2}$ and the corresponding angles in all subsequent revolutions.

Mathematicians use trigonometric functions to model and solve problems involving naturally occurring periodic phenomena. Examples of periodic phenomena found in nature include all forms of radiation (ultraviolet rays, visible light, microwaves, etc.), sound waves and pendulums. Additionally, trigonometric functions often approximate fluctuations in temperature, employment and consumer behavior (business models).The following are examples of the use of the sine function to model problems.

Example 1:

Consider the average monthly temperatures for a hypothetical location.

Month	Avg. Temp. (F)
Jan	40
March	48
May	65
July	81
Sept	80
Nov	60

Note that the graph of the average temperatures resembles the graph of a trigonometric function with a period of one year. We can use the periodic nature of seasonal temperature fluctuation to predict weather patterns.

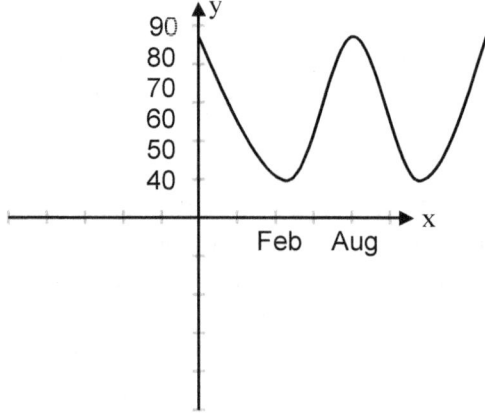

Example 2:

The general form of the sine function that is useful in modeling problems involving time is:

$$y = A[\sin \omega(t - \alpha)] + C = A[\sin(\omega t - \alpha \omega)] + C$$

where A is the amplitude, C is the vertical offset, ω is the angular frequency ($\frac{2\pi}{P}$, P is period), t is the time in years and α is the horizontal offset or phase shift.

Consider the following situation. An economist at a temporary employment agency reports that the demand for temporary employment (as measured by thousands of applications for week) varies according to the following model, where t is the time in years, starting with January, 2002.

Demand (d) = 4.7sin(0.75t + 0.4) + 7.7

From this model, we can calculate the characteristics of the sine function and interpret the cyclical nature of demand for temporary employment. Applying the general sine function formula to the model:

A = 4.7
C = 7.7
ω = 0.75

$\omega\alpha$ = 0.4 ➔ α = 0.4/0.75 = 0.53

P (period) = $\frac{2\pi}{\omega}$ = 8.4

Thus, we interpret the model as follows.

The demand for temporary employment fluctuates in cycles of 8.4 years (period) about a baseline of 7,700 job applications per week (vertical offset). The peak of each cycle is approximately 12,400 job applications per week and the low point of each cycle is 3,000 (vertical offset ± amplitude).

Competency 9 Understand principles and applications of differential and integral calculus.

The limit of a function is the *y* value that the graph approaches as the *x* values approach a certain number. To find a limit there are two points to remember.

1. Factor the expression completely and cancel all common factors in fractions.
2. Substitute the number to which the variable is approaching. In most cases this produces the value of the limit.

If the variable in the limit is approaching ∞, factor and simplify first; then examine the result. If the result does not involve a fraction with the variable in the denominator, the limit is usually also equal to ∞. If the variable is in the denominator of the fraction, the denominator is getting larger which makes the entire fraction smaller. In other words the limit is zero.

Examples:

1. $\lim\limits_{x \to ^-3} \dfrac{x^2+5x+6}{x+3} + 4x$ Factor the numerator.

   $\lim\limits_{x \to ^-3} \dfrac{(x+3)(x+2)}{(x+3)} + 4x$ Cancel the common factors.

   $\lim\limits_{x \to ^-3} (x+2) + 4x$ Substitute $^-3$ for x.

   $(^-3+2) + 4(^-3)$ Simplify.

   $^-1 + ^-12$

   $^-13$

2. $\lim\limits_{x \to \infty} \dfrac{2x^2}{x^5}$ Cancel the common factors.

   $\lim\limits_{x \to \infty} \dfrac{2}{x^3}$

       Since the denominator is getting larger, the entire fraction is getting smaller. The fraction is getting close to zero.

   $\dfrac{2}{\infty^3}$

Practice problems:

1. $\lim\limits_{x \to \pi} 5x^2 + \sin x$

2. $\lim\limits_{x \to -4} = \dfrac{x^2+9x+20}{x+4}$

After simplifying an expression to evaluate a limit, substitute the value that the variable approaches. If the substitution results in either $0/0$ or ∞/∞, use L'Hopital's rule to find the limit.

L'Hopital's rule states that you can find such limits by taking the derivative of the numerator and the derivative of the denominator, and then finding the limit of the resulting quotient.

Examples:

1. $\lim\limits_{x \to \infty} \dfrac{3x-1}{x^2 + 2x + 3}$ No factoring is possible.

$\dfrac{3\infty - 1}{\infty^2 + 2\infty + 3}$ Substitute ∞ for x.

$\dfrac{\infty}{\infty}$ Since a constant times infinity is still a large number, $3(\infty) = \infty$.

$\lim\limits_{x \to \infty} \dfrac{3}{2x+2}$ To find the limit, take the derivative of the numerator and denominator.

$\dfrac{3}{2(\infty)+2}$ Substitute ∞ for x again.

$\dfrac{3}{\infty}$

0 Since the denominator is a very large number, the fraction is getting smaller. Thus the limit is zero.

2. $\lim_{x \to 1} \dfrac{\ln x}{x-1}$ Substitute 1 for x.

$\dfrac{\ln 1}{1-1}$ The $\ln 1 = 0$

$\dfrac{0}{0}$

To find the limit, take the derivative of the numerator and denominator.

$\lim_{x \to 1} \dfrac{\frac{1}{x}}{1}$ Substitute 1 for x again.

$\dfrac{\frac{1}{1}}{1}$ Simplify. The limit is one.

1

Practice problems:

1. $\lim_{x \to \infty} \dfrac{x^2 - 3}{x}$

2. $\lim_{x \to \frac{\pi}{2}} \dfrac{\cos x}{x - \frac{\pi}{2}}$

The concept of **limit** applies when examining the way a function behaves close to a particular point of interest. Evaluating the continuity of a function and determining the nature of discontinuous functions is one application of the concept of limit. We also use limits to determine the asymptotes of the graph of a function.

If the limit of a function as x approaches a equals the value of the function at a, then the function is continuous at a. In other words, a function is continuous at a number a if

$$\lim_{x \to a} f(x) = f(a).$$

The function f is continuous at a if the function satisfies the following three criteria.

1. f(a) is defined
2. The limit of f(x) as x approaches a exists.
3. The limit of f(x) as x approaches a equals f(a).

Example 1: $f(x) = \dfrac{x}{x-2}$

This function is discontinuous at x = 2 because f(2) is not defined.

Example 2: $f(x) = \dfrac{x^2 - x - 2}{x+1}$ if x ≠ -1, and 1 if x = -1.

This function is discontinuous at x = -1 even though f(-1) is defined and the limit as x approaches -1 exists.

$$\lim_{x \to -1} f(x) = \frac{x^2 - x - 2}{x+1} = \lim_{x \to -1} \frac{(x-2)(x+1)}{x+1} = \lim_{x \to -1} (x-2) = -3$$

The function is discontinuous because $\lim_{x \to -1} f(x) \neq f(-1)$. The function does not satisfy all three necessary criteria.

Discontinuous functions have breaks in their graphs. In other words, we cannot sketch the graph of a discontinuous function without lifting the pen off the paper.

The **difference quotient** is the average rate of change over an interval. For a function f, the **difference quotient** is represented by the formula:

$$\frac{f(x+h) - f(x)}{h}.$$

This formula computes the slope of the secant line through two points on the graph of f. These are the points with x-coordinates x and $x+h$.

Example: Find the difference quotient for the function $f(x) = 2x^2 + 3x - 5$.

$$\frac{f(x+h) - f(x)}{h} = \frac{2(x+h)^2 + 3(x+h) - 5 - (2x^2 + 3x - 5)}{h}$$

$$= \frac{2(x^2 + 2hx + h^2) + 3x + 3h - 5 - 2x^2 - 3x + 5}{h}$$

$$= \frac{2x^2 + 4hx + 2h^2 + 3x + 3h - 5 - 2x^2 - 3x + 5}{h}$$

$$= \frac{4hx + 2h^2 + 3h}{h}$$

$$= 4x + 2h + 3$$

A. Derivative of a constant--for any constant, the derivative is always zero.

B. Derivative of a variable--the derivative of a variable (i.e. x) is one.

C. Derivative of a variable raised to a power--for variable expressions with rational exponents (i.e. $3x^2$) multiply the coefficient (3) by the exponent (2) then subtract one (1) from the exponent to arrive at the derivative $(3x^2) = (6x)$

Example:

1. $y = 5x^4$ Take the derivative.

   $\dfrac{dy}{dx} = (5)(4)x^{4-1}$ Multiply the coefficient by the exponent and subtract 1 from the exponent.

   $\dfrac{dy}{dx} = 20x^3$ Simplify.

2. $y = \dfrac{1}{4x^3}$ Rewrite using negative exponent.

   $y = \dfrac{1}{4}x^{-3}$ Take the derivative.

   $\dfrac{dy}{dx} = \left(\dfrac{1}{4} \cdot {-3}\right)x^{-3-1}$

   $\dfrac{dy}{dx} = \dfrac{-3}{4}x^{-4} = \dfrac{-3}{4x^4}$ Simplify.

3. $y = 3\sqrt{x^5}$ Rewrite using $\sqrt[z]{x^n} = x^{n/z}$.

   $y = 3x^{5/2}$ Take the derivative.

   $\dfrac{dy}{dx} = (3)\left(\dfrac{5}{2}\right)x^{5/2-1}$

   $\dfrac{dy}{dx} = \left(\dfrac{15}{2}\right)x^{3/2}$ Simplify.

   $\dfrac{dy}{dx} = 7.5\sqrt{x^3} = 7.5x\sqrt{x}$

A. sin x --the derivative of the sine of x is simply the cosine of x.

B. cos x --the derivative of the cosine of x is negative one ($^-1$) times the sine of x.

C. tan x --the derivative of the tangent of x is the square of the secant of x.

If the object of the trig. function is an expression other than x, follow the above rules substituting the expression for x. The only additional step is to multiply the result by the derivative of the expression.

Examples:

1. $y = \pi \sin x$ Carry the coefficient (π) throughout the problem.

    $\dfrac{dy}{dx} = \pi \cos x$

2. $y = \dfrac{2}{3} \cos x$

    Do not forget to multiply the coefficient by negative one when taking the derivative of a cosine function.

    $\dfrac{dy}{dx} = \dfrac{^-2}{3} \sin x$

3. $y = 4\tan(5x^3)$

    $\dfrac{dy}{dx} = 4\sec^2(5x^3)(5 \bullet 3x^{3-1})$ The derivative of $\tan x$ is $\sec^2 x$.

    $\dfrac{dy}{dx} = 4\sec^2(5x^3)(15x^2)$ Carry the $(5x^3)$ term throughout the problem.

    $\dfrac{dy}{dx} = 4 \bullet 15x^2 \sec^2(5x^3)$ Multiply $4\sec^2(5x^3)$ by the derivative of $5x^3$.

    $\dfrac{dy}{dx} = 60x^2 \sec^2(5x^3)$ Rearrange the terms and simplify.

$f(x) = e^x$ is an **exponential function**. The derivative of e^x is exactly the same thing $\rightarrow e^x$. If instead of x, the exponent on e is an expression, the derivative is the same e raised to the algebraic exponent multiplied by the derivative of the algebraic expression.

If a base other than e is used, the derivative is the natural log of the base times the original exponential function times the derivative of the exponent.

Examples:

1. $y = e^x$

   $\dfrac{dy}{dx} = e^x$

2. $y = e^{3x}$

   $\dfrac{dy}{dx} = e^{3x} \bullet 3 = 3e^{3x}$ Multiply e^{3x} by the derivative of $3x$ which is 3.

   $\dfrac{dy}{dx} = 3e^{3x}$ Rearrange the terms.

3. $y = \dfrac{5}{e^{\sin x}}$

   $y = 5e^{-\sin x}$ Rewrite using negative exponents

   $\dfrac{dy}{dx} = 5e^{-\sin x} \bullet (^-\cos x)$

       Multiply $5e^{-\sin x}$ by the derivative of $^-\sin x$ which is $^-\cos x$.

   $\dfrac{dy}{dx} = \dfrac{^-5 \cos x}{e^{\sin x}}$ Use the definition of negative exponents to simplify.

4. $y = {}^-2 \bullet \ln 3^{4x}$

   $\dfrac{dy}{dx} = {}^-2 \bullet (\ln 3)(3^{4x})(4)$ The natural log of the base is ln3.

       The derivative of $4x$ is 4.

   $\dfrac{dy}{dx} = {}^-8 \bullet 3^{4x} \ln 3$ Rearrange terms to simplify.

MATHEMATICS (Secondary)

The most common logarithmic function on the Exam is the natural logarithmic function ($\ln x$). The derivative of $\ln x$ is simply $1/x$. If x is replaced by an algebraic expression, the derivative is the fraction one divided by the expression multiplied by the derivative of the expression.

For all other logarithmic functions, the derivative is 1 over the argument of the logarithm multiplied by 1 over the natural logarithm (ln) of the base multiplied by the derivative of the argument.
Examples:

1. $y = \ln x$

   $\dfrac{dy}{dx} = \dfrac{1}{x}$

2. $y = 3\ln(x^{-2})$

   $\dfrac{dy}{dx} = 3 \bullet \dfrac{1}{x^{-2}} \bullet \left(^-2x^{-2-1}\right)$

   Multiply one over the argument (x^{-2}) by the derivative of x^{-2} which is $^-2x^{-2-1}$.

   $\dfrac{dy}{dx} = 3 \bullet x^2 \bullet \left(^-2x^{-3}\right)$

   $\dfrac{dy}{dx} = \dfrac{^-6x^2}{x^3}$

   Simplify using the definition of negative exponents.

   $\dfrac{dy}{dx} = \dfrac{^-6}{x}$

   Cancel common factors to simplify.

3. $y = \log_5(\tan x)$

   $\dfrac{dy}{dx} = \dfrac{1}{\tan x} \bullet \dfrac{1}{\ln 5} \bullet (\sec^2 x)$ The derivative of $\tan x$ is $\sec^2 x$.

   $\dfrac{dy}{dx} = \dfrac{\sec^2 x}{(\tan x)(\ln 5)}$

Implicitly defined functions are ones where both variables (usually x and y) appear in the function. All of the rules for finding the derivative still apply to both variables. The only difference is that, while the derivative of x is one (1) and typically not even mentioned, the derivative of y must be written y' or dy/dx. Work these problems just like the other derivative problems, just remember to include the extra step of multiplying by dy/dx in the result.

If the question asks for the derivative of y, given an equation with x and y on both sides, find the derivative of each side. Then solve the new equation for dy/dx just as you would an algebra problem.

Examples:

1. $\dfrac{d}{dx}(y^3) = 3y^{3-1} \cdot \dfrac{dy}{dx}$

    Recall the derivative of x^3 is $3x^{3-1}$. Follow the same rule, but also multiply by the derivative of y which is dy/dx.

    $\dfrac{d}{dx}(y^3) = 3y^2 \dfrac{dy}{dx}$

2. $\dfrac{d}{dx}(3\ln y) = 3 \cdot \dfrac{1}{y} \cdot \dfrac{dy}{dx}$

3. $\dfrac{d}{dx}(^-2\cos y) =\ ^- 2(^-1 \sin y)\dfrac{dy}{dx}$

    Recall the derivative of $\cos x$ is $^-\sin x$.

    $\dfrac{d}{dx}(^-2\cos y) = 2\sin y \dfrac{dy}{dx}$

4. $2y = e^{3x}$

    Solve for after taking the derivative.

    $2 \cdot \dfrac{dy}{dx} = e^{3x} \cdot 3$

    The derivative of e^{3x} is $e^{3x} \cdot 3$.

    $\dfrac{dy}{dx} = \dfrac{3}{2}e^{3x}$

    Divide both sides by 2 to solve for the derivative dy/dx.

A. Derivative of a sum--find the derivative of each term separately and add the results.

B. Derivative of a product--multiply the derivative of the first factor by the second factor and add to it the product of the first factor and the derivative of the second factor.

Remember the phrase "first times the derivative of the second plus the second times the derivative of the first."

C. Derivative of a quotient--use the rule "bottom times the derivative of the top minus the top times the derivative of the bottom all divided by the bottom squared."

Examples:

1. $y = 3x^2 + 2\ln x + 5\sqrt{x}$ $\qquad \sqrt{x} = x^{1/2}$.

$\dfrac{dy}{dx} = 6x^{2-1} + 2 \cdot \dfrac{1}{x} + 5 \cdot \dfrac{1}{2} x^{1/2-1}$

$\dfrac{dy}{dx} = 6x + \dfrac{2}{x} + \dfrac{5}{2} \cdot \dfrac{1}{\sqrt{x}} = \dfrac{12x^2 + 4 + 5\sqrt{x}}{2x}$

$= \dfrac{12x^2 + 5\sqrt{x} + 4}{2x}$

$x^{1/2-1} = x^{-1/2} = 1/\sqrt{x}$.

2. $y = 4e^{x^2} \cdot \sin x$

$\dfrac{dy}{dx} = 4(e^{x^2} \cdot \cos x + \sin x \cdot e^{x^2} \cdot 2x)$

The derivative of e^{x^2} is $e^{x^2} \cdot 2$.

$\dfrac{dy}{dx} = 4(e^{x^2} \cos x + 2xe^{x^2} \sin x)$

$\dfrac{dy}{dx} = 4e^{x^2} \cos x + 8xe^{x^2} \sin x$

3. $y = \dfrac{\cos x}{x}$

$\dfrac{dy}{dx} = \dfrac{x(^-\sin x) - \cos x \cdot 1}{x^2}$

The derivative of x is 1.
The derivative of $\cos x$ is $^-\sin x$.

$\dfrac{dy}{dx} = \dfrac{^-x \sin x - \cos x}{x^2}$

A **composite function** is made up of two or more separate functions such as $\sin(\ln x)$ or $x^2 e^{3x}$. To find the derivatives of these composite functions requires two steps. First identify the predominant function in the problem. For example, in $\sin(\ln x)$ the major function is the sine function. In $x^2 e^{3x}$ the major function is a product of two expressions (x^2 and e^{3x}). Once the predominant function is identified, apply the appropriate differentiation rule. Be certain to include the step of taking the derivative of every part of the functions which comprise the composite function. Use parentheses as much as possible.

Examples:

1. $y = \sin(\ln x)$ The major function is a sine function.

   $\dfrac{dy}{dx} = [\cos(\ln x)] \cdot \left[\dfrac{1}{x}\right]$ The derivative of $\sin x$ is $\cos x$.

   The derivative of $\ln x$ is $1/x$.

2. $y = x^2 \cdot e^{3x}$ The major function is a product.

   $\dfrac{dy}{dx} = x^2\left(e^{3x} \cdot 3\right) + e^{3x} \cdot 2x$

   The derivative of a product is "First $\dfrac{dy}{dx} = 3x^2 e^{3x} + 2x e^{3x}$ times the derivative of second plus the second times the derivative of the first."

3. $y = \tan^2\left(\dfrac{\ln x}{\cos x}\right)$

   This function is made of several functions. The major function is a power function.

   $\dfrac{dy}{dx} = \left[2\tan^{2-1}\left(\dfrac{\ln x}{\cos x}\right)\right]\left[\sec^2\left(\dfrac{\ln x}{\cos x}\right)\right]\left[\dfrac{d}{dx}\left(\dfrac{\ln x}{\cos x}\right)\right]$

The derivative of $\tan x$ is $\sec^2 x$. Hold off one more to take the derivative of $\ln x/\cos x$.

$$\frac{dy}{dx} = \left[2\tan\left(\frac{\ln x}{\cos x}\right)\sec^2\left(\frac{\ln x}{\cos x}\right)\right]\left[\frac{(\cos x)(1/x) - \ln x(^-\sin x)}{\cos^2 x}\right]$$

$$\frac{dy}{dx} = \left[2\tan\left(\frac{\ln x}{\cos x}\right)\sec^2\left(\frac{\ln x}{\cos x}\right)\right]\left[\frac{(\cos x)(1/x) + \ln x(\sin x)}{\cos^2 x}\right]$$

The derivative of a quotient is "Bottom times the derivative of the top minus the top times the derivative of the bottom all divided by the bottom squared."

Higher order derivatives

If a question simply asks for the **derivative of a function**, the question is asking for the first derivative. To find the second derivative of a function, take the derivative of the first derivative. To find the third derivative, take the derivative of the second derivative; and so on. All of the regular derivative rules still apply.

Examples:

1. Find the second derivative $\left(\frac{d^2y}{dx^2} \text{ or } y''\right)$ of the following function:

$$y = 5x^2$$

$\frac{dy}{dx} = 2 \bullet 5x^{2-1} = 10$ Take the first derivative.

$\frac{d^2y}{dx^2} = 10$ The derivative of $10x$ is 10.

2. Find the third derivative (y''') of $f(x) = 4x^{3/2}$:

$$y' = \left(4 \bullet \frac{3}{2}\right)x^{\left(\frac{3}{2}-1\right)} = 6x^{\frac{1}{2}}$$

$$y'' = \left(6 \bullet \frac{1}{2}\right)x^{\left(\frac{1}{2}-1\right)} = 3x^{-\frac{1}{2}}$$

$$y''' = \left[3 \bullet \left(-\frac{1}{2}\right)\right]x^{\left(-\frac{1}{2}-1\right)} = -\frac{3}{2}x^{-\frac{3}{2}}$$

Derivative Interpretation

The derivative of a function has two basic interpretations.

    I.   Instantaneous rate of change
    II.   Slope of a tangent line at a given point

If a question asks for the rate of change of a function, take the derivative to find the equation for the rate of change. Then plug in for the variable to find the instantaneous rate of change.

The following is a list summarizing some of the more common quantities referred to in rate of change problems.

area	height	profit
decay	population growth	sales
distance	position	temperature
frequency	pressure	volume

Pick a point, say $x = {}^-3$, on the graph of a function. Draw a tangent line at that point. Find the derivative of the function and plug in $x = {}^-3$. The result will be the slope of the tangent line.

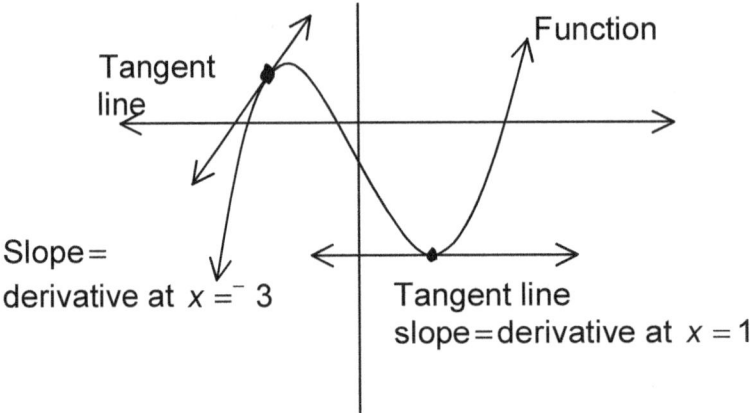

To find the **slope of a curve** at a point, there are two steps to follow.

1. Take the derivative of the function.
2. Plug in the value to find the slope.

If plugging into the derivative yields a value of zero, the tangent line is horizontal at that point.

If plugging into the derivative produces a fraction with zero in the denominator, the tangent line at this point has an undefined slope and is thus a vertical line.

Examples:

1. Find the slope of the tangent line for the given function at the given point.

$y = \dfrac{1}{x-2}$ at $(3,1)$

$y = (x-2)^{-1}$ Rewrite using negative exponents.

$\dfrac{dy}{dx} = {}^-1(x-2)^{-1-1}(1)$ Use the Chain rule. The derivative of $(x-2)$ is 1.

$\dfrac{dy}{dx} = {}^-1(x-2)^{-2}$

$\dfrac{dy}{dx}\bigg|_{x=3} = {}^-1(3-2)^{-2}$ Evaluate at $x=3$.

$\dfrac{dy}{dx}\bigg|_{x=3} = {}^-1$

The slope of the tangent line is $^-1$ at $x=3$.

2. Find the points where the tangent to the curve $f(x) = 2x^2 + 3x$ is parallel to the line $y = 11x - 5$.

$f'(x) = 2 \bullet 2x^{2-1} + 3$ Take the derivative of $f(x)$ to get the slope of a tangent line.

$f'(x) = 4x + 3$

$4x + 3 = 11$ Set the slope expression $(4x+3)$ equal to the slope of $y = 11x - 5$.

$x = 2$ Solve for the x value of the point.

$f(2) = 2(2)^2 + 3(2)$ The y value is 14.

$f(2) = 14$ So $(2,14)$ is the point on $f(x)$ where the tangent line is parallel to $y = 11x - 5$.

To write an equation of a tangent line at a point, two things are needed.

1. A point--the problem will usually provide a point, (x, y). If the problem only gives an x value, plug the value into the original function to get the y coordinate.

2. The slope--to find the slope, take the derivative of the original function. Then plug in the x value of the point to get the slope.

After obtaining a point and a slope, use the Point-Slope form for the equation of a line:

$$(y - y_1) = m(x - x_1)$$

where m is the slope and (x_1, y_1) is the point.

Example:
Find the equation of the tangent line to $f(x) = 2e^{x^2}$ at $x = {}^-1$.

$f({}^-1) = 2e^{({}^-1)^2}$	Plug in the x coordinate to obtain the y coordinate.
$= 2e^1$	The point is $({}^-1, 2e)$.
$f'(x) = 2e^{x^2} \bullet (2x)$	
$f'({}^-1) = 2e^{({}^-1)^2} \bullet (2 \bullet {}^-1)$	
$f'({}^-1) = 2e^1({}^-2)$	
$f'({}^-1) = {}^-4e$	The slope at $x = {}^-1$ is ${}^-4e$.
$(y - 2e) = {}^-4e(x - {}^-1)$	Plug in the point $({}^-1, 2e)$ and the slope $m = {}^-4e$. Use the point slope form of a line.
$y = {}^-4ex - 4e + 2e$	
$y = {}^-4ex - 2e$	Simplify to obtain the equation for the tangent line.

MATHEMATICS (Secondary)

A **normal line** is a line which is perpendicular to a tangent line at a given point. Perpendicular lines have slopes which are negative reciprocals of each other. To find the equation of a normal line, first get the slope of the tangent line at the point. Find the negative reciprocal of this slope. Next, use the new slope and the point on the curve, both the x_1 and y_1 coordinates, and substitute into the Point-Slope form of the equation for a line:

$$(y - y_1) = slope \bullet (x - x_1)$$

Examples:

1. Find the equation of the normal line to the tangent to the curve $y = (x^2 - 1)(x - 3)$ at $x = {}^-2$.

$f(-2) = (({}^-2)^2 - 1)({}^-2 - 3)$ First find the y coordinate of the point on the curve. Here,

$f(-2) = {}^-15$ $y = {}^-15$ when $x = {}^-2$.

$y = x^3 - 3x^2 - x + 3$ Before taking the derivative, multiply the expression first. The derivative of a sum is easier to find than the derivative of a product.

$y' = 3x^2 - 6x - 1$ Take the derivative to find the slope of the tangent line.

$y'_{x={}^-2} = 3({}^-2)^2 - 6({}^-2) - 1$

$y'_{x={}^-2} = 23$

slope of normal $= \dfrac{{}^-1}{23}$

    For the slope of the normal line, take the negative reciprocal of the tangent line's slope.

$(y - {}^-15) = \dfrac{{}^-1}{23}(x - {}^-2)$ Plug (x_1, y_1) into the point-slope equation.

$(y + 15) = \dfrac{{}^-1}{23}(x + 2)$

$y = -\dfrac{1}{23}x - 14\dfrac{21}{23}$

$y = -\dfrac{1}{23}x + \dfrac{2}{23} - 15 = \dfrac{1}{23}x - 14\dfrac{21}{23}$

2. Find the equation of the normal line to the tangent to the curve $y = \ln(\sin x)$ at $x = \pi$.

$f(\pi) = \ln(\sin \pi)$
$f(\pi) = \ln(1) = 0$
$y' = \dfrac{1}{\sin x} \bullet \cos x$

$\sin \pi = 1$ and $\ln(1) = 0$ (recall $e^0 = 1$).
So $x_1 = \pi$ and $y_1 = 0$.

Take the derivative to find the slope of the tangent line.

$y'_{x=\pi} = \dfrac{\cos \pi}{\sin \pi} = \dfrac{0}{1}$

Slope of normal does not exist. $\dfrac{-1}{0}$ does not exist. So the normal line is vertical at $x = \pi$.

A function is said to be increasing if it is rising from left to right and decreasing if it is falling from left to right. Lines with positive slopes are increasing, and lines with negative slopes are decreasing. If the function in question is something other than a line, simply refer to the slopes of the tangent lines as the test for increasing or decreasing. Take the derivative of the function and plug in an x value to get the slope of the tangent line; a positive slope means the function is increasing and a negative slope means it is decreasing. If an interval for x values is given, just pick any point between the two values to substitute.

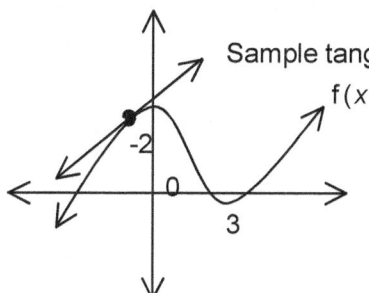

Sample tangent line on $(^-2,0)$

On the interval $(^-2,0)$, $f(x)$ is increasing. The tangent lines on this part of the graph have positive slopes.

Example:

The growth of a certain bacteria is given by $f(x) = x + \dfrac{1}{x}$. Determine if the rate of growth is increasing or decreasing on the time interval $(^-1,0)$.

$f'(x) = 1 + \dfrac{^-1}{x^2}$

To test for increasing or decreasing, find the slope of the tangent line by taking the derivative.

$f'\left(\dfrac{^-1}{2}\right) = 1 + \dfrac{^-1}{(^-1/2)^2}$

Pick any point on $(^-1,0)$ and substitute into the derivative.

$f'\left(\dfrac{^-1}{2}\right) = 1 + \dfrac{^-1}{1/4}$

$= 1 - 4$

$= {}^-3$

The slope of the tangent line at $x = \dfrac{^-1}{2}$ is $^-3$. The exact value of the slope is not important. The important fact is that the slope is negative.

Substituting an x value into a function produces a corresponding y value. The coordinates of the point (x,y), where y is the largest of all the y values, is said to be a **maximum point**. The coordinates of the point (x,y), where y is the smallest of all the y values, is said to be a **minimum point**. To find these points, only a few x values must be tested. First, find all of the x values that make the derivative either zero or undefined. Substitute these values into the original function to obtain the corresponding y values. Compare the y values. The largest y value is a maximum; the smallest y value is a minimum. If the question asks for the maxima or minima on an interval, be certain to also find the y values that correspond to the numbers at either end of the interval.

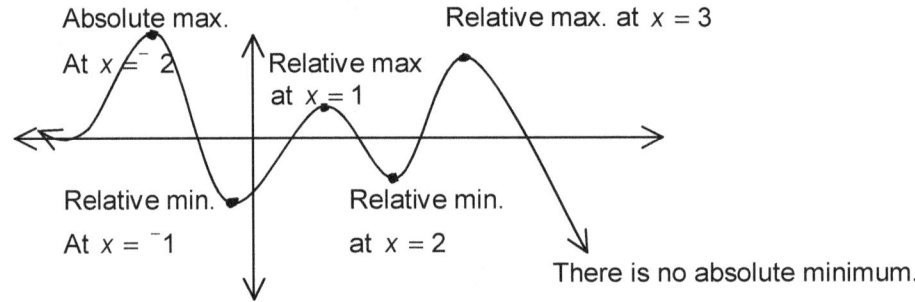

Example:

Find the maxima and minima of $f(x) = 2x^4 - 4x^2$ at the interval $(^-2, 1)$.

$f'(x) = 8x^3 - 8x$	Take the derivative first. Find all the x values (critical values) that make the derivative zero or undefined. In this case, there are no x values that make the derivative undefined.
$8x^3 - 8x = 0$	
$8x(x^2 - 1) = 0$	
$8x(x - 1)(x + 1) = 0$	Substitute the critical values into the original function. Also, plug in the endpoint of the interval. Note that 1 is a critical point and an endpoint.
$x = 0, x = 1,$ or $x = ^-1$	
$f(0) = 2(0)^4 - 4(0)^2 = 0$	
$f(1) = 2(1)^4 - 4(1)^2 = ^-2$	
$f(^-1) = 2(^-1)^4 - 4(^-1)^2 = ^-2$	
$f(^-2) = 2(^-2)^4 - 4(^-2)^2 = 16$	

The maximum is at (–2, 16) and there are minima at (1, –2) and (–1, –2). (0,0) is neither the maximum or minimum on (–2, 1) but it is still considered a relative extra point.

The first derivative reveals whether a curve is rising or falling **(increasing or decreasing)** from the left to the right. In much the same way, the second derivative relates whether the curve is concave up or concave down. Curves which are concave up are said to "collect water;" curves which are concave down are said to "dump water." To find the intervals where a curve is concave up or concave down, follow the following steps.

1. Take the second derivative (i.e. the derivative of the first derivative).
2. Find the critical x values.
   - Set the second derivative equal to zero and solve for critical x values.
   - Find the x values that make the second derivative undefined (i.e. make the denominator of the second derivative equal to zero).
   Such values may not always exist.
3. Pick sample values which are both less than and greater than each of the critical values.
4. Substitute each of these sample values into the second derivative and determine whether the result is positive or negative.
   - If the sample value yields a positive number for the second derivative, the curve is concave up on the interval where the sample value originated.
   - If the sample value yields a negative number for the second derivative, the curve is concave down on the interval where the sample value originated.

Example:

Find the intervals where the curve is concave up and concave down for $f(x) = x^4 - 4x^3 + 16x - 16$.

$f'(x) = 4x^3 - 12x^2 + 16$
$f''(x) = 12x^2 - 24x$

Take the second derivative.

$12x^2 - 24x = 0$
$12x(x - 2) = 0$
$x = 0$ or $x = 2$

Find the critical values by setting the second derivative equal to zero.

There are no values that make the second derivative undefined. Set up a number line with the critical values.

Sample values: ⁻1, 1, 3

$f''(-1) = 12(-1)^2 - 24(-1) = 36$
$f''(1) = 12(1)^2 - 24(1) = -12$
$f''(3) = 12(3)^2 - 24(3) = 36$

Pick sample values in each of the 3 intervals. If the sample value produces a negative number, the function is concave down.

If the value produces a positive number, the curve is concave up. If the value produces a zero, the function is linear.

Therefore when $x < 0$ the function is concave up,
when $0 < x < 2$ the function is concave down,
when $x > 2$ the function is concave up.

A **point of inflection** is a point where a curve changes from being concave up to concave down or vice versa. To find these points, follow the steps for finding the intervals where a curve is concave up or concave down. A critical value is part of an inflection point if the curve is concave up on one side of the value and concave down on the other. The critical value is the x coordinate of the inflection point. To get the y coordinate, plug the critical value into the original function.

Example: Find the inflection points of $f(x) = 2x - \tan x$ where $\frac{-\pi}{2} < x < \frac{\pi}{2}$.

$(x) = 2x - \tan x$ $\quad \frac{-\pi}{2} < x < \frac{\pi}{2}$ $\quad$ Note the restriction on x.

$f'(x) = 2 - \sec^2 x$ $\quad$ Take the second derivative.

$f''(x) = 0 - 2 \bullet \sec x \bullet (\sec x \tan x)$ $\quad$ Use the Power rule.

$= -2 \bullet \dfrac{1}{\cos x} \bullet \dfrac{1}{\cos x} \bullet \dfrac{\sin x}{\cos x}$

The derivative of $\sec x$ is $(\sec x \tan x)$.

$f''(x) = \dfrac{-2 \sin x}{\cos^3 x}$

Find critical values by solving for the second derivative equal to zero.

$0 = \dfrac{-2 \sin x}{\cos^3 x}$

No x values on $\left(\dfrac{-\pi}{2}, \dfrac{\pi}{2}\right)$ make the denominator zero.

$^-2\sin x = 0$

$\sin x = 0$

$x = 0$

←——|——→
      0

Pick sample values on each side of the critical value $x = 0$.

Sample values: $x = \dfrac{^-\pi}{4}$ and $x = \dfrac{\pi}{4}$

$$f''\left(\dfrac{^-\pi}{4}\right) = \dfrac{^-2\sin(^-\pi/4)}{\cos^3(\pi/4)} = \dfrac{^-2(^-\sqrt{2}/2)}{(\sqrt{2}/2)^3} = \dfrac{\sqrt{2}}{(\sqrt{8}/8)} = \dfrac{8\sqrt{2}}{\sqrt{8}} = \dfrac{8\sqrt{2}}{\sqrt{8}} \cdot \dfrac{\sqrt{8}}{\sqrt{8}}$$

$$= \dfrac{8\sqrt{16}}{8} = 4$$

$$f''\left(\dfrac{\pi}{4}\right) = \dfrac{^-2\sin(\pi/4)}{\cos^3(\pi/4)} = \dfrac{^-2(\sqrt{2}/2)}{(\sqrt{2}/2)^3} = \dfrac{^-\sqrt{2}}{(\sqrt{8}/8)} = \dfrac{^-8\sqrt{2}}{\sqrt{8}} = -4$$

The second derivative is positive on $(0, \infty)$ and negative on $(^-\infty, 0)$. So the curve changes concavity at $x = 0$. Use the original equation to find the y value that inflection occurs at.

$f(0) = 2(0) - \tan 0 = 0 - 0 = 0$ The inflection point is (0,0).

Taking the integral of a function and evaluating it from one x value to another provides the total **area under the curve** (i.e. between the curve and the x axis). Remember, though, that regions above the x axis have "positive" area and regions below the x axis have "negative" area. You must account for these positive and negative values when finding the area under curves. Follow these steps.

1. Determine the x values that will serve as the left and right boundaries of the region.
2. Find all x values between the boundaries that are either solutions to the function or are values which are not in the domain of the function. These numbers are the interval numbers.
3. Integrate the function.
4. Evaluate the integral once for each of the intervals using the boundary numbers.
5. If any of the intervals evaluates to a negative number, make it positive (the negative simply tells you that the region is below the x axis).
6. Add the value of each integral to arrive at the area under the curve.

Example:

Find the area under the following function on the given intervals.
$f(x) = \sin x$; $(0, 2\pi)$

$\sin x = 0$ Find any roots to f(x) on $(0, 2\pi)$.
$x = \pi$
$(0, \pi)$ $(\pi, 2\pi)$ Determine the intervals using the boundary numbers and the roots.

$\int \sin x \, dx = {}^{-}\cos x$ Integrate f(x). We can ignore the constant c because we have numbers to use to evaluate the integral.

${}^{-}\cos x \big]_{x=0}^{x=\pi} = {}^{-}\cos \pi - ({}^{-}\cos 0)$

${}^{-}\cos x \big]_{x=0}^{x=\pi} = {}^{-}(-1) + (1) = 2$

${}^{-}\cos x \big]_{x=\pi}^{x=2\pi} = {}^{-}\cos 2\pi - ({}^{-}\cos \pi)$

${}^{-}\cos x \big]_{x=\pi}^{x=2\pi} = {}^{-}1 + ({}^{-}1) = {}^{-}2$ The ${}^{-}2$ means that for $(\pi, 2\pi)$, the region is below the x axis, but the area is still 2.

Area $= 2 + 2 = 4$ Add the 2 integrals together to get the area.

Extreme value problems are also known as max-min problems. Extreme value problems require using the first derivative to find values which either maximize or minimize some quantity such as area, profit, or volume. Follow these steps to solve an extreme value problem.

1. Write an equation for the quantity to be maximized or minimized.
2. Use the other information in the problem to write secondary equations.
3. Use the secondary equations for substitutions, and rewrite the original equation in terms of only one variable.
4. Find the derivative of the primary equation (step 1) and the critical values of this derivative.
5. Substitute these critical values into the primary equation.

The value which produces either the largest or smallest value is used to find the solution.

Example:

A manufacturer wishes to construct an open box from the piece of metal shown below by cutting squares from each corner and folding up the sides. The square piece of metal is 12 feet on a side. What are the dimensions of the squares to be cut out which will maximize the volume?

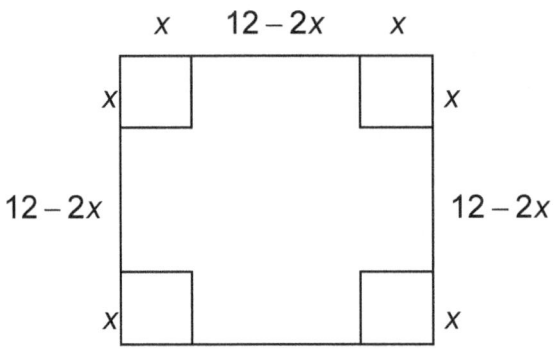

Volume = lwh Primary equation.
$l = 12 - 2x$
$w = 12 - 2x$ Secondary equations.
$h = x$
$V = (12 - 2x)(12 - 2x)(x)$ Make substitutions.
$V = (144x - 48x^2 + 4x^3)$ Take the derivative.
$\dfrac{dV}{dx} = 144 - 96x + 12x^2$

Find critical values by setting the derivative equal to zero.
$0 = 12(x^2 - 8x + 12)$
$0 = 12(x - 6)(x - 2)$
$x = 6$ and $x = 2$ Substitute critical values into volume equation.

$V = 144(6) - 48(6)^2 + 4(6)^3$ $V = 144(2) - 48(2)^2 + 4(2)^3$
$V = 0$ ft^3 when $x = 6$ $V = 128$ ft^3 when $x = 2$

Therefore, the manufacturer can maximize the volume if the squares to be cut out are 2 feet by 2 feet ($x = 2$).

Velocity and acceleration of a particle moving along a line

If a particle (or a car, a bullet, etc.) is moving along a line, then the distance that the particle travels can be expressed by a function in terms of time.

1. The first derivative of the distance function will provide the velocity function for the particle. Substituting a value for time into this expression will provide the instantaneous velocity of the particle at the time. Velocity is the rate of change of the distance traveled by the particle. Taking the absolute value of the derivative provides the speed of the particle. A positive value for the velocity indicates that the particle is moving forward, and a negative value indicates the particle is moving backwards.
2. The second derivative of the distance function (which would also be the first derivative of the velocity function) provides the acceleration function. The acceleration of the particle is the rate of change of the velocity. If a value for time produces a positive acceleration, the particle is speeding up; if it produces a negative value, the particle is slowing down. If the acceleration is zero, the particle is moving at a constant speed.

To find the time when a particle stops, set the first derivative (i.e. the velocity function) equal to zero and solve for time. This time value is also the instant when the particle changes direction.

Example:

The motion of a particle moving along a line is according to the equation:

$s(t) = 20 + 3t - 5t^2$ where s is in meters and t is in seconds. Find the position, velocity, and acceleration of a particle at $t = 2$ seconds.

$s(2) = 20 + 3(2) - 5(2)^2$ $= 6$ meters	Plug $t = 2$ into the original equation to find the position.
$s'(t) = v(t) = 3 - 10t$	The derivative of the first function gives the velocity.
$v(2) = 3 - 10(2) = {}^-17$ m/s	Plug $t = 2$ into the velocity function to find the velocity. ${}^-17$ m/s indicates the particle is moving backwards.
$s''(t) = a(t) = {}^-10$ $a(2) = {}^-10$ m/s²	The second derivation of position gives the acceleration. Substitute $t = 2$, yields an acceleration of ${}^-10$ m/s², which indicates the particle is slowing down.

Finding the **rate of change** of one quantity (for example distance, volume, etc.) with respect to time it is often referred to as a rate of change problem. To find an instantaneous rate of change of a particular quantity, write a function in terms of time for that quantity; then take the derivative of the function. Substitute in the values at which the instantaneous rate of change is sought.

Functions which are in terms of more than one variable may be used to find related rates of change. These functions are often not written in terms of time. To find a related rate of change, follow these steps.

1. Write an equation which relates all the quantities referred to in the problem.
2. Take the derivative of both sides of the equation with respect to time.
   Follow the same steps as used in implicit differentiation. This means take the derivative of each part of the equation remembering to multiply each term by the derivative of the variable involved with respect to time. For example, if a term includes the variable v for volume, take the derivative of the term remembering to multiply by dv/dt for the derivative of volume with respect to time. dv/dt is the rate of change of the volume.
3. Substitute the known rates of change and quantities, and solve for the desired rate of change.

Example:

1. What is the instantaneous rate of change of the area of a circle where the radius is 3 cm?

$A(r) = \pi r^2$	Write an equation for area.
$A'(r) = 2\pi r$	Take the derivative to find the rate of change.
$A'(3) = 2\pi(3) = 6\pi$	Substitute in $r = 3$ to arrive at the instantaneous rate of change.

Antiderivatives

Taking the antiderivative of a function is the opposite of taking the derivative of the function--much in the same way that squaring an expression is the opposite of taking the square root of the expression. For example, since the derivative of x^2 is $2x$ then the antiderivative of 2x is x^2. The key to being able to take antiderivatives is being as familiar as possible with the derivative rules.

To take the antiderivative of an algebraic function (the sum of products of coefficients and variables raised to powers other than negative one), take the antiderivative of each term in the function by following these steps.

1. Take the antiderivative of each term separately.
2. The coefficient of the variable should be equal to one plus the exponent.
3. If the coefficient is not one more than the exponent, put the correct coefficient on the variable and also multiply by the reciprocal of the number put in.

   Ex. For $4x^5$, the coefficient should be 6 not 4. So put in 6 and the reciprocal 1/6 to achieve $(4/6)6x^5$.

4. Finally take the antiderivative by replacing the coefficient and variable with just the variable raised to one plus the original exponent.

   Ex. For $(4/6)6x^5$, the antiderivative is $(4/6)x^6$.

   You have to add in constant c because there is no way to know if a constant was originally present since the derivative of a constant is zero.

5. Check your work by taking the first derivative of your answer. You should get the original algebraic function.

Examples: Take the antiderivative of each function.

1. $f(x) = 5x^4 + 2x$ The coefficient of each term is already 1 more than the exponent.

   $F(x) = x^5 + x^2 + c$ $F(x)$ is the antiderivative of $f(x)$

   $F'(x) = 5x^4 + 2x$ Check by taking the derivative of $F(x)$.

2. $f(x) = {}^-2x^{-3}$

   $F(x) = x^{-2} + c = \dfrac{1}{x^2} + c$ $F(x)$ is the antiderivative of $f(x)$.

   $F'(x) = {}^-2x^{-3}$ Check.

3. $f(x) = {}^-4x^2 + 2x^7$ Neither coefficient is correct.

   $f(x) = {}^-4 \bullet \dfrac{1}{3} \bullet 3x^2 + 2 \bullet \dfrac{1}{8} \bullet 8x^7$

   Put in the correct coefficient along with its reciprocal.

   $F(x) = {}^-4 \bullet \dfrac{1}{3} x^3 + 2 \bullet \dfrac{1}{8} x^8 + c$ $F(x)$ is the antiderivative of $f(x)$.

   $F(x) = \dfrac{{}^-4}{3} x^3 + \dfrac{1}{4} x^8 + c$

   $F'(x) = {}^-4x^2 + 2x^7$ Check.

Antiderivatives for trigonometric functions

The rules for taking antiderivatives of trigonometric functions follow, but be aware that these can get very confusing to memorize because they are very similar to the derivative rules. Check the antiderivative you get by taking the derivative and comparing it to the original function.

1. $\sin x$ the antiderivative for $\sin x$ is $^-\cos x + c$.
2. $\cos x$ the antiderivative for $\cos x$ is $\sin x + c$.
3. $\tan x$ the antiderivative for $\tan x$ is $-\ln|\cos x| + c$.
4. $\sec^2 x$ the antiderivative for $\sec^2 x$ is $\tan x + c$.
5. $\sec x \tan x$ the antiderivative for $\sec x \tan x$ is $\sec x + c$.

If the trigonometric function has a coefficient, simply keep the coefficient and multiply the antiderivative by it.

Examples: Find the antiderivatives for the following functions.

1. $f(x) = 2\sin x$ Carry the 2 throughout the problem.

   $F(x) = 2(^-\cos x) = ^-2\cos x + c$ $F(x)$ is the antiderivative.

   $F'(x) = ^-2(^-\sin x) = 2\sin x$ Check by taking the derivative of $F(x)$.

2. $f(x) = \dfrac{\tan x}{5}$

   $F(x) = \dfrac{-\ln|\cos x|}{5} + c$ $F(x)$ is the antiderivative of $f(x)$.

   $F'(x) = \dfrac{1}{5}\left(-\dfrac{1}{|\cos x|}\right)(-\sin x) = \dfrac{1}{5}\tan x$ Check by taking the derivative of $F(x)$.

Practice problems: Find the antiderivative of each function.

1. $f(x) = ^-20\cos x$ 2. $f(x) = \pi \sec x \tan x$

Antiderivatives of exponential functions

Use the following rules when finding the antiderivative of an exponential function.

1. e^x The antiderivative of e^x is the same $e^x + c$.
2. a^x The antiderivative of a^x, where a is any number, is $a^x / \ln a + c$.

Examples: Find the antiderivatives of the following functions:

1. $f(x) = 10e^x$

$F(x) = 10e^x + c$ $F(x)$ is the antiderivative.

$F'(x) = 10e^x$ Check by taking the derivative of $F(x)$.

2. $f(x) = \dfrac{2^x}{3}$

$F(x) = \dfrac{1}{3} \cdot \dfrac{2^x}{\ln 2} + c$ $F(x)$ is the antiderivative.

$F'(x) = \dfrac{1}{3\ln 2} \ln 2 (2^x)$ Check by taking the derivative of $F(x)$.

$F'(x) = \dfrac{2^x}{3}$

Velocity problems

The derivative of a distance function provides a velocity function, and the derivative of a velocity function provides an acceleration function. Therefore taking the antiderivative of an acceleration function yields the velocity function, and the antiderivative of the velocity function yields the distance function.

Example:

A particle moves along the x axis with acceleration $a(t) = 3t - 1$ cm/sec/sec. At time $t = 4$, the particle is moving to the left at 3 cm per second. Find the velocity of the particle at time $t = 2$ seconds.

$a(t) = 3t - 1$ Before taking the antiderivative, make sure the correct coefficients are present.

$a(t) = 3 \bullet \dfrac{1}{2} \bullet 2t - 1$

$v(t) = \dfrac{3}{2}t^2 - 1 \bullet t + c$ $v(t)$ is the antiderivative of $a(t)$.

$v(4) = \dfrac{3}{2}(4)^2 - 1(4) + c = {}^-3$

Use the given information that $v(4) = {}^-3$ to find c.

$24 - 4 + c = {}^-3$
$20 + c = {}^-3$
$c = {}^-23$ The constant is ${}^-23$.

$v(t) = \dfrac{3}{2}t^2 - 1t + {}^-23$ Rewrite $v(t)$ using $c = {}^-23$.

$v(2) = \dfrac{3}{2}2^2 - 1(2) + {}^-23$ Solve $v(t)$ at $t=2$.

$v(2) = 6 + 2 + {}^-23 = {}^-15$ the velocity at $t = 2$ is -15 cm/sec.

Practice problem:

A particle moves along a line with acceleration $a(t) = 5t + 2$. The velocity after 2 seconds is ${}^-10$ m/sec.

1. Find the initial velocity.
2. Find the velocity at $t = 4$.

Distance problems

To find the distance function, take the antiderivative of the velocity function. And to find the velocity function, find the antiderivative of the acceleration function. Use the information in the problem to solve for the constants that result from taking the antiderivatives.

Example:

A particle moves along the x axis with acceleration $a(t) = 6t - 6$. The initial velocity is 0 m/sec and the initial position is 8 cm to the right of the origin. Find the velocity and position functions.

$v(0) = 0$
$s(0) = 8$
$a(t) = 6t - 6$ Interpret the given information.

Put in the coefficients needed to take the antiderivative.

$a(t) = 6 \cdot \dfrac{1}{2} \cdot 2t - 6$

$v(t) = \dfrac{6}{2}t^2 - 6t + c$

Take the antiderivative of $a(t)$ to get $v(t)$.

$v(0) = 3(0)^2 - 6(0) + c = 0$ Use $v(0) = 0$ to solve for c.
$0 - 0 + c = 0$
$c = 0$ $c = 0$

$v(t) = 3t^2 - 6t + 0$ Rewrite $v(t)$ using $c = 0$.

$v(t) = 3t^2 - 6\dfrac{1}{2} \cdot 2t$

Put in the coefficients needed to take the antiderivative.

$s(t) = t^3 - \dfrac{6}{2}t^2 + c$

Take the antiderivative of $v(t)$ to get $s(t)$ → the distance function.

$s(0) = 0^3 - 3(0)^2 + c = 8$ Use $s(0) = 8$ to solve for c.
$c = 8$
$s(t) = t^3 - 3t^2 + 8$

TEACHER CERTIFICATION STUDY GUIDE

Integral evaluation - fundamental theorem of calculus

An integral is almost the same thing as an antiderivative, the only difference is the notation.

$\int_{-2}^{1} 2x\,dx$ is the integral form of the antiderivative of $2x$. The numbers at the top and bottom of the integral sign (1 and $^-2$) are the numbers used to find the exact value of this integral. If these numbers are used the integral is said to be *definite* and does not have an unknown constant c in the answer.

The fundamental theorem of calculus states that an integral such as the one above is equal to the antiderivative of the function inside (here $2x$) evaluated from $x = {}^-2$ to $x = 1$. To do this, follow these steps.

1. Take the antiderivative of the function inside the integral.

2. Plug in the upper number (here $x = 1$) and plug in the lower number (here $x = {}^- 2$), giving two expressions.

3. Subtract the second expression from the first to achieve the integral value.

Examples:

1. $\int_{-2}^{1} 2x\,dx = x^2 \Big]_{-2}^{1}$ Take the antiderivative.

   $\int_{-2}^{1} 2x\,dx = 1^2 - (^-2)^2$ Substitute in $x = 1$ and $x = {}^-2$ and subtract the results.

   $\int_{-2}^{1} 2x\,dx = 1 - 4 = {}^- 3$ The integral has the value $^-3$.

2. $\int_{0}^{\pi/2} \cos x\,dx = \sin x\Big]_{0}^{\pi/2}$

   The antiderivative of $\cos x$ is $\sin x$.

   $\int_{0}^{\pi/2} \cos x\,dx = \sin\frac{\pi}{2} - \sin 0$ Substitute in $x = \frac{\pi}{2}$ and $x = 0$. Subtract the results.

   $\int_{0}^{\pi/2} \cos x\,dx = 1 - 0 = 1$ The integral has the value 1.

MATHEMATICS (Secondary)

A list of integration formulas follows. In each case the letter u is used to represent either a single variable or an expression. Note that also in each case du is required. du is the derivative of whatever u stands for. If u is sin x then du is cosx, which is the derivative of sinx. If the derivative of u is not entirely present, remember you can put in constants as long as you also insert the reciprocal of any such constants. n is a natural number.

$$\int u^n du = \frac{1}{n+1} u^{n+1} + c \text{ if } n \neq {}^-1$$

$$\int \frac{1}{u} du = \ln|u| + c$$

$$\int e^u du = e^u + c$$

$$\int a^u du = \frac{1}{\ln a} a^u + c$$

$$\int \sin u\, du = {}^-\cos u + c$$

$$\int \cos u\, du = \sin u + c$$

$$\int \sec^2 u\, du = \tan u + c$$

$$\int \csc^2 u\, du = {}^-\cot u + c$$

Example:

1. $\int \frac{6}{x} dx = 6 \int \frac{1}{x} dx$ You can pull any constants outside the integral.

   $\int \frac{6}{x} dx = 6\ln|x| + c$

Sometimes an integral does not always look exactly like the forms above. But with a simple substitution (sometimes called a u substitution), the integral can be made to look like one of the general forms.

You might need to experiment with different u substitutions before you find the one that works. Follow these steps.

1. If the object of the integral is a sum or difference, first split the integral up.
2. For each integral, see if it fits one of the general forms from the previous pg.
3. If the integral does not fit one of the forms, substitute the letter u in place of one of the expressions in the integral.
4. Off to the side, take the derivative of u, and see if that derivative exists inside the original integral. If it does, replace that derivative expression with du. If it does not, try another u substitution.
5. Now the integral should match one of the general forms, including both the u and the du.
6. Take the integral using the general forms, and substitute for the value of u.

Examples:

1. $\int(\sin x^2 \cdot 2x + \cos x^2 \cdot 2x)dx$ Split the integral up.

$\int \sin(x^2) \cdot 2x\,dx + \int \cos(x^2) 2x\,dx$

$u = x^2, \quad du = 2x\,dx$ If you let $u = x^2$, the derivative of u, du, is $2x\,dx$.

$\int \sin u\,du + \int \cos u\,du$ Make the u and du substitutions.

$^-\cos u + \sin u + c$ Use the formula for integrating $\sin u$ and $\cos u$.

$^-\cos(x^2) + \sin(x^2) + c$ Substitute back in for u.

2. $\int e^{\sin x} \cos x\,dx$ Try letting $u = \cos x$. The

$u = \cos x, \, du = ^-\sin x\,dx$ derivative of u would be $^-\sin x\,dx$, which is not present.

$u = \sin x, \, du = \cos x\,dx$ Try another substitution: $u = \sin x, du = \cos x\,dx$. $du = \cos x\,dx$ is present.

$\int e^u\,du$ e^u is one of the general forms.

e^u The integral of e^u is e^u.

$e^{\sin x}$ Substitute back in for u.

Integration by parts should only be used if none of the other integration methods works. Integration by parts requires two substitutions (both *u* and *dv*).

1. Let *dv* be the part of the integral that you think can be integrated by itself.
2. Let *u* be the part of the integral which is left after the *dv* substitution is made.
3. Integrate the *dv* expression to arrive at just simply *v*.
4. Differentiate the *u* expression to arrive at *du*. If *u* is just *x*, then *du* is dx.
5. Rewrite the integral using $\int u\,dv = uv - \int v\,du$.
6. All that is left is to integrate $\int v\,du$.
7. If you cannot integrate *v du,* try a different set of substitutions and start the process over.

Examples:

1. $\int xe^{3x}\,dx$

$dv = e^{3x}\,dx \quad u = x$

$v = \frac{1}{3}e^{3x} \quad du = dx$

$\int xe^{3x}\,dx = x\left(\frac{1}{3}e^{3x}\right) - \int \frac{1}{3}e^{3x}\,dx$

$\int xe^{3x}\,dx = \frac{1}{3}xe^{3x} - \frac{1}{3} \cdot \frac{1}{3}\int e^{3x}\,3\,dx$

$\int xe^{3x}\,dx = \frac{1}{3}xe^{3x} - \frac{1}{9}e^{3x} + c$

Make *dv* and *u* substitutions.

Integrate the *dv* term to arrive at *v*.

Differentiate the *u* term to arrive at *du*.

Rewrite the integral using the above formula. Before taking the integral of $\frac{1}{3}e^{3x}\,dx$, you must put in a 3 and another $1/3$.

Integrate to arrive at the solution.

2. $\int \ln 4x \, dx$

Note that no other integration method will work.

$dv = dx \quad u = \ln 4x$

Make the *dv* and *u* substitutions.

$v = x \quad du = \dfrac{1}{4x} \cdot 4 = \dfrac{1}{x} dx$

Integrate *dx* to get *x*.

Differentiate ln4*x* to get $(1/x)\, dx$.

$\int \ln 4x \, dx = \ln 4x \cdot x - \int x \cdot \dfrac{1}{x} dx$

Rewrite the formula above.

$\int \ln 4x \, dx = \ln 4x \cdot x - \int dx$

Simplify the integral.

$\int \ln 4 \, dx = \ln 4x \cdot x - x + c$

Integrate *dx* to get the value $x + c$

Integration – area between two curves

Finding the area between two curves is much the same as finding the area under one curve. But instead of finding the roots of the functions, you need to find the *x* values which produce the same number from both functions (set the functions equal and solve). Use these numbers and the given boundaries to write the intervals.
On each interval you must pick sample values to determine which function is "on top" of the other. Find the integral of each function. For each interval, subtract the "bottom" integral from the "top" integral. Use the interval numbers to evaluate each of these differences. Add the evaluated integrals to get the total area between the curves.

Example:

Find the area of the regions bounded by the two functions on the indicated intervals.

$f(x) = x + 2$ and $g(x) = x^2$ $[^-2, 3]$ Set the functions equal and solve.

$x + 2 = x^2$
$0 = (x - 2)(x + 1)$
$x = 2$ or $x = {}^-1$
$({}^-2, {}^-1)$ $({}^-1, 2)$ $(2, 3)$

Use the solutions and the boundary numbers to write the intervals.

$f({}^-3/2) = \left(\dfrac{{}^-3}{2}\right) + 2 = \dfrac{1}{2}$

Pick sample values on the integral and evaluate each function as that number.

$g({}^-3/2) = \left(\dfrac{{}^-3}{2}\right)^2 = \dfrac{9}{4}$

$g(x)$ is "on top" on $[^-2, {}^-1]$.

$f(0) = 2$

$f(x)$ is "on top" on $[^-1, 2]$.

$g(0) = 0$

$f(5/2) = \dfrac{5}{2} + 2 = \dfrac{9}{2}$

$g(x)$ is "on top" on $[2, 3]$.

$g(5/2) = \left(\dfrac{5}{2}\right)^2 = \dfrac{25}{4}$

$\int f(x)dx = \int (x + 2)dx$

$\int f(x)dx = \int x\,dx + 2\int dx$

$\int f(x)dx = \dfrac{1}{1+1}x^{1+1} + 2x$

$\int f(x)dx = \dfrac{1}{2}x^2 + 2x$

$\int g(x)dx = \int x^2 dx$

$\int g(x)dx = \dfrac{1}{2+1}x^{2+1} = \dfrac{1}{3}x^3$

MATHEMATICS (Secondary)

$$\text{Area 1} = \int g(x)dx - \int f(x)dx \qquad g(x) \text{ is "on top" on } [^-2, ^-1].$$

$$\text{Area 1} = \frac{1}{3}x^3 - \left(\frac{1}{2}x^2 + 2x\right)\Big]_{-2}^{-1}$$

$$\text{Area 1} = \left[\frac{1}{3}(^-1)^3 - \left(\frac{1}{2}(^-1)^2 + 2(^-1)\right)\right] - \left[\frac{1}{3}(^-2)^3 - \left(\frac{1}{2}(^-2)^2 + 2(^-2)\right)\right]$$

$$\text{Area 1} = \left[\frac{-1}{3} - \left(\frac{-3}{2}\right)\right] - \left[\frac{-8}{3} - (^-2)\right]$$

$$\text{Area 1} = \left(\frac{7}{6}\right) - \left(\frac{-2}{3}\right) = \frac{11}{6}$$

$$\text{Area 2} = \int f(x)dx - \int g(x)dx \qquad f(x) \text{ is "on top" on } [^-1, 2].$$

$$\text{Area 2} = \frac{1}{2}x^2 + 2x - \frac{1}{3}x^3\Big]_{-1}^{2}$$

$$\text{Area 2} = \left(\frac{1}{2}(2)^2 + 2(2) - \frac{1}{3}(2)^3\right) - \left(\frac{1}{2}(^-1)^2 + 2(^-1) - \frac{1}{3}(^-1)^3\right)$$

$$\text{Area 2} = \left(\frac{10}{3}\right) - \left(\frac{1}{2} - 2 + \frac{1}{3}\right)$$

$$\text{Area 2} = \frac{27}{6}$$

$$\text{Area 3} = \int g(x)dx - \int f(x)dx \qquad g(x) \text{ is "on top" on } [2, 3].$$

$$\text{Area 3} = \frac{1}{3}x^3 - \left(\frac{1}{2}x^2 + 2x\right)\Big]_{2}^{3}$$

$$\text{Area 3} = \left[\frac{1}{3}(3)^3 - \left(\frac{1}{2}(3^2) + 2(3)\right)\right] - \left[\frac{1}{3}(2)^3 - \left(\frac{1}{2}(2)^2 + 2(2)\right)\right]$$

$$\text{Area 3} = \left(\frac{-3}{2}\right) - \left(\frac{-10}{3}\right) = \frac{11}{6}$$

$$\text{Total area} = \frac{11}{6} + \frac{27}{6} + \frac{11}{6} = \frac{49}{6} = 8\frac{1}{6}$$

Integration - volume of a solid of revolution

If you take the area bounded by a curve or curves and revolve it about a line, the result is a solid of revolution. To find the volume of such a solid, the Washer Method works in most instances. Imagine slicing through the solid perpendicular to the line of revolution. The "slice" should resemble a washer. Use an integral and the formula for the volume of disk.

$$Volume_{disk} = \pi \bullet radius^2 \bullet thickness$$

Depending on the situation, the radius is the distance from the line of revolution to the curve; or if there are two curves involved, the radius is the difference between the two functions. The thickness is *dx* if the line of revolution is parallel to the *x* axis and *dy* if the line of revolution is parallel to the *y* axis. Finally, integrate the volume expression using the boundary numbers from the interval.

Example:

Find the value of the solid of revolution found by revolving $f(x) = 9 - x^2$ about the *x* axis on the interval $[0, 4]$.

radius $= 9 - x^2$
thickness $= dx$

$$Volume = \int_0^4 \pi(9 - x^2)^2 dx$$

Use the formula for volume of a disk.

$$Volume = \pi \int_0^4 \left(81 - 18x^2 + x^4\right) dx$$

$$Volume = \pi \left(81x - \frac{18}{2+1}x^3 + \frac{1}{4+1}x^5 \right) \Big]_0^4$$

Take the integral.

$$Volume = \pi \left(81x - 6x^3 + \frac{1}{5}x^5 \right) \Big]_0^4$$

Evaluate the integral first and subtract. $x = 4$ then at $x = 0$

$$Volume = \pi \left[\left(324 - 384 + \frac{1024}{5} \right) - (0 - 0 + 0) \right]$$

$$Volume = \pi \left(144\frac{4}{5} \right) = 144\frac{4}{5}\pi = 454.9$$

MATHEMATICS (Secondary)

SUBAREA III.   **MEASUREMENT AND GEOMETRY**

Competency 10   Understand attributes of measurement and measuring units.

It is necessary to be familiar with the metric and customary system in order to estimate measurements.

Some common equivalents include:

ITEM	APPROXIMATELY EQUAL TO	
	METRIC	IMPERIAL
large paper clip	1 gram	1 ounce
1 quart	1 liter	
average sized man	75 kilograms	170 pounds
1 yard	1 meter	
math textbook	1 kilogram	2 pounds
1 mile	1 kilometer	
1 foot	30 centimeters	
thickness of a dime	1 millimeter	0.1 inches

Estimate the measurement of the following items:

The length of an adult cow = _____ meters
The thickness of a compact disc = _____ millimeters
Your height = _____ meters
length of your nose = _____ centimeters
weight of your math textbook = _____ kilograms
weight of an automobile = _____ kilograms
weight of an aspirin = _____ grams

TEACHER CERTIFICATION STUDY GUIDE

Solve the following problems.

1) Choose the correct unit of measure for a man that ran three laps around a football field.

A. minutes
B. degrees
C. kilograms
D. kilometers

Answer:

Only D is a unit of length or distance→Correct answer.

    A is a unit of time.
    B is a unit of angle.
    C is a unit of weight.

2) Choose the statement with an appropriate unit of measurement.

A. He ran out of paint while painting the wall. He only covered three yards of the wall.
B. He painted the wall very fast and covered the wall except 12 inches of it.
C. It took him 9 hours to paint 36 feet of the wall.
D. If he paints at a rate of 3 square feet per minute, he would complete painting the wall in 15 minutes.

Answer: D is the only correct answer, since the unit of area is "square" of length.

3) What unit of measurement would not be used to measure the weight of a small bird?

A. grams
B. ounces
C. pints
D. milligrams

Answer: C is not the appropriate measure. Pints is a measure of volume. All the other choices are units of weight measurement.

Distances, area, and volumes

A car skidded 170 yards on an icy road before coming to a stop. How long is the skid distance in kilometers?

Since 1 yard ≈ 0.9 meters, multiply 170 yards by 0.9.

$$170 \times 0.9 = 153 \text{ meters}$$

Since 1000 meters = 1 kilometer, divide 153 by 1000.

$$\frac{153}{1000} = 0.153 \text{ kilometers}$$

A dog house has the shape and dimensions shown. Find the perimeter of the dog house to the nearest foot.

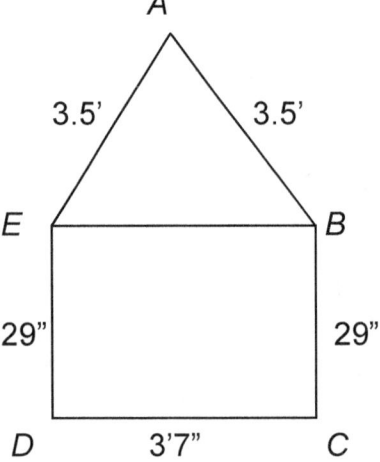

First, convert the dimensions to a common unit. Let's work in inches.

$AB = 3.5' = 3.5 \times 12$ (inches) $= 42"$
$BC = 29"$
$CD = 3'7" = (3 \times 12) + 7$ inches $= 36" + 7" = 43"$
$DE = 29"$
$EA = 42"$ (same as AB)

Perimeter (distance around) = $AB + BC + CD + DE + EA$

$$= 42 + 29 + 43 + 29 + 42 = 185"$$

In feet, the perimeter is $\dfrac{185}{12} = 15.416$ feet.

To the nearest foot, the perimeter is 15 feet.

Characteristics of a circle

1) The radius, r, of a circle is the length of a line segment from the center to a point on the circle.

2) The diameter, d, is the length of a line segment through the center of the circle with the end points on the circle.

3) The circumference, c, is the distance around the circle.

4) $d = 2r$

5) Circumference is given by $c = 2\pi r$. (π is approximately 3.14)

6) Area of the circle is given by $A = \pi r^2$.

Example: A city municipal pool has the shape and dimensions shown below.
It has a uniform depth of 6 feet.

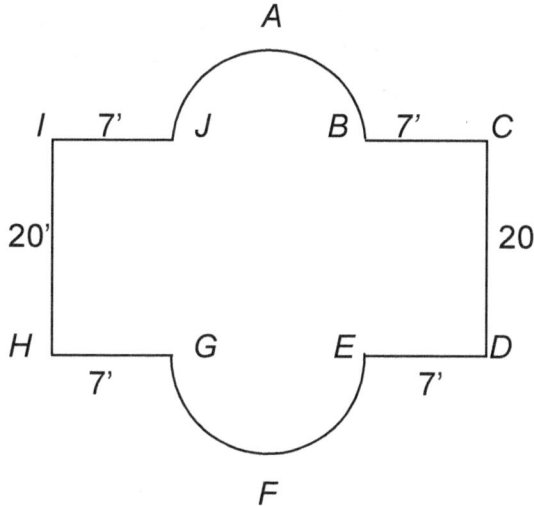

The radius of the half circle *JAB* and *EFG* is 4 ft.

a) Find the perimeter in feet of the pool.
b) Find the surface area of the pool in ft^2.
c) Find the volume of the pool in ft^3.

Answer a. Perimeter is the distance around the pool, or the total of $JAB + BC + CD + DE + EFG + GH + HI + IJ$.
JAB is half a circle with radius of 4 feet.

Circumference of $JAB = EFG = \frac{1}{2}(2\pi(4)) = 4\pi$

Perimeter $= 4\pi + 7 + 20 + 7 + 4\pi + 7 + 20 + 7 = 68' + 8\pi'$
Perimeter ≈ 93.135 feet.

Answer b. Area of the rectangle is length x width.
$$A = 20' \times 22' = 440 \text{ ft}^2$$
Area of one half circle $= \frac{1}{2}\pi r^2 = \frac{1}{2}\pi(4)^2 = 8\pi \text{ ft}^2$
Area of the other half circle is the same.

Total area $= 440 + 16\pi \approx 490.265 \text{ ft}^2$

Answer c. The volume of the pool is equal to the surface area times the height, or depth. From part b, we know the surface area is $440 \text{ ft}^2 + 8\pi \text{ ft}^2$.

Thus, the volume is:

$(440 + 16\pi) \times 6 = 2640 + 96\pi = 2941.5928$
The volume is 2941.593 ft^3.

Example: Mary wants to carpet her living room with dimensions as shown below. She is leaving a uniform space of 1.5 feet from each wall uncarpeted. The material and labor will cost $12.56 per square yard. Find the cost of the carpeting.

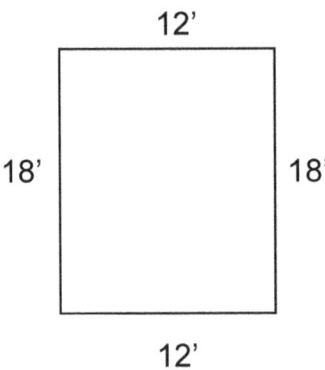

Length of the carpet area $= 18' - 2(1.5') = 18' - 3' = 15'$.
Width of carpet area $= 12' - 2(1.5') = 12' - 3' = 9'$.

Area of the carpet needed $= 15' \times 9' = 135 \text{ ft}^2$.
Note: 1 yd^2 is equal to 9 ft^2.

In square yards, the area that needs carpeting $= \frac{135}{9} = 15 \text{ yd}^2$.

The cost of carpeting $= 15 \text{ yd}^2 \times \$12.56$
The cost is $188.40.

Example: Mr. Jack wants to pave a walkway with a concrete uniform 4' width around his swimming pool (dimensions are shown below). 1 bag of concrete cost $10.85, and can pave and area of 4 square feet. Find the cost of the job.

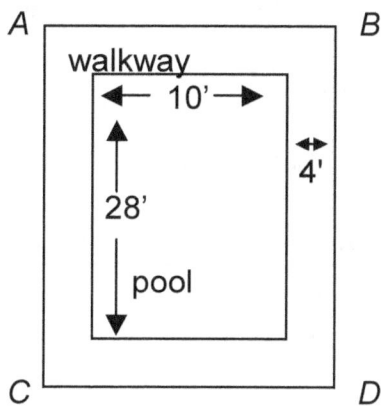

The area of the concrete walk = area *ABCD* − area of pool.

Length of area $ABCD = 28' + 4' + 4' = 36'$
Width of area $ABCD = 10' + 4' + 4' = 18'$
Area of $ABCD = 36' \times 18' = 648$ ft^2

Area of pool $= 28' \times 10' = 280$ ft^2
Subtract the area of the pool from the area of *ABCD* to determine the amount of concrete needed.

$$648 - 280 = 368 \text{ ft}^2$$

The number of concrete bags needed is:

$$\frac{368}{4} = 92 \text{ bags.}$$

Each back costs $10.85, so the cost of 92 bags is:

$$92 \times \$10.85 = \$998.20$$

There are many methods for converting measurements within a system. One method is to multiply the given measurement by a conversion factor. This conversion factor is the ratio of:

$$\frac{\text{new units}}{\text{old units}} \quad \text{OR} \quad \frac{\text{what you want}}{\text{what you have}}$$

Sample problems:

1. Convert 3 miles to yards.

$$\frac{3 \text{ miles}}{1} \times \frac{1{,}760 \text{ yards}}{1 \text{ mile}} = \underline{\qquad} \text{ yards}$$

= 5,280 yards

1. multiply by the conversion factor
2. cancel the miles units
3. solve

2. Convert 8,750 meters to kilometers.

$$\frac{8{,}750 \text{ meters}}{1} \times \frac{1 \text{ kilometer}}{1000 \text{ meters}} = \underline{\qquad} \text{ km}$$

= 8.75 kilometers

1. multiply by the conversion factor
2. cancel the meters units
3. solve

Examining the **change in area or volume** of a given figure requires first to find the existing area given the original dimensions and then finding the new area given the increased dimensions.

Sample problem:

Given the rectangle below determine the change in area if the length is increased by 5 and the width is increased by 7.

Draw and label a sketch of the new rectangle.

Find the areas.

Area of original = LW   Area of enlarged shape = LW
        = (7)(4)   = (12)(11)
        = 28 units^2 = 132 units^2

The change in area is 132 − 28 = 104 units^2.

Example:

The distance around a race course is exactly 1 mile, 17 feet, and 9¼ inches. Approximate this distance to the nearest tenth of a foot. Convert the distance to feet.

$$1 \text{ mile} = 1760 \text{ yards} = 1760 \times 3 \text{ feet} = 5280 \text{ feet.}$$

$$9\frac{1}{4} \text{ inches} = \frac{37}{4} \times \frac{1}{12} = \frac{37}{48} \approx 0.77083 \text{ feet}$$

So 1 mile, 17 feet and $9\frac{1}{4}$ inches = $5280 + 17 + 0.77083$ feet

$$= 5297.\underline{7}7083 \text{ feet.}$$

Now, we need to round to the nearest tenth digit. The underlined 7 is in the tenth place. The digit in the hundredth place, also a 7, is greater than 5, the 7 in the tenths place needs to be rounded up to 8 to get a final answer of 5297.8 feet.

We can use first-order differential equations to model and solve real-world problems. For example, we can solve the following problem involving the flow of water out of a tank using differential equations.

Example:

Let $y(t)$ be the height of the water in a tank at time t. Let $V(t)$ be the volume of water in a tank at time t. Water leaks through a hole of area a out of the bottom of the tank. The following equation defines the rate of change in the volume of water in the tank.

$$\frac{dV}{dt} = -a\sqrt{2gy}$$ where g is the acceleration due to gravity

Suppose the tank is a cylinder with height of 3 feet, a radius of 1 foot, and a circular hole with radius of 2 inches. Find the height of the water at time t, if the tank was full at $t=0$. Assume g equals 32 ft/s^2.

$V = 3\pi$ ft^3 $\quad a = 4\pi$ in$^2 = \dfrac{1}{36}\pi$ ft^2

Define volume of tank and area of hole.

$$\dfrac{dV}{dt} = -a\sqrt{2gy} = -\dfrac{1}{36}\pi\sqrt{64y} = -\dfrac{2}{9}\pi\sqrt{y}$$

Apply rate of change formula.

$$y(t) = \dfrac{V(t)}{\pi}$$

$$\dfrac{dy}{dt} = \dfrac{1}{\pi}\dfrac{dV}{dt} = (\dfrac{1}{\pi})(-\dfrac{2}{9}\pi\sqrt{y}) = -\dfrac{2}{9}\sqrt{y}$$

Define $y(t)$ and $\dfrac{dy}{dt}$.

$$\dfrac{-9}{2\sqrt{y}}dy = dt, \quad \int\dfrac{-9}{2\sqrt{y}}dy = \int dt$$

Solve and integrate.

$$t = \dfrac{(-9)2\sqrt{y}}{2} = (-9)\sqrt{y} + C$$

Solve for t.

at $t = 0$, $y = 3$ because the tank is full

$$0 = (-9)\sqrt{3} + C$$
$$C = 9\sqrt{3}$$

Find the constant.

$$t = \dfrac{(-9)2\sqrt{y}}{2} = (-9)\sqrt{y} + 9\sqrt{3}$$

$$y(t) = \dfrac{(t-9\sqrt{3})^2}{(-9)^2} = \dfrac{t^2 - 18\sqrt{3} + 243}{81}$$

Solve for $y(t)$.

Most numbers in mathematics are "exact" or "counted". Measurements are "approximate". They usually involve interpolation or figuring out which mark on the ruler is closest. Any measurement you get with a measuring device is approximate. Variations in measurement are called precision and accuracy.

Precision is a measurement of how exactly a measurement is made, without reference to a true or real value. If a measurement is precise it can be made again and again with little variation in the result. The precision of a measuring device is the smallest fractional or decimal division on the instrument. The smaller the unit or fraction of a unit on the measuring device, the more precisely it can measure.

The greatest possible error of measurement is always equal to one-half the smallest fraction of a unit on the measuring device.

Accuracy is a measure of how close the result of measurement comes to the "true" value.

If you are throwing darts, the true value is the bull's eye. If the three darts land on the bull's eye, the dart thrower is both precise (all land near the same spot) and accurate (the darts all land on the "true" value). The greatest measure of error allowed is called the tolerance. The least acceptable limit is called the lower limit and the greatest acceptable limit is called the upper limit. The difference between the upper and lower limits is called the tolerance interval. For example, a specification for an automobile part might be 14.625 ± 0.005 mm. This means that the smallest acceptable length of the part is 14.620 mm and the largest length acceptable is 14.630 mm. The tolerance interval is 0.010 mm. One can see how it would be important for automobile parts to be within a set of limits in terms of length. If the part is too long or too short it will not fit properly and vibrations will occur weakening the part and eventually causing damage to other parts.

Competency 11   **Apply measurement principles to analyze the spatial characteristics of two- and three-dimensional shapes.**

Cut the **compound shape** into smaller, more familiar shapes and then compute the total area by adding the areas of the smaller parts.

Sample problem:

Find the area of the given shape.

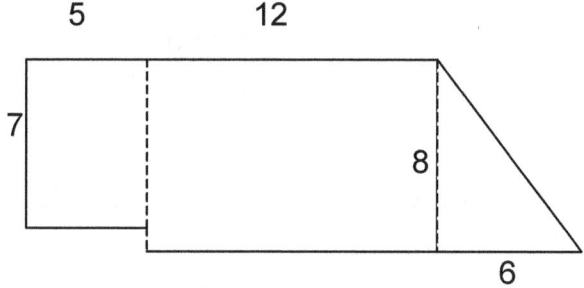

1. Using a dotted line we have cut the shape into smaller parts that are familiar.

2. Use the appropriate formula for each shape and find the sum of all areas.

Area 1 = LW	Area 2 = LW	Area 3 = ½bh
= (5)(7)	= (12)(8)	= ½(6)(8)
= 35 units²	= 96 units²	= 24 units²

Total area = Area 1 + Area 2 + Area 3
           = 35 + 96 + 24
           = 155 units²

The strategy for solving problems of this nature should be to identify the given shapes and choose the correct formulas. Subtract the smaller cut out shape from the larger shape.

Sample problems:

1. Find the area of one side of the metal in the circular flat washer shown below:

   1. the shapes are both circles.

   2. use the formula $A = \pi r^2$ for both.
      (Inside diameter is 3/8")

   Area of larger circle   Area of smaller circle
   $A = \pi r^2$ $A = \pi r^2$
   $A = \pi(.75^2)$ $A = \pi(.1875^2)$
   $A = 1.76625$ in^2 $A = .1103906$ in^2

   Area of metal washer = larger area − smaller area

   $= 1.76625$ in^2 $- .1103906$ in^2
   $= 1.6558594$ in^2

2. You have decided to fertilize your lawn. The shapes and dimensions of your lot, house, pool and garden are given in the diagram below. The shaded area will not be fertilized. If each bag of fertilizer costs $7.95 and covers 4,500 square feet, find the total number of bags needed and the total cost of the fertilizer.

Area of Lot	Area of House	Area of Driveway
$A = \frac{1}{2} h(b_1 + b_2)$	$A = LW$	$A = LW$
$A = \frac{1}{2}(100)(180 + 160)$	$A = (80)(50)$	$A = (10)(25)$
$A = 17{,}000$ sq ft	$A = 4{,}000$ sq ft	$A = 250$ sq ft

Area of Pool	Area of Garden
$A = \pi r^2$	$A = s^2$
$A = \pi(10)^2$	$A = (20)^2$
$A = 314.159$ sq. ft.	$A = 400$ sq. ft.

Total area to fertilize = Lot area − (House + Driveway + Pool + Garden)
= 17,000 − (4,000 + 250 + 314.159 + 400)
= 12,035.841 sq ft

Number of bags needed = Total area to fertilize / 4,500 sq.ft. bag
= 12,035.841 / 4,500
= 2.67 bags

Since we cannot purchase 2.67 bags we must purchase 3 full bags.

Total cost = Number of bags * $7.95
= 3 * $7.95
= $23.85

Surface Area and Volume of Regular and Solid Figures

Use the formulas to find the volume and surface area.

FIGURE	VOLUME	TOTAL SURFACE AREA
Right Cylinder	$\pi r^2 h$	$2\pi rh + 2\pi r^2$
Right Cone	$\dfrac{\pi r^2 h}{3}$	$\pi r \sqrt{r^2 + h^2} + \pi r^2$
Sphere	$\dfrac{4}{3}\pi r^3$	$4\pi r^2$
Rectangular Solid	LWH	$2LW + 2WH + 2LH$

Note: $\sqrt{r^2 + h^2}$ is equal to the slant height of the cone.

Sample problem:

1. Given the figure below, find the volume and surface area.

   $r = 5$ in $h = 6.2$ in

Volume $= \dfrac{\pi r^2 h}{3}$ First write the formula.

$\dfrac{1}{3}\pi(5^2)(6.2)$ Then substitute.

162.3 cubic inches   Finally solve the problem.

Surface area $= \pi r \sqrt{r^2 + h^2} + \pi r^2$ First write the formula.

$\pi 5 \sqrt{5^2 + 6.2^2} + \pi 5^2$ Then substitute.

203.6 square inches   Compute.

Note: volume is always given in cubic units and area is always given in square units.

Perimeter and area of polygons

FIGURE	AREA FORMULA	PERIMETER FORMULA
Rectangle	LW	$2(L+W)$
Triangle	$\dfrac{1}{2}bh$	$a+b+c$
Parallelogram	bh	sum of lengths of sides
Trapezoid	$\dfrac{1}{2}h(a+b)$	sum of lengths of sides

Sample problems:

1. Find the area and perimeter of a rectangle if its length is 12 inches and its diagonal is 15 inches.

1. Draw and label a sketch.

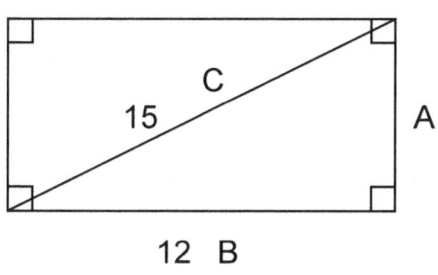

2. Since the height is still needed use Pythagorean formula to find missing leg of the triangle.

$$A^2 + B^2 = C^2$$
$$A^2 + 12^2 = 15^2$$
$$A^2 = 15^2 - 12^2$$
$$A^2 = 81$$
$$A = 9$$

Now use this information to find the area and perimeter.

$A = LW$	$P = 2(L + W)$	1. write formula
$A = (12)(9)$	$P = 2(12 + 9)$	2. substitute
$A = 108 \text{ in}^2$	$P = 42$ inches	3. solve

Circumferences and areas of circles

Given a circular figure the formulas are as follows:

$$A = \pi r^2 \qquad C = \pi d \text{ or } 2\pi r$$

Sample problem:

1. If the area of a circle is 50 cm^2, find the circumference.

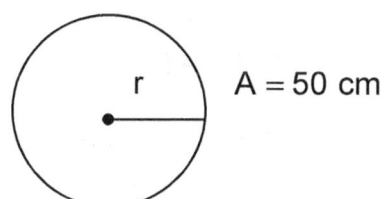

1. Draw a sketch.

$A = 50$ cm^2

2. Determine what is still needed.

MATHEMATICS (Secondary)

Use the area formula to find the radius.

$A = \pi r^2$	1. write formula
$50 = \pi r^2$	2. substitute
$\dfrac{50}{\pi} = r^2$	3. divide by π
$15.915 = r^2$	4. substitute
$\sqrt{15.915} = \sqrt{r^2}$	5. take square root of both sides
$3.989 \approx r$	6. compute

Use the approximate answer (due to rounding) to find the circumference.

$C = 2\pi r$	1. write formula
$C = 2\pi (3.989)$	2. substitute
$C \approx 25.064$	3. compute

Areas of parallelograms, triangles, and trapezoids

When using formulas to find each of the required items it is helpful to remember to always use the same strategies for problem solving. First, draw and label a sketch if needed. Second, write the formula down and then substitute in the known values. This will assist in identifying what is still needed (the unknown). Finally, solve the resulting equation.

Being consistent in the strategic approach to problem solving is paramount to teaching the concept as well as solving it.

Use appropriate problem solving strategies to find the solution.

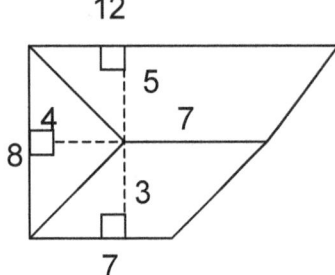

1. Find the area of the given figure.

2. Cut the figure into familiar shapes.

3. Identify what type figures are given and write the appropriate formulas.

Area of figure 1 (triangle)	Area of figure 2 (parallelogram)	Area of figure 3 (trapezoid)
$A=\frac{1}{2}bh$	$A=bh$	$A=\frac{1}{2}h(a+b)$
$A=\frac{1}{2}(8)(4)$	$A=(7)(3)$	$A=\frac{1}{2}(5)(12+7)$
$A=16$ sq. ft	$A=21$ sq. ft	$A=47.5$ sq. ft

Now find the total area by adding the area of all figures.

Total area $= 16+21+47.5$
Total area $= 84.5$ square ft

Given the figure below, find the area by dividing the polygon into smaller shapes.

1. divide the figure into two triangles and a rectangle.

2. find the missing lengths.

3. find the area of each part.

4. find the sum of all areas.

Find base of both right triangles using Pythagorean Formula:

$a^2 + b^2 = c^2$ $a^2 + b^2 = c^2$
$a^2 + 12^2 = 15^2$ $a^2 + 12^2 = 20^2$
$a^2 = 225 - 144$ $a^2 = 400 - 144$
$a^2 = 81$ $a^2 = 256$
$a = 9$ $a = 16$

Area of triangle 1	Area of triangle 2	Area of rectangle
$A=\frac{1}{2}bh$	$A=\frac{1}{2}bh$	$A=LW$
$A=\frac{1}{2}(9)(12)$	$A=\frac{1}{2}(16)(12)$	$A=(15)(12)$
$A=54$ sq. units	$A=96$ sq. units	$A=180$ sq. units

Find the sum of all three figures.

$54 + 96 + 180 = 330$ square units

FIGURE	LATERAL AREA	TOTAL AREA	VOLUME
Right prism	sum of area of lateral faces (rectangles)	lateral area plus 2 times the area of base	area of base times height
regular pyramid	sum of area of lateral faces (triangles)	lateral area plus area of base	1/3 times the area of the base times the height

Find the total area of the given figure:

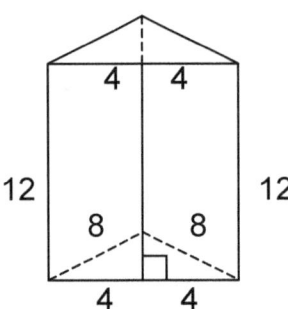

1. Since this is a triangular prism, first find the area of the bases.

2. Find the area of each rectangular lateral face.

3. Add the areas together.

$A = \frac{1}{2}bh$ $A = LW$ 1. write formula

$8^2 = 4^2 + h^2$
$h = 6.928$ 2. find the height of the base triangle

$A = \frac{1}{2}(8)(6.928)$ $A = (8)(12)$ 3. substitute known values

$A = 27.713$ sq. units $A = 96$ sq. units   4. compute

Total Area $= 2(27.713) + 3(96)$
$\phantom{\text{Total Area}} = 343.426$ sq. units

FIGURE	VOLUME	TOTAL SURFACE AREA	LATERAL AREA
Right Cylinder	$\pi r^2 h$	$2\pi rh + 2\pi r^2$	$2\pi rh$
Right Cone	$\dfrac{\pi r^2 h}{3}$	$\pi r\sqrt{r^2+h^2} + \pi r^2$	$\pi r\sqrt{r^2+h^2}$

Note: $\sqrt{r^2+h^2}$ is equal to the slant height of the cone.

Sample problem:

1. A water company is trying to decide whether to use traditional cylindrical paper cups or to offer conical paper cups since both cost the same. The traditional cups are 8 cm wide and 14 cm high. The conical cups are 12 cm wide and 19 cm high. The company will use the cup that holds the most water.

Draw and label a sketch of each.

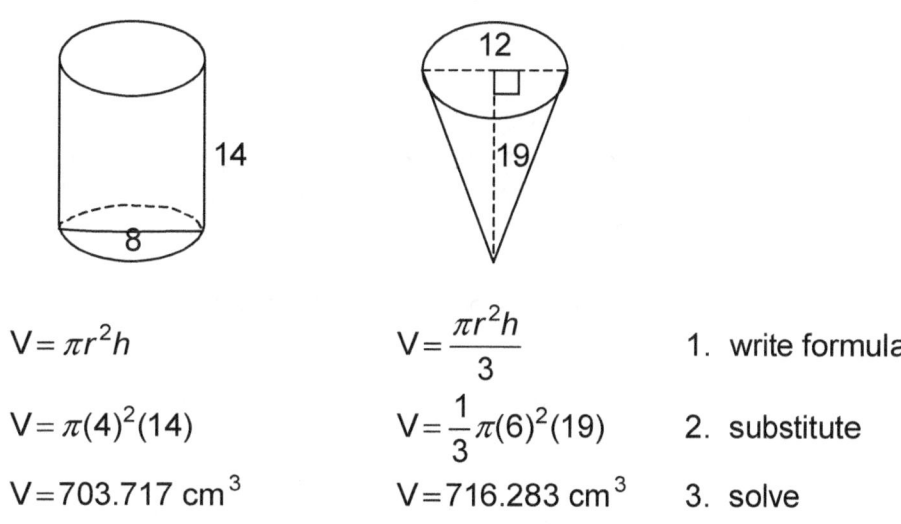

$V = \pi r^2 h$	$V = \dfrac{\pi r^2 h}{3}$	1. write formula
$V = \pi(4)^2(14)$	$V = \dfrac{1}{3}\pi(6)^2(19)$	2. substitute
$V = 703.717$ cm^3	$V = 716.283$ cm^3	3. solve

The choice should be the conical cup since its volume is more.

Surface area and volume of spheres

FIGURE	VOLUME	TOTAL SURFACE AREA
Sphere	$\dfrac{4}{3}\pi r^3$	$4\pi r^2$

Sample problem:

1. How much material is needed to make a basketball that has a diameter of 15 inches? How much air is needed to fill the basketball?

Draw and label a sketch:

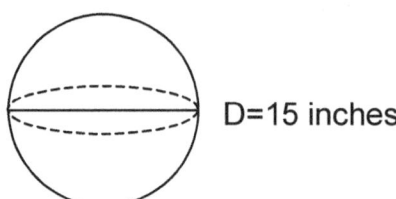 D=15 inches

Total surface area

$TSA = 4\pi r^2$

$= 4\pi(7.5)^2$

$= 706.9 \text{ in}^2$

Volume

$V = \dfrac{4}{3}\pi r^3$

$= \dfrac{4}{3}\pi(7.5)^3$

$= 1767.1 \text{ in}^3$

1. write formula
2. substitute
3. solve

Polygons are similar if and only if there is a one-to-one correspondence between their vertices such that the corresponding angles are congruent and the lengths of corresponding sides are proportional.

Given the rectangles below, compare the area and perimeter.

$A = LW$
$A = (6)(9)$

$A = 54$ sq. units

$P = 2(L+W)$
$P = 2(6+9)$

$P = 30$ units

$A = LW$
$A = (9)(13.5)$

$A = 121.5$ sq. units

$P = 2(L+W)$
$P = 2(9+13.5)$

$P = 45$ units

1. write formula
2. substitute known values
3. compute

1. write formula
2. substitute known values
3. compute

Notice that the areas relate to each other in the following manner:

Ratio of sides   9/13.5 = 2/3

Multiply the first area by the square of the reciprocal (3/2)² to get the second area.
$$54 \times (3/2)^2 = 121.5$$

The perimeters relate to each other in the following manner:

Ratio of sides   9/13.5 = 2/3

Multiply the perimeter of the first by the reciprocal of the ratio to get the perimeter of the second.
$$30 \times 3/2 = 45$$

State and apply the relationships that exist when the altitude is drawn to the hypotenuse of a right triangle.

A **right triangle** is a triangle with one right angle. The side opposite the right angle is called the **hypotenuse**. The other two sides are the **legs**. An **altitude** is a line drawn from one vertex, perpendicular to the opposite side.

When an altitude is drawn to the hypotenuse of a right triangle, then the two triangles formed are similar to the original triangle and to each other.

Example:

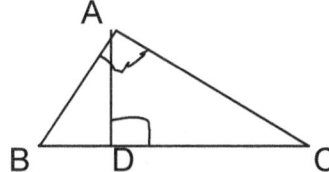

Given right triangle ABC with right angle at A, altitude AD drawn to hypotenuse BC at D.

△ABC ~ △ABD ~ △ACD   The triangles formed are similar to each other and to the original right triangle.

$$\frac{a}{b} = \frac{b}{c}$$

If a, b and c are positive numbers such that then b is called the **geometric mean** between a and c.

Example:

Find the geometric mean between 6 and 30.

$$\frac{6}{x} = \frac{x}{30}$$
$$x^2 = 180$$
$$x = \sqrt{180} = \sqrt{36 \cdot 5} = 6\sqrt{5}$$

The geometric mean is significant when the altitude is drawn to the hypotenuse of a right triangle.

The length of the altitude is the geometric mean between each segment of the hypotenuse,
    and
Each leg is the geometric mean between the hypotenuse and the segment of the hypotenuse that is adjacent to the leg.

Example:

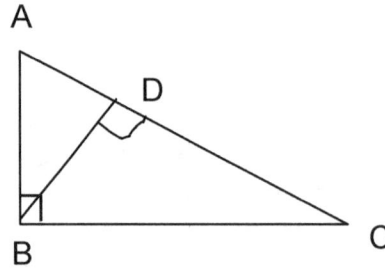

△ABC is a right △
BD is the altitude of △ABC
AB = 6
AC = 12
Find AD, CD, BD, and BC

$$\frac{12}{6} = \frac{6}{AD} \qquad \frac{3}{BD} = \frac{BD}{9} \qquad \frac{12}{BC} = \frac{BC}{9}$$

12(AD) = 36 $(BD)^2 = 27$ $(BC)^2 = 108$

AD = 3

BD = $\sqrt{27} = \sqrt{9 \cdot 3} = 3\sqrt{3}$

BC = $\sqrt{108} = \sqrt{36 \cdot 3} = 6\sqrt{3}$

CD = 12 - 3 = 9

Pythagorean theorem states that the square of the length of the hypotenuse is equal to the sum of the squares of the lengths of the legs. Symbolically, this is stated as:

$$c^2 = a^2 + b^2$$

Given the right triangle below, find the missing side.

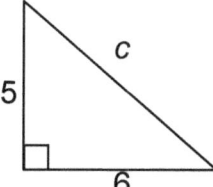

$c^2 = a^2 + b^2$ 1. write formula
$c^2 = 5^2 + 6^2$ 2. substitute known values
$c^2 = 61$ 3. take square root
$c = \sqrt{61}$ or 7.81   4. solve

The converse of the Pythagorean Theorem states that if the square of one side of a triangle is equal to the sum of the squares of the other two sides, then the triangle is a right triangle.

Example:
Given $\triangle XYZ$, with sides measuring 12, 16 and 20 cm. Is this a right triangle?

$$c^2 = a^2 + b^2$$
$$20^2 \; ? \; 12^2 + 16^2$$
$$400 \; ? \; 144 + 256$$
$$400 = 400$$

Yes, the triangle is a right triangle.

This theorem can be expanded to determine if triangles are obtuse or acute.

If the square of the longest side of a triangle is greater than the sum of the squares of the other two sides, then the triangle is an obtuse triangle.
    and
If the square of the longest side of a triangle is less than the sum of the squares of the other two sides, then the triangle is an acute triangle.

Example:
Given △LMN with sides measuring 7, 12, and 14 inches. Is the triangle right, acute, or obtuse?

$$14^2 \; ? \; 7^2 + 12^2$$
$$196 \; ? \; 49 + 144$$
$$196 > 193$$

Therefore, the triangle is obtuse.

Given the special right triangles below, we can find the lengths of other special right triangles.

Sample problems:

1. 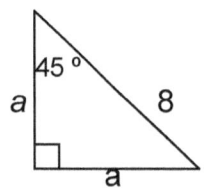 if $8 = a\sqrt{2}$ then $a = 8/\sqrt{2}$ or 5.657

2. 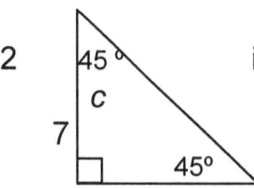 if $7 = a$ then $c = a\sqrt{2} = 7\sqrt{2}$ or 9.899

3. 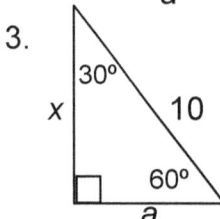 if $2a = 10$ then $a = 5$ and $x = a\sqrt{3} = 5\sqrt{3}$ or 8.66

MATHEMATICS (Secondary)

Given right triangle ABC, the adjacent side and opposite side can be identified for each angle A and B.

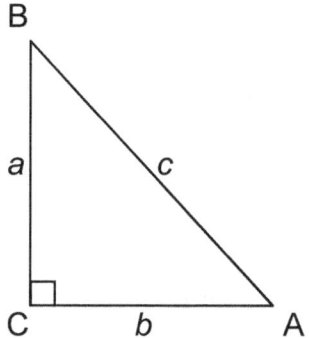

Looking at angle A, it can be determined that side *b* is adjacent to angle A and side *a* is opposite angle A.

If we now look at angle B, we see that side a is adjacent to angle b and side *b* is opposite angle B.

The longest side (opposite the 90 degree angle) is always called the hypotenuse.

The basic trigonometric ratios are listed below:

Sine = opposite / hypotenuse   Cosine = adjacent / hypotenuse   Tangent = opposite / adjacent

Sample problem:

1. Use triangle ABC to find the sin, cos and tan for angle A.

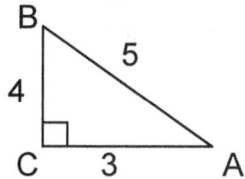

sin = 4/5
cos = 3/5
tan = 4/3

Use the basic trigonometric ratios of sine, cosine and tangent to solve for the missing sides of right triangles when given at least one of the acute angles.

In the triangle ABC, an acute angle of 63 degrees and the length of the hypotenuse (12). The missing side is the one adjacent to the given angle.

MATHEMATICS (Secondary)

The appropriate trigonometric ratio to use would be cosine since we are looking for the adjacent side and we have the length of the hypotenuse.

$Cos x = \dfrac{adjacent}{hypothesis}$ 1. Write formula.

$Cos\ 63 = \dfrac{x}{12}$ 2. Substitute known values.

$0.454 = \dfrac{x}{12}$

$x = 5.448$ 3. Solve.

We can represent any two-dimensional geometric figure in the **Cartesian** or **rectangular coordinate system**. The Cartesian or rectangular coordinate system is formed by two perpendicular axes (coordinate axes): the X-axis and the Y-axis. If we know the dimensions of a two-dimensional, or planar, figure, we can use this coordinate system to visualize the shape of the figure.

Example: Represent an isosceles triangle with two sides of length 4.

Draw the two sides along the x- and y- axes and connect the points (vertices).

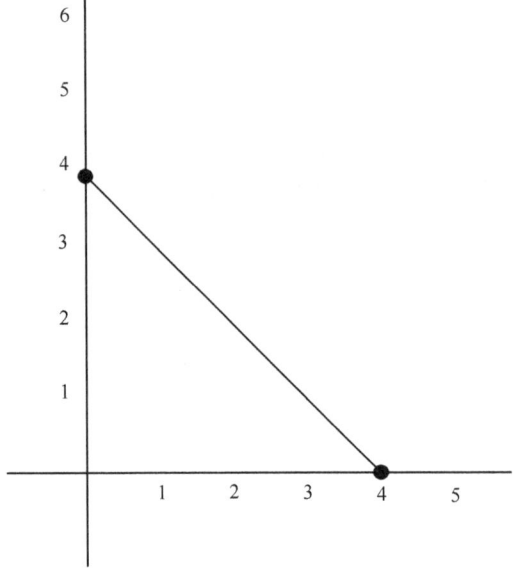

In order to represent three-dimensional figures, we need three coordinate axes (X, Y, and Z) which are all mutually perpendicular to each other. Since we cannot draw three mutually perpendicular axes on a two-dimensional surface, we use oblique representations.

Example: Represent a cube with sides of 2.

Once again, we draw three sides along the three axes to make things easier.

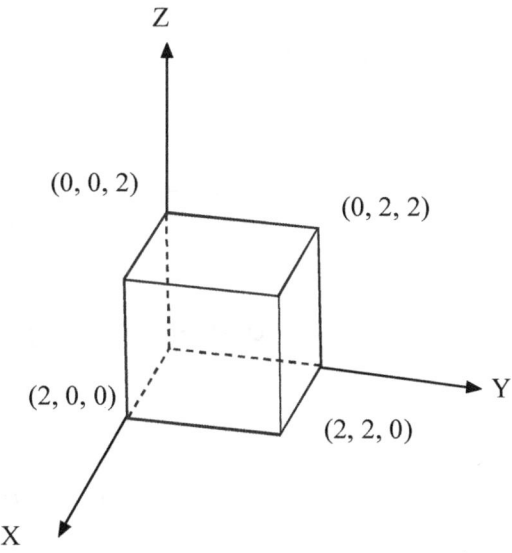

Each point has three coordinates (x, y, z).

The union of all points on a simple closed surface and all points in its interior form a space figure called a **solid**. The five regular solids, or **polyhedra**, are the cube, tetrahedron, octahedron, icosahedron, and dodecahedron. A **net** is a two-dimensional figure that can be cut out and folded up to make a three-dimensional solid. Below are models of the five regular solids with their corresponding face polygons and nets.

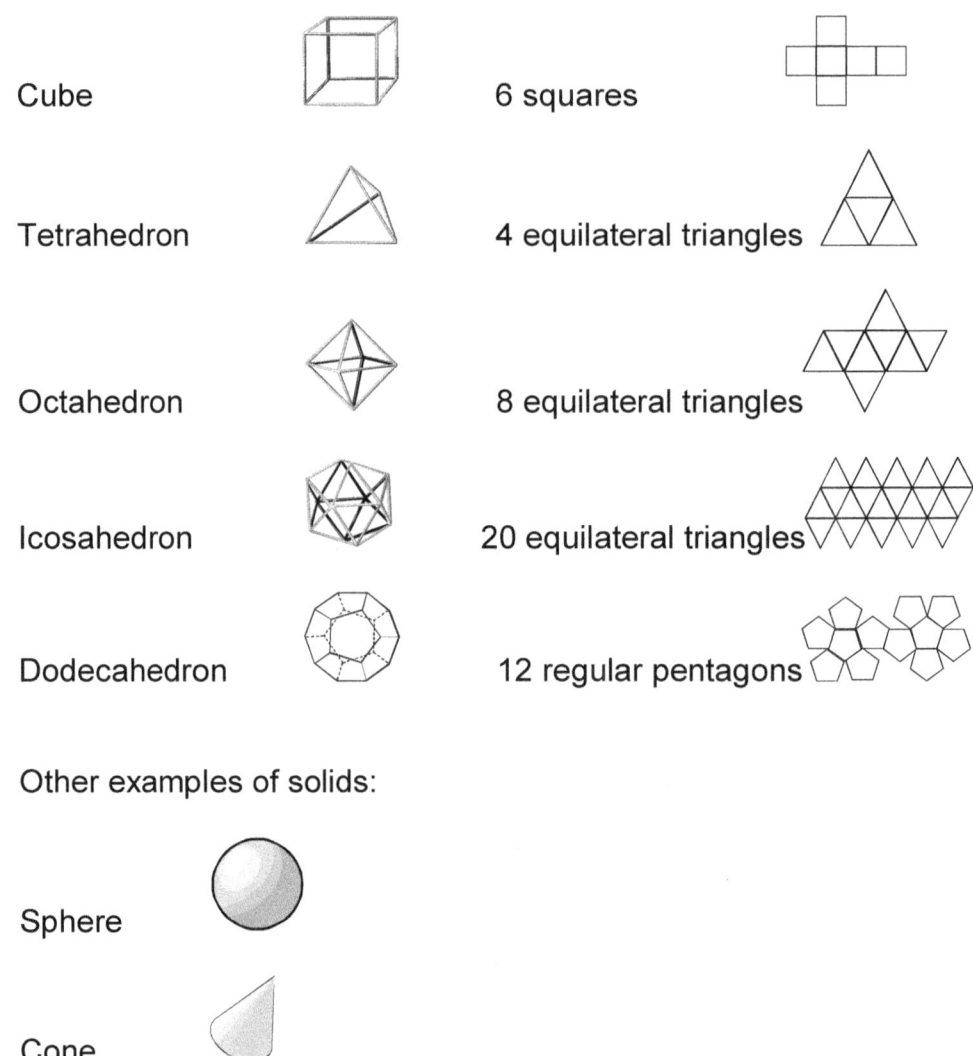

Other examples of solids:

Sphere

Cone

Competency 12   **Apply geometric principles of points, lines, angles, planes, congruence, and similarity to analyze the formal characteristics of two- and three-dimensional shapes.**

A **triangle** is a polygon with three sides.

Triangles can be classified by the types of angles or the lengths of their sides.

Classifying by angles:

An **acute** triangle has exactly three *acute* angles.
A **right** triangle has one *right* angle.
An **obtuse** triangle has one *obtuse* angle.

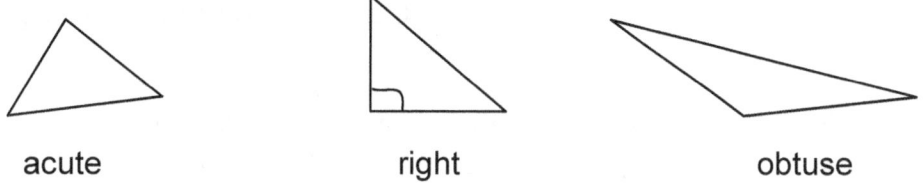

    acute   right   obtuse

Classifying by sides:

All *three* sides of an **equilateral** triangle are the same length.
Two sides of an **isosceles** triangle are the same length.
None of the sides of a **scalene** triangle are the same length.

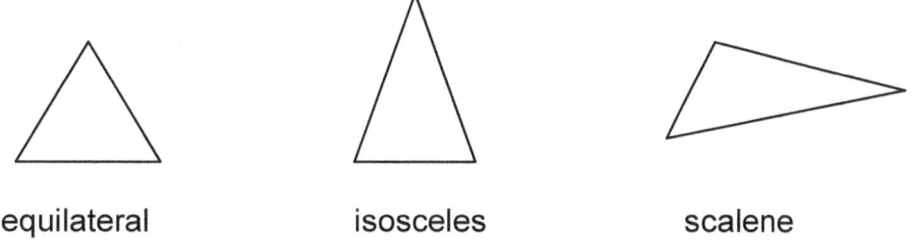

    equilateral   isosceles   scalene

A **quadrilateral** is a polygon with four sides.
The sum of the measures of the angles of a quadrilateral is 360°.

A **trapezoid** is a quadrilateral with exactly <u>one</u> pair of parallel sides.

In an **isosceles trapezoid**, the non-parallel sides are congruent.

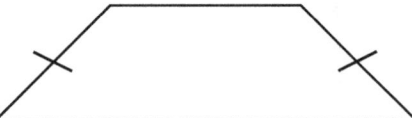

A **parallelogram** is a quadrilateral with two pairs of parallel sides.

A parallelogram exhibits these properties.

The diagonals bisect each other.
Each diagonal divides the parallelogram into two congruent triangles.
Both pairs of opposite sides are congruent.
Both pairs of opposite angles are congruent.
Two adjacent angles are supplementary.

A **rectangle** is a parallelogram with a right angle.

A **rhombus** is a parallelogram with all sides equal length.

A **square** is a rectangle with all sides equal length.

Since a **rectangle** is a special type of parallelogram, it exhibits all the properties of a parallelogram. All the angles of a rectangle are right angles because of congruent opposite angles. Additionally, the diagonals of a rectangle are congruent.

A **rhombus** also has all the properties of a parallelogram. Additionally, its diagonals are perpendicular to each other and they bisect its angles.

A **square** has all the properties of a rectangle and a rhombus.

Example 1:

	True or false?
All squares are rhombuses.	True
All parallelograms are rectangles.	False - <u>some</u> parallelograms are rectangles
All rectangles are parallelograms.	True
Some rhombuses are squares.	True
Some rectangles are trapezoids.	False - only <u>one</u> pair of parallel sides
All quadrilaterals are parallelograms.	False -some quadrilaterals are parallelograms
Some squares are rectangles.	False - all squares are rectangles
Some parallelograms are rhombuses.	True

A **trapezoid** is a quadrilateral with exactly <u>one</u> pair of parallel sides.

In an **isosceles trapezoid**, the non-parallel sides are congruent.

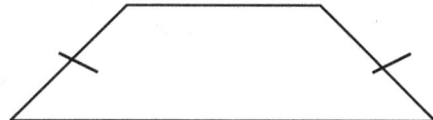

An isosceles trapezoid has the following properties:

The diagonals of an isosceles trapezoid are congruent.
The base angles of an isosceles trapezoid are congruent.

Euclid wrote a set of 13 books around 330 B.C. called the Elements. He outlined ten axioms and then deduced 465 theorems. Euclidean geometry is based on the undefined concept of the point, line and plane.

The fifth of Euclid's axioms (referred to as the parallel postulate) was not as readily accepted as the other nine axioms. Many mathematicians throughout the years have attempted to prove that this axiom is not necessary because it could be proved by the other nine. Among the many who attempted to prove this was Carl Friedrich Gauss. His works led to the development of hyperbolic geometry. Elliptical or Reimannian geometry was suggested by G.F. Berhard Riemann. He based his work on the theory of surfaces and used models as physical interpretations of the undefined terms that satisfy the axioms.

The chart below lists the fifth axiom (parallel postulate) as it is given in each of the three geometries.

EUCLIDEAN	ELLIPTICAL	HYPERBOLIC
Given a line and a point not on that line, one and only one line can be drawn through the given point parallel to the given line.	Given a line and a point not on that line, no line can be drawn through the given point parallel to the given line.	Given a line and a point not on that line, two or more lines can be drawn through the point parallel to the given line.

In geometry the **point, line and plane** are key concepts and can be discussed in relation to each other.

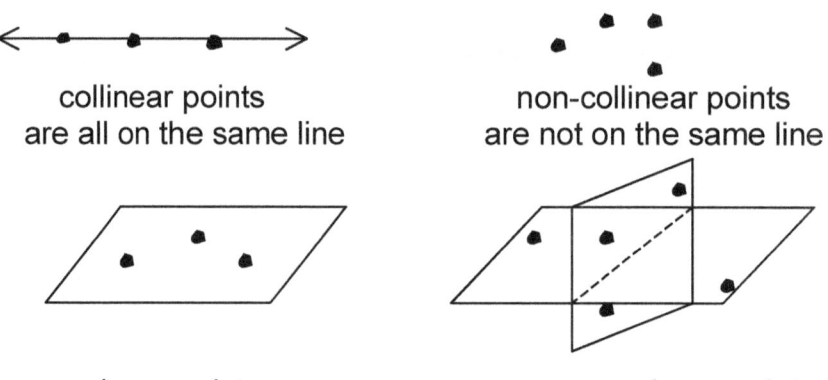

collinear points
are all on the same line

non-collinear points
are not on the same line

coplanar points
are on the same plane

non-coplanar points
are not on the same plane

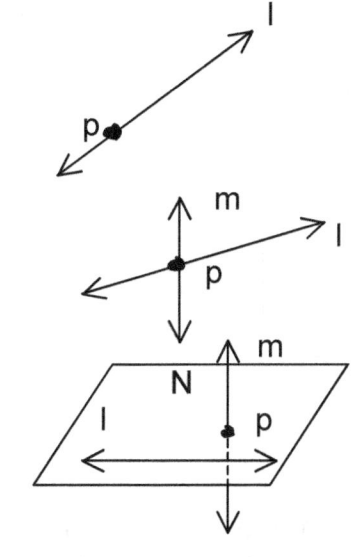

Point p is in line l
Point p is on line l
l contains P
l passes through P
l and m intersect at p
p is the intersection of l and m
l and p are in plane N
N contains p and l
m intersects N at p
p is the intersection of m and N

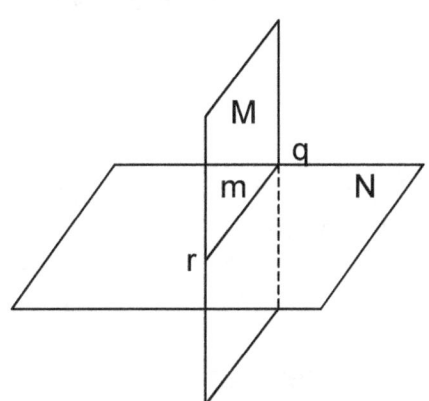

Planes M and N intersect at rq
rq is the intersection of M and N
rq is in M and N
M and N contain rQ

Parallel lines or planes do not intersect.

Perpendicular lines or planes form a 90 degree angle to each other.

Intersecting lines share a common point and intersecting planes share a common set of points or line.

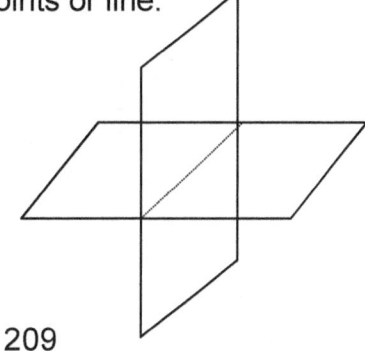

Skew lines do not intersect and do not lie on the same plane.

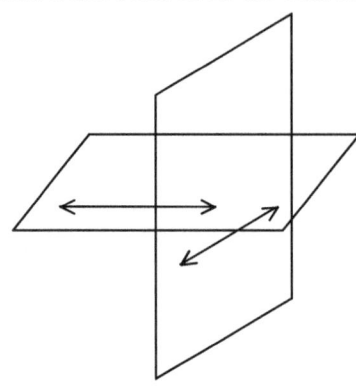

Label and Classify Angles

The classifying of angles refers to the angle measure. The naming of angles refers to the letters or numbers used to label the angle.

Sample Problem:

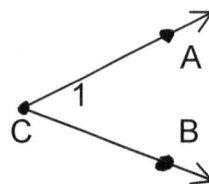

$\overrightarrow{CA}$ (read ray CA) and $\overrightarrow{CB}$ are the sides of the angle.
The angle can be called $\angle ACB$, $\angle BCA$, $\angle C$ or $\angle 1$.

Angles are classified according to their size as follows:

>acute: greater than 0 and less than 90 degrees.
>right: exactly 90 degrees.
>obtuse: greater than 90 and less than 180 degrees.
>straight: exactly 180 degrees

Angles can be classified in a number of ways. Some of those classifications are outlined here.

Adjacent angles have a common vertex and one common side but no interior points in common.

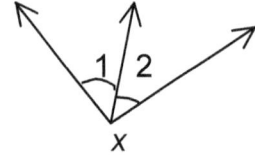

Complimentary angles add up to 90 degrees.

Supplementary angles add up to 180 degrees.

Vertical angles have sides that form two pairs of opposite rays.

Corresponding angles are in the same corresponding position on two parallel lines cut by a transversal.

Alternate interior angles are diagonal angles on the inside of two parallel lines cut by a transversal.

Alternate exterior angles are diagonal angles on the outside of two parallel lines cut by a transversal.

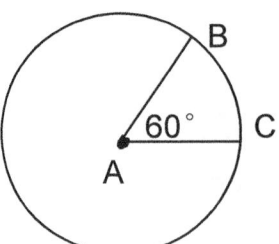

Central angle BAC = 60°
Minor arc BC = 60°
Major arc BC = 360 − 60 = 300°

If you draw **two radii** in a circle, the angle they form with the center as the vertex is a central angle. The piece of the circle "inside" the angle is an arc. Just like a central angle, an arc can have any degree measure from 0 to 360. The measure of an arc is equal to the measure of the central angle which forms the arc. Since a diameter forms a semicircle and the measure of a straight angle like a diameter is 180°, the measure of a semicircle is also 180°.

Given two points on a circle, there are two different arcs which the two points form. Except in the case of semicircles, one of the two arcs will always be greater than 180° and the other will be less than 180°. The arc less than 180° is a minor arc and the arc greater than 180° is a major arc.

Examples:

1.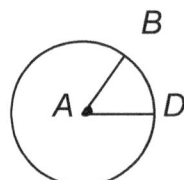

   $m\angle BAD = 45°$
   What is the measure of the major arc BD?

$\angle BAD$ = minor arc BD	The measure of the central angle is the same as the measure of the arc it forms.
45° = minor arc BD	
360 − 45 = major arc BD	A major and minor arc always add to 360°.
315° = major arc BD	

2.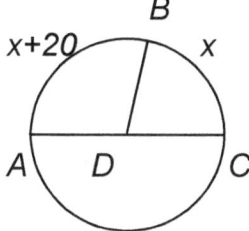

$\overline{AC}$ is a diameter of circle D.
What is the measure of $\angle BDC$?

$m\angle ADB + m\angle BDC = 180°$ A diameter forms a semicircle
$x + 20 + x = 180$ which has a measure of $180°$.
$2x + 20 = 180$
$2x = 160$
$x = 80$

minor arc $BC = 80°$ A central angle has the same
$m\angle BDC = 80°$ measure as the arc it forms.

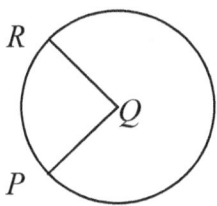

$$\frac{\angle PQR}{360°} = \frac{\text{length of arc } RP}{\text{circumference of } \odot Q} = \frac{\text{area of sector } PQR}{\text{area of } \odot Q}$$

While an arc has a measure associated to the degree measure of a central angle, it also has a length which is a fraction of the circumference of the circle.

For each central angle and its associated arc, there is a sector of the circle which resembles a pie piece. The area of such a sector is a fraction of the area of the circle.

The fractions used for the area of a sector and length of its associated arc are both equal to the ratio of the central angle to $360°$.

Examples:

1.

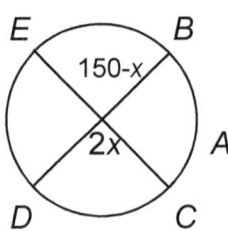

⊙ A has a radius of 4 cm. What is the length of arc ED?

$$2x + 150 - x = 180$$
$$x + 150 = 180$$
$$x = 30$$

Arc BE and arc DE make a semicircle.

Arc ED = 2(30) = 60°   The ratio 60° to 360° is equal to the ratio of arch length ED to the circumference of ⊙ A.

$$\frac{60}{360} = \frac{\text{arc length } ED}{2\pi 4}$$

$$\frac{1}{6} = \frac{\text{arc length}}{8\pi}$$

Cross multiply and solve for the arc length.

$$\frac{8\pi}{6} = \text{arc length}$$

arc length $ED = \frac{4\pi}{3}$ cm.

2.

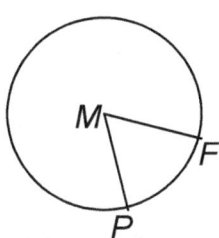

The radius of ⊙M is 3 cm. The length of arc PF is 2π cm. What is the area of sector PMF?

Circumference of ⊙$M = 2\pi(3) = 6\pi$	Find the circumference
Area of ⊙$M = \pi(3)^2 = 9\pi$	and area of the circle.
$\dfrac{\text{area of } PMF}{9\pi} = \dfrac{2\pi}{6\pi}$	The ratio of the sector area to the circle area is the same as the arc length to the circumference.
$\dfrac{\text{area of } PMF}{9\pi} = \dfrac{1}{3}$	
area of $PMF = \dfrac{9\pi}{3}$	
area of $PMF = 3\pi$	Solve for the area of the sector.

Angles with their vertices on the circle:

An inscribed angle is an angle whose vertex is on the circle. Such an angle could be formed by two chords, two diameters, two secants, or a secant and a tangent. An inscribed angle has one arc of the circle in its interior. The measure of the inscribed angle is one-half the measure of this intercepted arc. If two inscribed angles intercept the same arc, the two angles are congruent (i.e. their measures are equal). If an inscribed angle intercepts an entire semicircle, the angle is a right angle.

Angles with their vertices in a circle's interior:

When two chords intersect inside a circle, two sets of vertical angles are formed. Each set of vertical angles intercepts two arcs which are across from each other. The measure of an angle formed by two chords in a circle is equal to one-half the sum of the angle intercepted by the angle and the arc intercepted by its vertical angle.

Angles with their vertices in a circle's exterior:

If an angle has its vertex outside of the circle and each side of the circle intersects the circle, then the angle contains two different arcs. The measure of the angle is equal to one-half the difference of the two arcs.

Examples:
1.

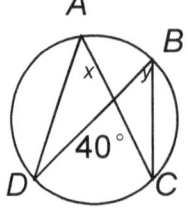

Find x and y.
arc $DC = 40°$

$m\angle DAC = \dfrac{1}{2}(40) = 20°$

$m\angle DBC = \dfrac{1}{2}(40) = 20°$

$x = 20°$ and $y = 20°$

$\angle DAC$ and $\angle DBC$ are both inscribed angles, so each one has a measure equal to one-half the measure of arc DC.

A **tangent line** intersects a circle in exactly one point. If a radius is drawn to that point, the radius will be perpendicular to the tangent.

A **chord** is a segment with endpoints on the circle. If a radius or diameter is perpendicular to a chord, the radius will cut the chord into two equal parts.

If **two chords** in the same circle have the same length, the two chords will have arcs that are the same length, and the two chords will be equidistant from the center of the circle. Distance from the center to a chord is measured by finding the length of a segment from the center perpendicular to the chord.

Examples:

1.

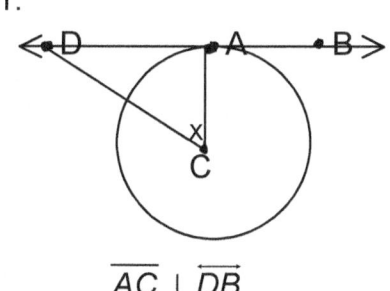

$\overrightarrow{DB}$ is tangent to ⊙C at A.

m∠ADC = 40°. Find x.

$\overline{AC} \perp \overrightarrow{DB}$ A radius is ⊥ to a tangent at the point of tangency.

m∠DAC = 90°   Two segments that are ⊥ form a 90° angle.

40 + 90 + x = 180   The sum of the angles of a triangle is 180°.

x = 50°   Solve for x.

Intersecting chords:

If two chords intersect inside a circle, each chord is divided into two smaller segments. The product of the lengths of the two segments formed from one chord equals the product of the lengths of the two segments formed from the other chord.

Intersecting tangent segments:

If two tangent segments intersect outside of a circle, the two segments have the same length.

Intersecting secant segments:

If two secant segments intersect outside a circle, a portion of each segment will lie inside the circle and a portion (called the exterior segment) will lie outside the circle. The product of the length of one secant segment and the length of its exterior segment equals the product of the length of the other secant segment and the length of its exterior segment.

Tangent segments intersecting secant segments:

If a tangent segment and a secant segment intersect outside a circle, the square of the length of the tangent segment equals the product of the length of the secant segment and its exterior segment.

Examples:

1.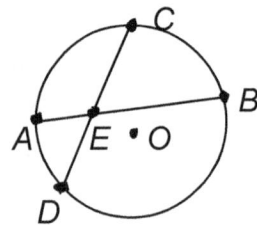

$\overline{AB}$ and $\overline{CD}$ are chords.
$CE=10$, $ED=x$, $AE=5$, $EB=4$

$(AE)(EB) = (CE)(ED)$ Since the chords intersect in the circle, the products of the segment pieces are equal.

$5(4) = 10x$
$20 = 10x$
$x = 2$ Solve for x.

2.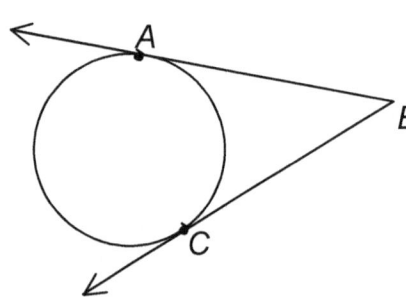

$\overline{AB}$ and $\overline{CD}$ are chords.
$\overline{AB} = x^2 + x - 2$
$\overline{BC} = x^2 - 3x + 5$
Find the length of
$\overline{AB}$ and $\overline{BC}$.

$\overline{AB} = x^2 + x - 2$
$\overline{BC} = x^2 - 3x + 5$ Given

$\overline{AB} = \overline{BC}$ Intersecting tangents are equal.

$x^2 + x - 2 = x^2 - 3x + 5$ Set the expressions equal to each other and solve.

$4x = 7$
$x = 1.75$ Substitute and solve.

$(1.75)^2 + 1.75 - 2 = \overline{AB}$

The sum of the measures of the angles of a triangle is 180°.

Example 1:
Can a triangle have two right angles?
No. A right angle measures 90°, therefore the sum of two right angles would be 180° and there could not be third angle.

Example 2:
Can a triangle have two obtuse angles?
No. Since an obtuse angle measures more than 90° the sum of two obtuse angles would be greater than 180°.

Example 3:
Can a right triangle be obtuse?
No. Once again, the sum of the angles would be more than 180°.

Example 4:
In a triangle, the measure of the second angle is three times the first. The third angle equals the sum of the measures of the first two angles. Find the number of degrees in each angle.

Let x = the number of degrees in the first angle
$3x$ = the number of degrees in the second angle
$x + 3x$ = the measure of the third angle

Since the sum of the measures of all three angles is 180°.

$$x + 3x + (x + 3x) = 180$$
$$8x = 180$$
$$x = 22.5$$
$$3x = 67.5$$
$$x + 3x = 90$$

Thus the angles measure 22.5°, 67.5°, and 90°. Additionally, the triangle is a right triangle.

Two adjacent angles form a linear pair when they have a common side and their remaining sides form a straight angle. Angles in a linear pair are supplementary. An **exterior angle** of a triangle forms a linear pair with an angle of the triangle.

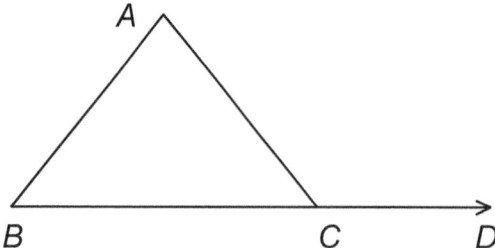

∠ACD is an exterior angle of triangle ABC, forming a linear pair with ∠ACB.

The measure of an exterior angle of a triangle is equal to the sum of the measures of the two non-adjacent interior angles.

Example:
In triangle ABC, the measure of ∠A is twice the measure of ∠B. ∠C is 30° more than their sum. Find the measure of the exterior angle formed at ∠C.

$$\text{Let } x = \text{the measure of } \angle B$$
$$2x = \text{the measure of } \angle A$$
$$x + 2x + 30 = \text{the measure of } \angle C$$
$$x + 2x + x + 2x + 30 = 180$$
$$6x + 30 = 180$$
$$6x = 150$$
$$x = 25$$
$$2x = 50$$

It is not necessary to find the measure of the third angle, since the exterior angle equals the sum of the opposite interior angles. Thus the exterior angle at ∠C measures 75°.

A **polygon** is a simple closed figure composed of line segments. In a **regular polygon** all sides are the same length and all angles are the same measure.

The sum of the measures of the **interior angles** of a polygon can be determined using the following formula, where n represents the number of angles in the polygon.

$$\text{Sum of } \angle s = 180(n - 2)$$

The measure of each angle of a regular polygon can be found by dividing the sum of the measures by the number of angles.

$$\text{Measure of } \angle = \frac{180(n-2)}{n}$$

Example: Find the measure of each angle of a regular octagon. Since an octagon has eight sides, each angle equals:

$$\frac{180(8-2)}{8} = \frac{180(6)}{8} = 135°$$

The sum of the measures of the **exterior angles** of a polygon, taken one angle at each vertex, equals 360°.

The measure of each exterior angle of a regular polygon can be determined using the following formula, where n represents the number of angles in the polygon.

$$\text{Measure of exterior } \angle \text{ of regular polygon} = 180 - \frac{180(n-2)}{n}$$

$$\text{or, more simply} = \frac{360}{n}$$

Example: Find the measure of the interior and exterior angles of a regular pentagon.

Since a pentagon has five sides, each exterior angle measures:

$$\frac{360}{5} = 72°$$

Since each exterior angle is supplementary to its interior angle, the interior angle measures 180 - 72 or 108°.

Parallelogram Applications

Example 1:
Find the measures of the other three angles of a parallelogram if one angle measures 38°.

Since opposite angles are equal, there are two angles measuring 38°.

Since adjacent angles are supplementary, 180 - 38 = 142 so the other two angles measure 142° each.

$$\begin{array}{r} 38 \\ 38 \\ 142 \\ + \ 142 \\ \hline 360 \end{array}$$

Example 2:
The measures of two adjacent angles of a parallelogram are $3x + 40$ and $x + 70$.

Find the measures of each angle.

$$2(3x + 40) + 2(x + 70) = 360$$
$$6x + 80 + 2x + 140 = 360$$
$$8x + 220 = 360$$
$$8x = 140$$
$$x = 17.5$$
$$3x + 40 = 92.5$$
$$x + 70 = 87.5$$

Thus the angles measure 92.5°, 92.5°, 87.5°, and 87.5°.

Rhombus Applications

Example 2:
In rhombus ABCD side $AB = 3x - 7$ and side $CD = x + 15$. Find the length of each side.
Since all the sides are the same length, $3x - 7 = x + 15$
$$2x = 22$$
$$x = 11$$

Since 3(11) - 7 = 25 and 11 + 15 = 25, each side measures 26 units.

Trapezoid Applications

Example:

An isosceles trapezoid has a diagonal of 10 and a base angle measure of 30°. Find the measure of the other 3 angles.

Based on the properties of trapezoids, the measure of the other base angle is 30° and the measure of the other diagonal is 10.

The other two angles have a measure of:

$$360 = 30(2) + 2x$$
$$x = 150°$$

The other two angles measure 150° each.

Congruence

Congruent figures have the same size and shape. If one is placed above the other, it will fit exactly. Congruent lines have the same length. Congruent angles have equal measures.

The symbol for congruent is $\cong$.

Polygons (pentagons) *ABCDE* and *VWXYZ* are congruent. They are exactly the same size and shape.

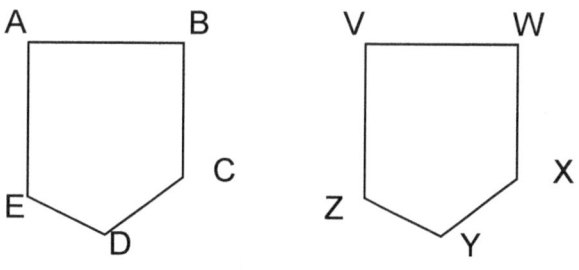

$$ABCDE \cong VWXYZ$$

Corresponding parts are those congruent angles and congruent sides, that is:

corresponding angles	corresponding sides
$\angle A \leftrightarrow \angle V$	$AB \leftrightarrow VW$
$\angle B \leftrightarrow \angle W$	$BC \leftrightarrow WX$
$\angle C \leftrightarrow \angle X$	$CD \leftrightarrow XY$
$\angle D \leftrightarrow \angle Y$	$DE \leftrightarrow YZ$
$\angle E \leftrightarrow \angle Z$	$AE \leftrightarrow VZ$

Two triangles can be proven congruent by comparing pairs of appropriate congruent corresponding parts.

SSS POSTULATE

If three sides of one triangle are congruent to three sides of another triangle, then the two triangles are congruent.

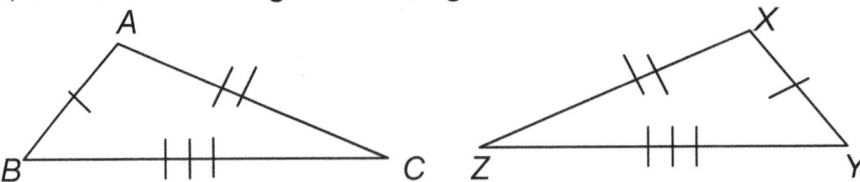

Since $AB \cong XY$, $BC \cong YZ$ and $AC \cong XZ$, then $\triangle ABC \cong \triangle XYZ$.

Example: Given isosceles triangle ABC with D the midpoint of base AC, prove the two triangles formed by AD are congruent.

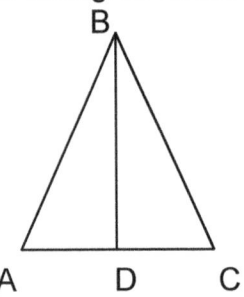

Proof:
1. Isosceles triangle ABC,
   D midpoint of base AC Given
2. $AB \cong BC$ An isosceles $\triangle$ has two congruent sides
3. $AD \cong DC$ Midpoint divides a line into two equal parts
4. $BD \cong BD$ Reflexive
5. $\triangle ABD \cong \triangle BCD$ SSS

SAS POSTULATE

If two sides and the included angle of one triangle are congruent to two sides and the included angle of another triangle, then the two triangles are congruent.

Example:

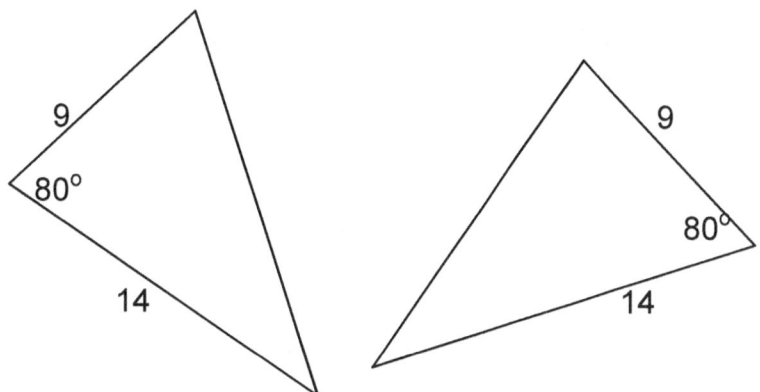

The two triangles are congruent by SAS.

ASA POSTULATE

If two angles and the included side of one triangle are congruent to two angles and the included side of another triangle, the triangles are congruent.

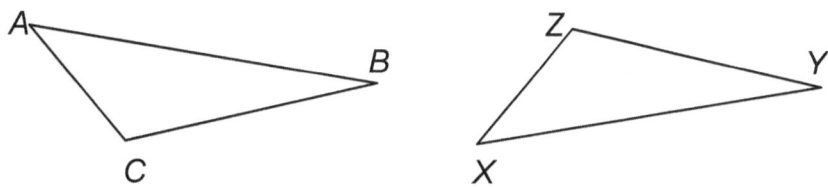

$\angle A \cong \angle X$, $\angle B \cong \angle Y$, $AB \cong XY$ then $\triangle ABC \cong \triangle XYZ$ by ASA

Example: Given two right triangles with one leg of each measuring 6 cm and the adjacent angle 37°, prove the triangles are congruent.

   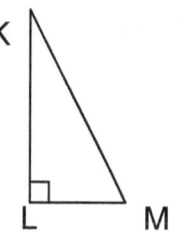

1. Right triangles ABC and KLM   Given
   $AB = KL = 6$ cm
   $\angle A = \angle K = 37°$
2. $AB \cong KL$ Figures with the same
   $\angle A \cong \angle K$ measure are congruent
3. $\angle B \cong \angle L$ All right angles are
                                       congruent.
4. $\triangle ABC \cong \triangle KLM$ ASA

Example:
What method would you use to prove the triangles congruent?

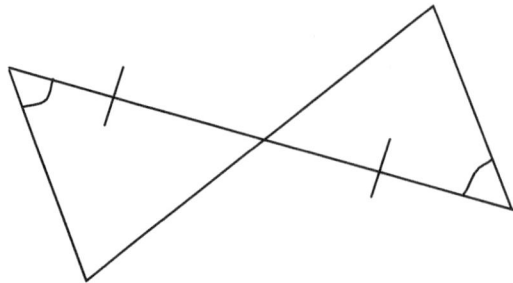

ASA because vertical angles are congruent.

AAS THEOREM

If two angles and a non-included side of one triangle are congruent to the corresponding parts of another triangle, then the triangles are congruent.

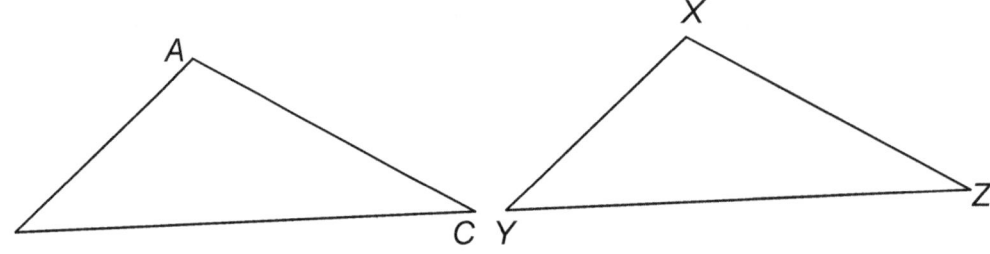

$\angle B \cong \angle Y$, $\angle C \cong \angle Z$, $AC \cong XZ$, then $\triangle ABC \cong \triangle XYZ$ by AAS.
We can derive this theorem because if two angles of the triangles are congruent, then the third angle must also be congruent. Therefore, we can use the ASA postulate.

HL THEOREM

If the hypotenuse and a leg of one right triangle are congruent to the corresponding parts of another right triangle, the triangles are congruent.

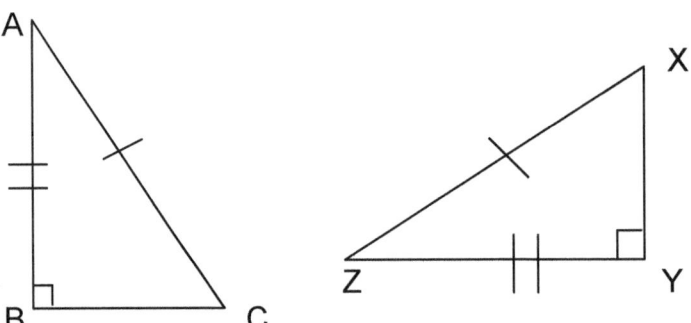

Since $\angle B$ and $\angle Y$ are right angles and $AC \cong XZ$ (hypotenuse of each triangle), $AB \cong YZ$ (corresponding leg of each triangle), then $\triangle ABC \cong \triangle XYZ$ by HL.

Example: What method would you use to prove the triangles congruent?

AAS

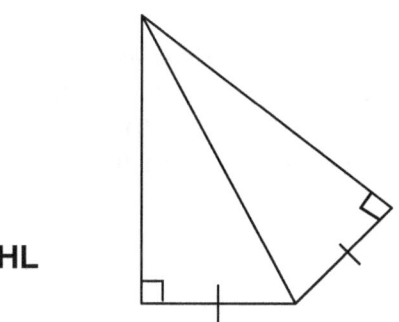

HL

Similarity

Two figures that have the **same shape** are **similar**. Two polygons are similar if corresponding angles are congruent and corresponding sides are in proportion. Corresponding parts of similar polygons are proportional.

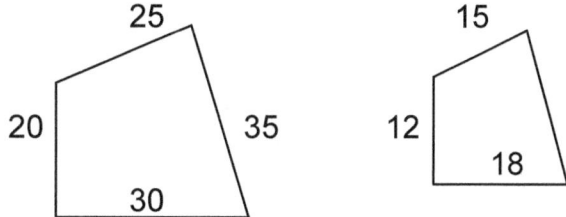

SIMILAR TRIANGLES

AA Similarity Postulate

If two angles of one triangle are congruent to two angles of another triangle, then the triangles are similar.

SAS Similarity Theorem

If an angle of one triangle is congruent to an angle of another triangle and the sides adjacent to those angles are in proportion, then the triangles are similar.

SSS Similarity Theorem

If the sides of two triangles are in proportion, then the triangles are similar.

Angle Bisector Theorem Proof

For a triangle **ABC** let the angle bisector of angle **A** intersect side **BC** at a point **D**. The angle bisector theorem states that the ratio of the length of the line segment **BD** to the length of segment **DC** is equal to the ratio of the length of side **AB** to the length of side **AC**.

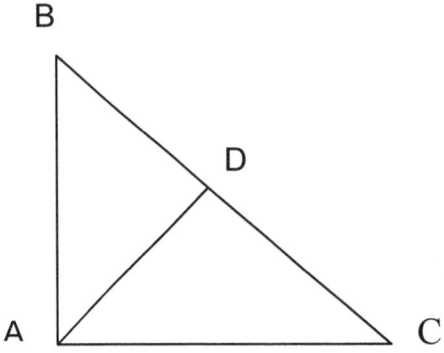

We refer to three-dimensional figures in geometry as **solids**. A solid is the union of all points on a simple closed surface and all points in its interior. A **polyhedron** is a simple closed surface formed from planar polygonal regions. Each polygonal region is called a **face** of the polyhedron.

The vertices and edges of the polygonal regions are called the **vertices** and **edges** of the polyhedron.

We may form a cube from three congruent squares. However, if we tried to put four squares about a single vertex, their interior angle measures would add up to 360°; i.e., four edge-to-edge squares with a common vertex lie in a common plane and therefore cannot form a corner figure of a regular polyhedron.

There are five ways to form corner figures with congruent regular polygons:

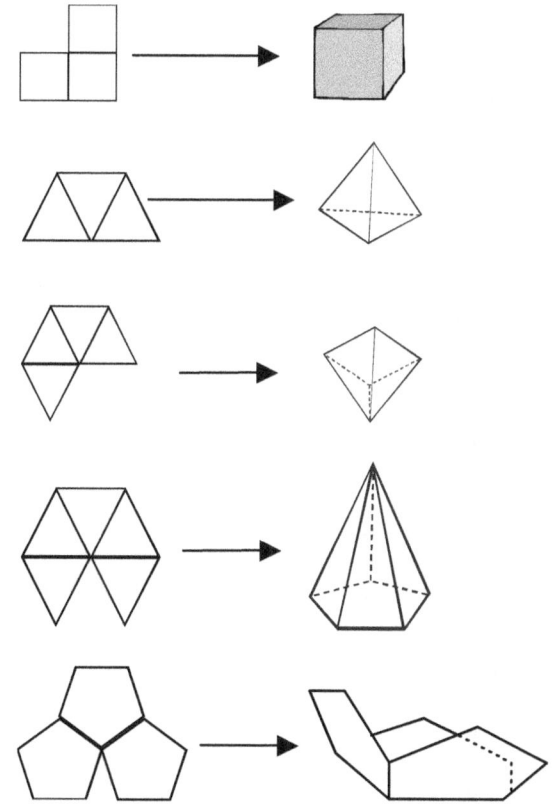

When creating a three-dimensional figure, if we know any two values of the vertices, faces, and edges, we can find the remaining value by using **Euler's Formula**: $V + F = E + 2$.

For example:

We want to create a pentagonal pyramid, and we know it has six vertices and six faces. Using Euler's Formula, we compute:

$$V + F = E + 2$$
$$6 + 6 = E + 2$$
$$12 = E + 2$$
$$10 = E$$

Thus, we know that our figure should have 10 edges.

Competency 13 Apply properties of geometric transformations and coordinate and vector methods to describe geometric objects in two and three dimensions.

A **transformation** is a change in the position, shape, or size of a geometric figure. **Transformational geometry** is the study of manipulating objects by flipping, twisting, turning and scaling. **Symmetry** is exact similarity between two parts or halves, as if one were a mirror image of the other.

There are four basic transformational symmetries that can be used: **translation, rotation, reflection,** and **glide reflection**. The transformation of an object is called its image. If the original object was labeled with letters, such as $ABCD$, the image may be labeled with the same letters followed by a prime symbol, $A'B'C'D'$.

A **translation** is a transformation that "slides" an object a fixed distance in a given direction. The original object and its translation have the same shape and size, and they face in the same direction.

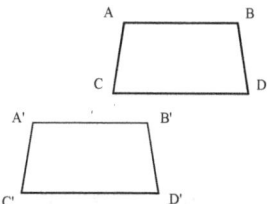

An example of a translation in architecture would be stadium seating. The seats are the same size and the same shape and face in the same direction.

A **rotation** is a transformation that turns a figure about a fixed point called the center of rotation. An object and its rotation are the same shape and size, but the figures may be turned in different directions. Rotations can occur in either a clockwise or a counterclockwise direction.

Rotations can be seen in wallpaper and art, and a Ferris wheel is an example of rotation.

An object and its **reflection** have the same shape and size, but the figures face in opposite directions.

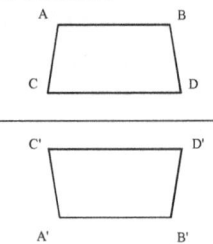

The line (where a mirror may be placed) is called the **line of reflection**. The distance from a point to the line of reflection is the same as the distance from the point's image to the line of reflection.

A **glide reflection** is a combination of a reflection and a translation.

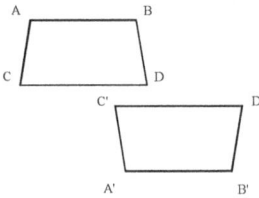

Another type of transformation is **dilation**. A dilation is a transformation that "shrinks" or "makes it bigger."

Example:

Using dilation to transform a diagram.

Starting with a triangle whose center of dilation is point P,

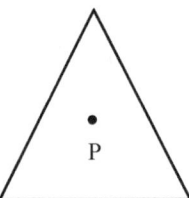

we dilate the lengths of the sides by the same factor to create a new triangle.

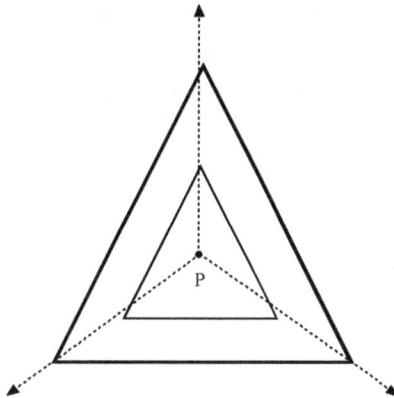

Example:

Using transformational methods, prove the Pythagorean Theorem.

Assume you have a right triangle with legs b and a, and hypotenuse c. Construct a segment subdivided into two parts of lengths a and b.

Using several rotations, construct a square on side a and a square on side b to create two regions whose total area is $a^2 + b^2$.

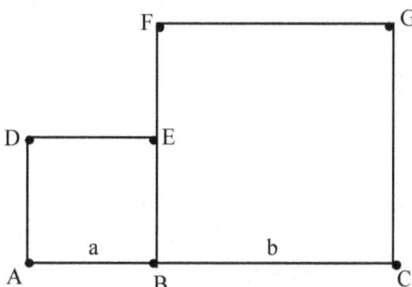

Define a translation from B to A and translate point C to get point H. Connect H to D and H to G, resulting in two right triangles.

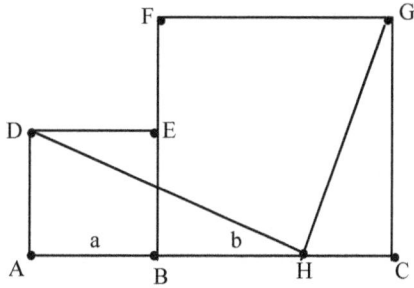

MATHEMATICS (Secondary)

Hide segment BC and create segments BH and HC. This is so that we have well-defined triangle sides for the next step – rotating right triangle ADH 90 degrees about its top vertex, and right triangle HGC 90 degrees about its top vertex.

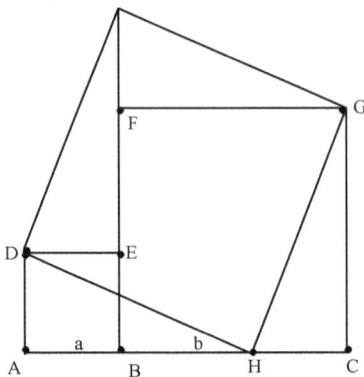

Note: Figure not drawn to scale.

Now prove that this construction yields a square (on DH) of side length c, and thus, since the area of this square is clearly equal to the sum of the areas of the original two squares, we have $a^2 + b^2 = c^2$, and the proof will be complete.

By SAS, triangle HCG must be congruent to the original right triangle, and thus its hypotenuse must be c. Also, by SAS, triangle DAH is also congruent to the original triangle, and so its hypotenuse is also c. Then, angles AHD and CHG (=ADH) must sum to 90 degrees, and the angle DHG is a right angle. Thus, you have shown that the construction yields a square on DH of side length c, and the proof is complete.

A **transformation matrix** defines how to map points from one coordinate space into another coordinate space. The matrix used to accomplish two-dimensional transformations is described mathematically by a 3-by-3 matrix.

Example:
A point transformed by a 3-by-3 matrix

$$[x \ y \ 1] \times \begin{pmatrix} a & b & u \\ c & d & v \\ t_x & t_y & w \end{pmatrix} = [x' \ y' \ 1]$$

A 3-by-3 matrix transforms a point (x, y) into a point (x', y') by means of the following equations:

$$x' = ax + cy + t_x$$

$$y' = bx + dy + t_y$$

A **locus** is the set of all points that satisfy a given condition. The solution to a locus problem is both a figure showing the locus and a statement or equation that names the locus and defines its position.

Sample Problem:

What is the locus of points 6 cm from a fixed point (0,0) in a plane?

1. Draw figure.

2. Write statement to name locus and define its position.

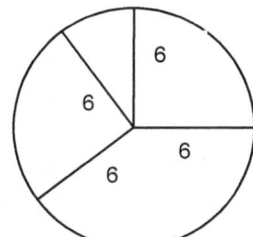

The locus is a circle with (0,0) as the center and a radius of 6 centimeters. The equation of this circle would be $x^2 + y^2 = 36$.

Practice problem:

1. Describe the locus of points equidistant from two given parallel lines $y = 3x + 1$ and $^-3x + y = {}^-5$.

Distance between a point and a line

In order to accomplish the task of finding the distance from a given point to another given line the perpendicular line that intersects the point and line must be drawn and the equation of the other line written. From this information the point of intersection can be found. This point and the original point are used in the distance formula given below:

$$D = \sqrt{(x_2 - x_1)^2 + (y_2 - y_1)^2}$$

Sample Problem:

1. Given the point $(^-4,3)$ and the line $y = 4x + 2$, find the distance from the point to the line.

$y = 4x + 2$	1. Find the slope of the given line by solving for y.
$y = 4x + 2$	2. The slope is 4/1, the perpendicular line will have a slope of $^-1/4$.
$y = \left(^-1/4\right)x + b$	3. Use the new slope and the given point to find the equation of the perpendicular line.
$3 = \left(^-1/4\right)\left(^-4\right) + b$	4. Substitute $(^-4,3)$ into the equation.
$3 = 1 + b$	5. Solve.
$2 = b$	6. Given the value for b, write the equation of the perpendicular line.
$y = \left(^-1/4\right)x + 2$	7. Write in standard form.
$x + 4y = 8$	8. Use both equations to solve by elimination to get the point of intersection.
$^-4x + y = 2$	
$x + 4y = 8$	9. Multiply the bottom row by 4.
$^-4x + y = 2$	
$4x + 16y = 32$	10. Solve.
$17y = 34$	
$y = 2$	
$y = 4x + 2$	11. Substitute to find the x value.
$2 = 4x + 2$	12. Solve.
$x = 0$	

MATHEMATICS (Secondary)

(0,2) is the point of intersection. Use this point on the original line and the original point to calculate the distance between them.

$$D = \sqrt{(x_2 - x_1)^2 + (y_2 - y_1)^2}$$ where points are (0,2) and (-4,3).

$$D = \sqrt{(^-4 - 0)^2 + (3 - 2)^2}$$ 1. Substitute.

$$D = \sqrt{(16) + (1)}$$ 2. Simplify.
$$D = \sqrt{17}$$

Distance between two parallel lines

The distance between two parallel lines, such as line *AB* and line *CD* as shown below is the line segment *RS*, the perpendicular between the two parallels.

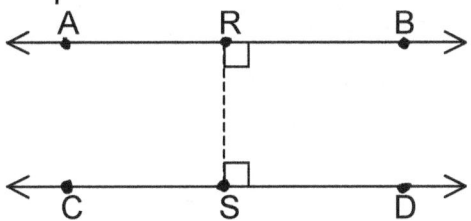

Sample Problem:

Given the geometric figure below, find the distance between the two parallel sides *AB* and *CD*.

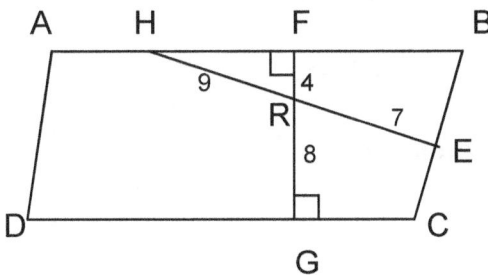

The distance *FG* is 12 units.

Distance formula applications

The key to applying the distance formula is to understand the problem before beginning.

$$D = \sqrt{(x_2 - x_1)^2 + (y_2 - y_1)^2}$$

Sample Problem:

1. Find the perimeter of a figure with vertices at (4,5), (⁻4,6) and (⁻5,⁻8).

The figure being described is a triangle. Therefore, the distance for all three sides must be found. Carefully, identify all three sides before beginning.

Side 1 = (4,5) to (⁻4,6)
Side 2 = (⁻4,6) to (⁻5,⁻8)
Side 3 = (⁻5,⁻8) to (4,5)

$$D_1 = \sqrt{(^-4 - 4)^2 + (6 - 5)^2} = \sqrt{65}$$

$$D_2 = \sqrt{((^-5 - (^-4))^2 + (^-8 - 6)^2} = \sqrt{197}$$

$$D_3 = \sqrt{((4 - (^-5))^2 + (5 - (^-8)^2))} = \sqrt{250} \text{ or } 5\sqrt{10}$$

$$\text{Perimeter} = \sqrt{65} + \sqrt{197} + 5\sqrt{10}$$

Midpoint formula applications

Midpoint Definition:

If a line segment has endpoints of (x_1, y_1) and (x_2, y_2), then the midpoint can be found using:

$$\left(\frac{x_1 + x_2}{2}, \frac{y_1 + y_2}{2} \right)$$

Sample problems:

1. Find the center of a circle with a diameter whose endpoints are (3,7) and (⁻4,⁻5).

$$\text{Midpoint} = \left(\frac{3+(^-4)}{2}, \frac{7+(^-5)}{2} \right)$$

$$\text{Midpoint} = \left(\frac{-1}{2}, 1 \right)$$

2. Find the midpoint given the two points $\left(5, 8\sqrt{6}\right)$ and $\left(9, ^-4\sqrt{6}\right)$.

$$\text{Midpoint} = \left(\frac{5+9}{2}, \frac{8\sqrt{6}+(^-4\sqrt{6})}{2} \right)$$

$$\text{Midpoint} = \left(7, 2\sqrt{6}\right)$$

Conic Sections

<u>PARABOLAS</u>-A parabola is a set of all points in a plane that are equidistant from a fixed point (focus) and a line (directrix).

FORM OF EQUATION $y = a(x-h)^2 + k$ $x = a(y-k)^2 + h$

IDENTIFICATION x^2 term, y not squared y^2 term, x not squared

SKETCH OF GRAPH

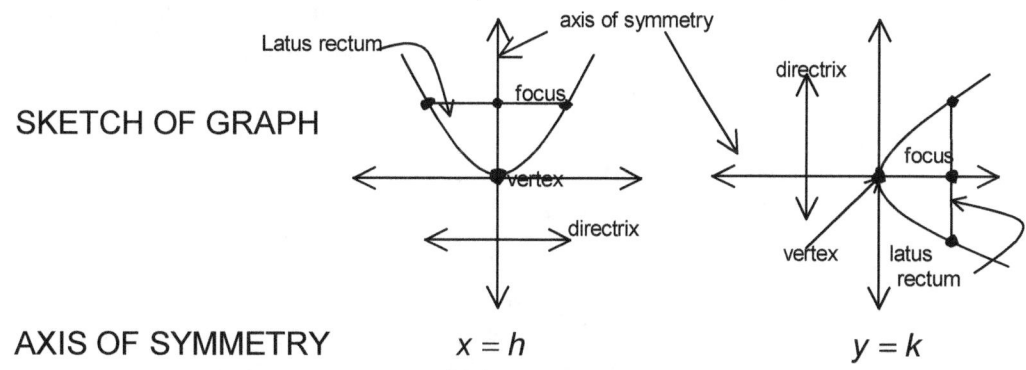

AXIS OF SYMMETRY $x = h$ $y = k$

-A line through the vertex and focus upon which the parabola is symmetric.

VERTEX	(h,k)	(h,k)

-The point where the parabola intersects the axis of symmetry.

FOCUS	$(h, k+1/4a)$	$(h+1/4a, k)$
DIRECTRIX	$y = k - 1/4a$	$x = h - 1/4a$
DIRECTION OF OPENING	up if $a > 0$, down if $a < 0$	right if $a > 0$, left if $a < 0$
LENGTH OF LATUS RECTUM	$\|1/a\|$	$\|1/a\|$

-A chord through the focus, perpendicular to the axis of symmetry, with endpoints on the parabola.

Sample Problem:

1. Find all identifying features of $y = {}^-3x^2 + 6x - 1$.

First, the equation must be put into the general form $y = a(x-h)^2 + k$.

$y = {}^-3x^2 + 6x - 1$ 1. Begin by completing the square.
$= {}^-3(x^2 - 2x + 1) - 1 + 3$
$= {}^-3(x-1)^2 + 2$ 2. Using the general form of the equation to identify known variables.

$a = {}^-3 \quad h = 1 \quad k = 2$

axis of symmetry: $x = 1$
vertex: $(1, 2)$
focus: $(1, 1\frac{1}{4})$
directrix: $y = 2\frac{3}{4}$
direction of opening: down since $a < 0$
length of latus rectum: $1/3$

ELLIPSE

FORM OF EQUATION $\dfrac{(x-h)^2}{a^2}+\dfrac{(y-k)^2}{b^2}=1$ $\dfrac{(x-h)^2}{b^2}+\dfrac{(y-k)^2}{a^2}=1$

(for ellipses where   where $b^2=a^2-c^2$ where $b^2=a^2-c^2$
$a^2>b^2$).

IDENTIFICATION   horizontal major axis   vertical major axis

SKETCH

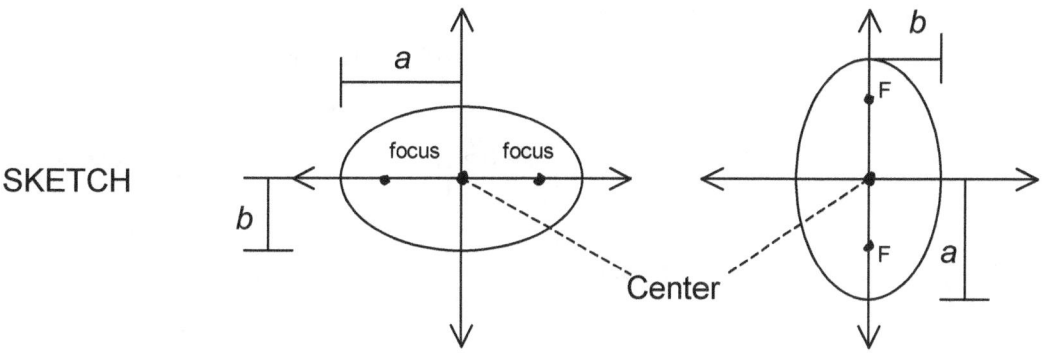

	horizontal	vertical
CENTER	(h,k)	(h,k)
FOCI	$(h\pm c, k)$	$(h, k\pm c)$
MAJOR AXIS LENGTH	$2a$	$2a$
MINOR AXIS LENGTH	$2b$	$2b$

Sample Problem:

Find all identifying features of the ellipse $2x^2+y^2-4x+8y-6=0$.

First, begin by writing the equation in standard form for an ellipse.

$2x^2+y^2-4x+8y-6=0$ 1. Complete the square for each variable.

$2(x^2-2x+1)+(y^2+8y+16)=6+2(1)+16$
$2(x-1)^2+(y+4)^2=24$ 2. Divide both sides by 24.
$\dfrac{(x-1)^2}{12}+\dfrac{(y+4)^2}{24}=1$

3. Now the equation is in standard form.

Identify known variables: $h = 1$ $k = ^-4$ $a = \sqrt{24}$ or $2\sqrt{6}$
$b = \sqrt{12}$ or $2\sqrt{3}$ $c = 2\sqrt{3}$

Identification: vertical major axis
Center: $(1, ^-4)$
Foci: $(1, ^-4 \pm 2\sqrt{3})$
Major axis: $4\sqrt{6}$
Minor axis: $4\sqrt{3}$

HYPERBOLA

FORM OF EQUATION

$$\frac{(x-h)^2}{a^2} - \frac{(y-k)^2}{b^2} = 1 \qquad \frac{(y-k)^2}{a^2} - \frac{(x-h)^2}{b^2} = 1$$

where $c^2 = a^2 + b^2$ where $c^2 = a^2 + b^2$

IDENTIFICATION   horizontal transverse   vertical transverse
axis (y^2 is negative)   axis (x^2 is negative)

SKETCH

 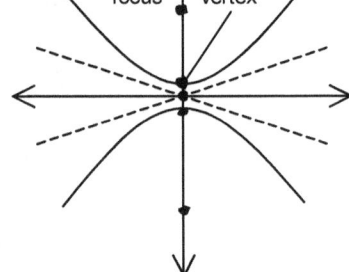

SLOPE OF ASYMPTOTES	$\pm(b/a)$	$\pm(a/b)$
TRANSVERSE AXIS (endpoints are vertices of the hyperbola and go through the center)	$2a$ -on y axis	$2a$ -on x axis
CONJUGATE AXIS (perpendicular to transverse axis at center)	$2b$, -on y axis	$2b$, -on x axis
CENTER	(h,k)	(h,k)
FOCI	$(h \pm c, k)$	$(h, k \pm c)$
VERTICES	$(h \pm a, k)$	$(h, k \pm a)$

Sample Problem:

Find all the identifying features of a hyperbola given its equation.

$$\frac{(x+3)^2}{4} - \frac{(y-4)^2}{16} = 1$$

Identify all known variables: $h = {}^-3 \quad k = 4 \quad a = 2 \quad b = 4 \quad c = 2\sqrt{5}$

Slope of asymptotes: $\pm 4/2$ or ± 2
Transverse axis: 4 units long
Conjugate axis: 8 units long
Center: $({}^-3, 4)$
Foci: $({}^-3 \pm 2\sqrt{5}, 4)$
Vertices: $({}^-1, 4)$ and $({}^-5, 4)$

Circles

The equation of a circle with its center at (h, k) and a radius r units is:

$$(x-h)^2 + (y-k)^2 = r^2$$

Sample Problem:

1. Given the equation $x^2 + y^2 = 9$, find the center and the radius of the circle. Then graph the equation.

First, writing the equation in standard circle form gives:

$$(x-0)^2 + (y-0)^2 = 3^2$$

therefore, the center is (0,0) and the radius is 3 units.

Sketch the circle:

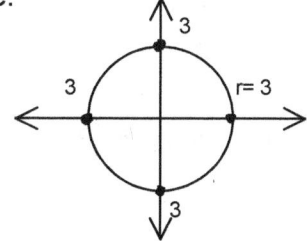

2. Given the equation $x^2 + y^2 - 3x + 8y - 20 = 0$, find the center and the radius. Then graph the circle.

First, write the equation in standard circle form by completing the square for both variables.

$x^2 + y^2 - 3x + 8y - 20 = 0$ 1. Complete the squares.

$(x^2 - 3x + 9/4) + (y^2 + 8y + 16) = 20 + 9/4 + 16$

$(x - 3/2)^2 + (y + 4)^2 = 153/4$

The center is $(3/2, {}^-4)$ and the radius is $\dfrac{\sqrt{153}}{2}$ or $\dfrac{3\sqrt{17}}{2}$.

Graph the circle.

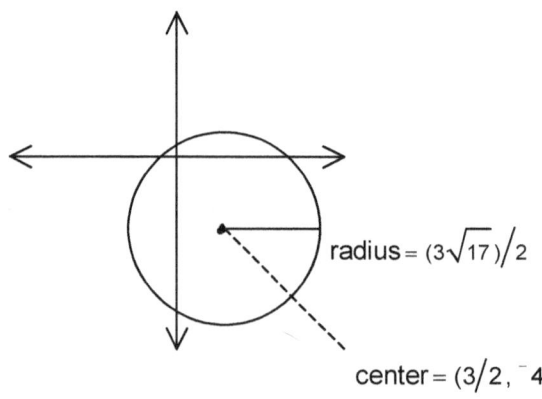

To write the equation given the center and the radius use the standard form of the equation of a circle:

$(x - h)^2 + (y - k)^2 = r^2$

Sample problems:

Given the center and radius, write the equation of the circle.

1. Center $({}^-1, 4)$; radius 11

    $(x - h)^2 + (y - k)^2 = r^2$ 1. Write standard equation.
    $(x - ({}^-1))^2 + (y - (4))^2 = 11^2$ 2. Substitute.
    $(x + 1)^2 + (y - 4)^2 = 121$ 3. Simplify.

2. Center $(\sqrt{3}, {}^-1/2)$; radius $= 5\sqrt{2}$

    $(x - h)^2 + (y - k)^2 = r^2$ 1. Write standard equation.
    $(x - \sqrt{3})^2 + (y - ({}^-1/2))^2 = (5\sqrt{2})^2$ 2. Substitute.
    $(x - \sqrt{3})^2 + (y + 1/2)^2 = 50$ 3. Simplify.

| SUBAREA IV. | DATA ANALYSIS, STATISTICS, PROBABILITY, AND DISCRETE MATHEMATICS |

Competency 14   **Understand methods of collecting, organizing, and displaying data.**

The **questioning technique** is a mathematic process skill in which students devise questions to clarify the problem, eliminate possible solutions, and simplify the problem solving process. By developing and attempting to answer simple questions, students can tackle difficult and complex problems.

Random sampling is the process of studying an aspect of a population by selecting and gathering data from a segment of the population and making inferences and generalizations based on the results. Two main types of random sampling are simple and stratified. With simple random sampling, each member of the population has an equal chance of selection to the sample group. With stratified random sampling, each member of the population has a known but unequal chance of selection to the sample group, as the study selects a random sample from each population demographic. In general, stratified random sampling is more accurate because it provides a more representative sample group. Sample statistics are important generalizations about the entire sample such as mean, median, mode, range, and sampling error (standard deviation). Various factors affect the accuracy of sample statistics and the generalizations made from them about the larger population.

Sample size is one important factor in the accuracy and reliability of sample statistics. As sample size increases, sampling error (standard deviation) decreases. Sampling error is the main determinant of the size of the confidence interval. Confidence intervals decrease in size as sample size increases. A confidence interval gives an estimated range of values, which is likely to include a particular population parameter. The confidence level associated with a confidence interval is the probability that the interval contains the population parameter. For example, a poll reports 60% of a sample group prefers candidate A with a margin of error of $\pm$ 3% and a confidence level of 95%. In this poll, there is a 95% chance that the preference for candidate A in the whole population is between 57% and 63%.

The ultimate goal of sampling is to make generalizations about a population based on the characteristics of a random sample. Estimators are sample statistics used to make such generalizations. For example, the mean value of a sample is the estimator of the population mean. Unbiased estimators, on average, accurately predict the corresponding population characteristic. Biased estimators, on the other hand, do not exactly mirror the corresponding population characteristic. While most estimators contain some level of bias, limiting bias to achieve accurate projections is the goal of statisticians.

A relationship between two quantities can be shown using a table, graph or rule. In this example, the rule y= 9x describes the relationship between the total amount earned, y, and the total amount of $9 sunglasses sold, x.

A table using this data would appear as:

number of sunglasses sold	1	5	10	15
total dollars earned	9	45	90	135

There are many graphical ways in which to represent data: line plots, line graphs, scatter plots, stem and leaf plots, histograms, bar graphs, pie charts, and pictographs.

A **line plot** organizes data in numerical order along a number line. An x is placed above the number line for each occurrence of the corresponding number. Line plots allow you to see at a glance a range of data and where typical and atypical data falls. They are generally used to summarize relatively small sets of data.

two variables, and each variable is plotted... highlights trends by drawing connecting lines between data points. They are particularly appropriate for representing data that varies continuously. Line graphs are sometimes referred to as **frequency polygons**.

Scatter plots compare two characteristics of the same group of things or people and usually consist of a large body of data. They show how much one variable is affected by another. The relationship between the two variables is their **correlation**. The closer the data points come to making a straight line when plotted, the closer the correlation.

Stem and leaf plots are visually similar to line plots. The **stems** are the digits in the greatest place value of the data values, and the **leaves** are the digits in the next greatest place values. Stem and leaf plots are best suited for small sets of data and are especially useful for comparing two sets of data. The following is an example using test scores:

4	9
5	4 9
6	1 2 3 4 6 7 8 8
7	0 3 4 6 6 6 7 7 7 8 8 8 8
8	3 5 5 7 8
9	0 0 3 4 5
10	0 0

Bar graphs are similar to histograms. However, bar graphs are often used to convey information about categorical data where the horizontal scale represents a non-numeric attributes such as cities or years. Another difference is that the bars in bar graphs rarely touch. Bar graphs are also useful in comparing data about two or more similar groups of items.

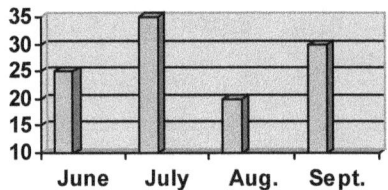

A **pie chart**, also known as a **circle graph**, is used to represent relative amounts of a whole.

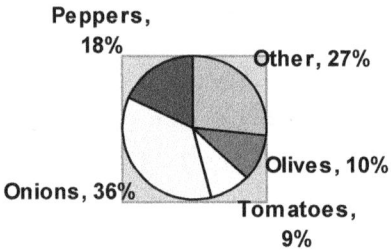

A **pictograph** uses small figures or icons to represent data. Pictographs are used to summarize relative amounts, trends, and data sets. They are useful in comparing quantities.

Monarch Butterfly Migration to the U.S.
in millions

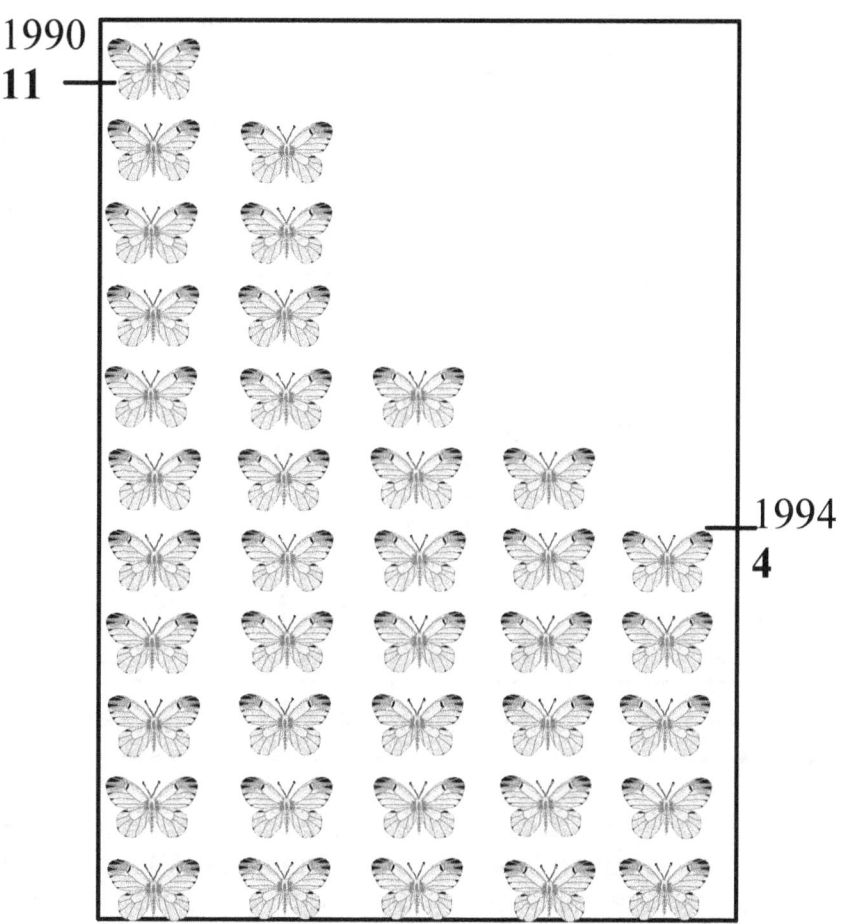

The data in this graph is not accurate. It is for illustration purposes only.

Using graphing calculators or computer software has many advantages. The technology is better able to handle large data sets, such as the results of a science experiment and it is much easier to edit and sort the data and change the style of the graph to find its best representation. Furthermore, graphing calculators also provide a tool to plot statistics.

Competency 15 Understand methods of describing, analyzing, and interpreting data.

Percentiles divide data into 100 equal parts. A person whose score falls in the 65th percentile has outperformed 65 percent of all those who took the test. This does not mean that the score was 65 percent out of 100 nor does it mean that 65 percent of the questions answered were correct. It means that the grade was higher than 65 percent of all those who took the test.

Stanine "standard nine" scores combine the understandability of percentages with the properties of the normal curve of probability. Stanines divide the bell curve into nine sections, the largest of which stretches from the 40th to the 60th percentile and is the "Fifth Stanine" (the average of taking into account error possibilities).

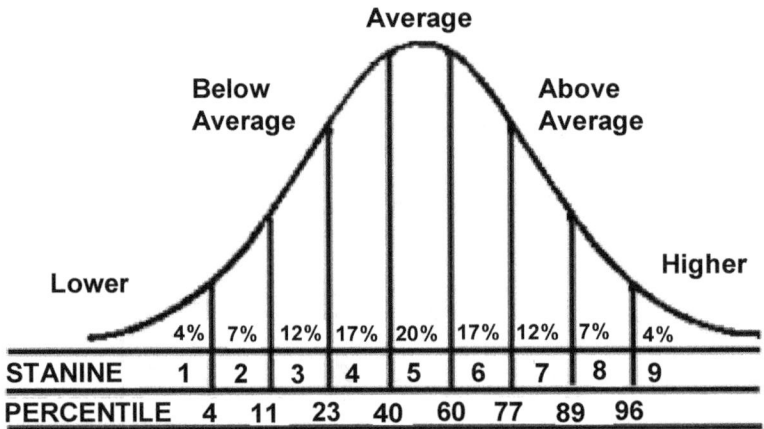

Quartiles divide the data into 4 parts. First find the median of the data set (Q2), then find the median of the upper (Q3) and lower (Q1) halves of the data set. If there are an odd number of values in the data set, include the median value in both halves when finding quartile values. For example, given the data set: {1, 4, 9, 16, 25, 36, 49, 64, 81} first find the median value, which is 25 this is the second quartile. Since there are an odd number of values in the data set (9), we include the median in both halves. To find the quartile values, we much find the medians of: {1, 4, 9, 16, 25} and {25, 36, 49, 64, 81}. Since each of these subsets had an odd number of elements (5), we use the middle value. Thus the first quartile value is 9 and the third quartile value is 49. If the data set had an even number of elements, average the middle two values. The quartile values are always either one of the data points, or exactly half way between two data points.

Sample problem:

1. Given the following set of data, find the percentile of the score 104.

    70, 72, 82, 83, 84, 87, 100, 104, 108, 109, 110, 115

Solution: Find the percentage of scores below 104.

7/12 of the scores are less than 104. This is 58.333%; therefore, the score of 104 is in the 58th percentile.

2. Find the first, second and third quartile for the data listed.

6, 7, 8, 9, 10, 12, 13, 14, 15, 16, 18, 23, 24, 25, 27, 29, 30, 33, 34, 37

Quartile 1: The 1st Quartile is the median of the lower half of the data set, which is 11.

Quartile 2: The median of the data set is the 2nd Quartile, which is 17.

Quartile 3: The 3rd Quartile is the median of the upper half of the data set, which is 28.

Mean, median and mode are three measures of central tendency. The **mean** is the average of the data items. The **median** is found by putting the data items in order from smallest to largest and selecting the item in the middle (or the average of the two items in the middle). The **mode** is the most frequently occurring item.

Range is a measure of variability. It is found by subtracting the smallest value from the largest value.

Sample problem:

Find the mean, median, mode and range of the test scores listed below:

85	77	65
92	90	54
88	85	70
75	80	69
85	88	60
72	74	95

Mean (X) = sum of all scores ÷ number of scores
= 78

Median = put numbers in order from smallest to largest. Pick middle number.

54, 60, 65, 69, 70, 72, 74, 75, 77, 80, 85, 85, 85, 88, 88, 90, 92, 95

both in middle

Therefore, median is average of two numbers in the middle or 78.5

Mode = most frequent number
= 85

Range = largest number minus the smallest number
= 95 − 54
= 41

Different situations require different information. If we examine the circumstances under which an ice cream store owner may use statistics collected in the store, we find different uses for different information.

Example:

Over a 7-day period, a store owner collected data on the ice cream flavors sold. He found the mean number of scoops sold was 174 per day. The most frequently sold flavor was vanilla. This information was useful in determining how much ice cream to order in all and in what amounts for each flavor.

In the case of the ice cream store, the median and range had little business value for the owner.

Consider the set of test scores from a math class: 0, 16, 19, 65, 65, 65, 68, 69, 70, 72, 73, 73, 75, 78, 80, 85, 88, and 92.

The mean is 64.06 and the median is 71. Since there are only three scores less than the mean out of the eighteen scores, the median (71) would be a more descriptive score.

Retail store owners may be most concerned with the most common dress size so they may order more of that size than any other.

An understanding of the definitions is important in determining the validity and uses of statistical data. All definitions and applications on the following page apply to ungrouped data.

Data item: each piece of data is represented by the letter X.

Mean: the average of all data represented by the symbol $\overline{X}$.

Range: difference between the highest and lowest value of data items.

Sum of the Squares: sum of the squares of the differences between each item and the mean.

$$Sx^2 = (X - \overline{X})^2$$

Variance: the sum of the squares quantity divided by the number of Items (the lower case Greek letter sigma squared (σ^2) represents variance).

$$\frac{Sx^2}{N} = \sigma^2$$

The larger the value of the variance the larger the spread

small variation   larger variation

Standard Deviation: the square root of the variance. The lower case Greek letter sigma (σ) is used to represent standard deviation.

$$\sigma = \sqrt{\sigma^2}$$

Most statistical calculators have standard deviation keys on them and should be used when asked to calculate statistical functions. It is important to become familiar with the calculator and the location of the keys needed.

Sample Problem:

Given the ungrouped data below, calculate the mean, range, standard deviation and the variance.

15   22   28   25   34   38
18   25   30   33   19   23

Mean ($\overline{X}$) = 25.8333333
Range: $38 - 15 = 23$
standard deviation (σ) = 6.99137
Variance (σ^2) = 48.87879

Statisticians use linear transformations of data sets to facilitate comparisons between data sets and equalize aberrant differences at very large and very small values. For example, to compare scores from different intelligence tests we transform raw test scores (i.e. number of correct answers) into scaled scores with uniform means and standard deviations. Linear transformations take the form

$$X' = a + bX_0.$$

X' is the transformed value, X_0 is the original value, *a* is the additive component and *b* is the multiplicative component.

The additive component of the transformation, *a*, shifts the original distribution to the right, if *a* is positive, or to the left, if *a* is negative. The additive component increases or decreases the mean of the distribution by *a* units, but does not affect the standard deviation. The following is an example of an additive transformation of a data set and a generic graphical representation.

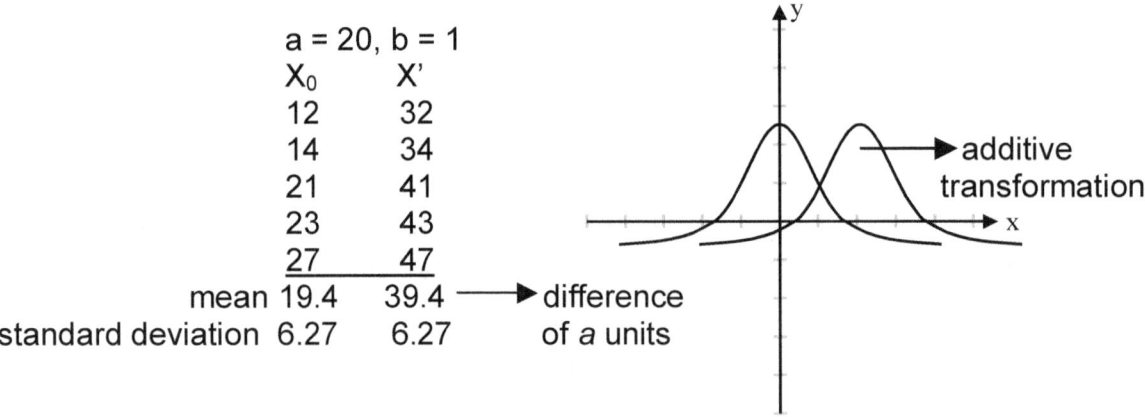

	X_0	X'
	12	32
	14	34
	21	41
	23	43
	27	47
mean	19.4	39.4
standard deviation	6.27	6.27

a = 20, b = 1

difference of *a* units

The multiplicative component of a linear transformation, *b*, horizontally stretches the distribution, if *b* is greater than one, and shrinks the distribution, if *b* is between zero and one. The multiplicative component increases or decreases the mean and standard deviation of a data set by a factor of *b*. The following is an example of a multiplicative transformation of a data set and a generic graphical representation.

$a = 0, b = 3$

X_0	X'
12	36
14	42
21	63
23	69
27	81

mean   19.4   58.2 ⟶ increase by factor of b units
standard deviation   6.27   18.8 ⟶

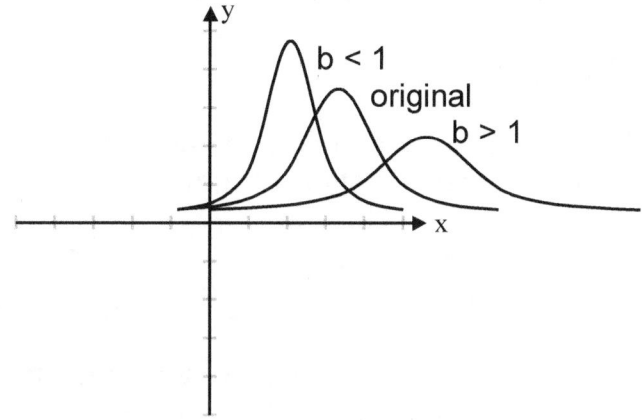

A **linear regression** equation is of the form: $Y = a + bX$.

Example:

A teacher wanted to determine how a practice test influenced a student's performance on the actual test. The practice test grade and the subsequent actual test grade for each student are given in the table below:

Practice Test (x)	Actual Test (y)
94	98
95	94
92	95
87	89
82	85
80	78
75	73
65	67
50	45
20	40

We determine the equation for the linear regression line to be
$y = 14.650 + 0.834x$.

A new student comes into the class and scores 78 on the practice test. Based on the equation obtained above, what would the teacher predict this student would get on the actual test?

$$y = 14.650 + 0.834(78)$$
$$y = 14.650 + 65.052$$
$$y = 80$$

A **logarithmic regression** equation is of the form: $y = a + b \ln x$.

Example:

The water, w, in an open container is evaporating. The number of ounces remaining after h hours is shown in the table below:

Hours (h)	2	5	10	15	19	30
Water (w)	13	11	9	8.5	7.5	6.5

We construct a scatter plot for this data and find a logarithmic regression equation to model the data.

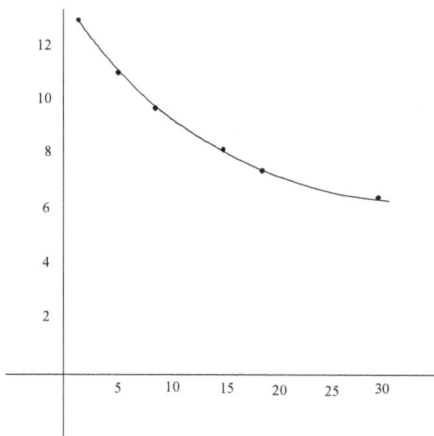

$$w = 14.71 - 2.41 \ln h$$

Using this regression equation predict how many ounces of water are remaining in the container after 48 hours.

$$w = 14.71 - 2.41 \ln(48)$$
$$w = 14.71 - 2.41(3.87)$$
$$w = 14.71 - 9.33$$
$$w = 5.4$$

An **exponential regression** equation is of the form: $y = a(b)^x$. An exponential function may be used to model either growth or decay, depending on the value of b. When $b > 1$ the function models exponential growth. When $0 < b < 1$ the function models exponential decay. You may fit an exponential curve to data and find the exponential function.

Example:

For the data in the table below, determine the exponential regression equation.

x	y
-5	10.22
1	7.98
2	6.63
5	5.51
8	4.57

$$y = 7.502(.94)^x$$

Using this equation predict what y will be when $x = 12$.

$$y = 7.502(.94)^{12}$$
$$y = 7.502(.476)$$
$$y = 3.57$$

Power regression is a functional form used for nonlinear regression. The formula is: $Y = ab^X$.

Example:

On a newly discovered planet the weight, w, of an object and the distance, d, this object is from the surface of the planet were recorded and are shown in the table below (Weight is in pounds and distance in miles).

d	w
2	116
3	58
4	36
5	24
6	18

We construct a scatter plot for the given data using distance as the independent variable (x) and find a power regression equation to model this data.

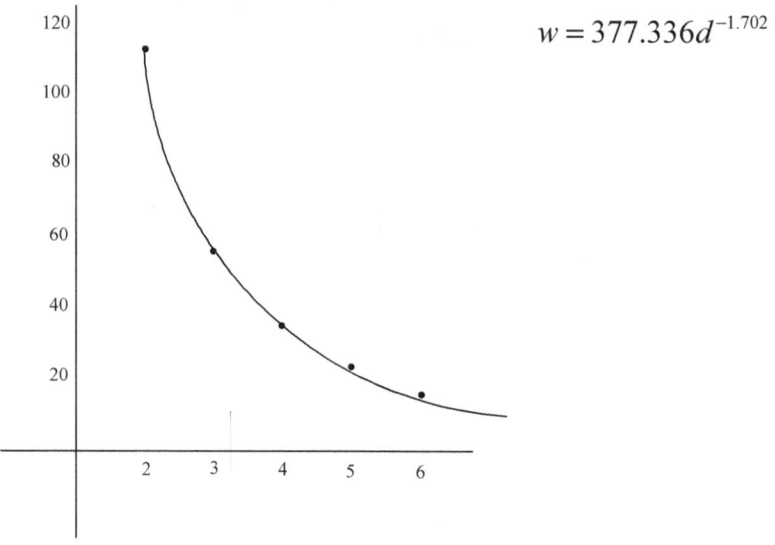

$$w = 377.336 d^{-1.702}$$

Using the regression equation we find the predicted weight of the object to the nearest pound when it is 20 miles from the surface of the planet.

$$w = 377.336(20)^{-1.702}$$
$$= 377.336(.006)$$
$$= 2$$

Observation-inference is another mathematic process skill that used regularly in statistics. We can use the data gathered or observed from a sample of the population to make inferences about traits and qualities of the population as a whole. For example, if we observe that 40% of voters in our sample favors Candidate A, then we can infer that 40% of the entire voting population favors Candidate A. Successful use of observation-inference depends on accurate observation and representative sampling.

Competency 16   Understand methods of making prediction and inferences based on data.

The four main types of measurement scales used in statistical analysis are nominal, ordinal, interval, and ratio. The type of variable measured and the research questions asked determine the appropriate measurement scale. The different measurement scales have distinctive qualities and attributes.

The nominal measurement scale is the most basic measurement scale. When measuring using the nominal scale, we simply label or classify responses into categories. Examples of variables measured on the nominal scale are gender, religion, ethnicity, and marital status. The essential attribute of the nominal scale is that the classifications have no numerical or comparative value. For example, when classifying people by marital status, there is no sense in which "single" is greater or less than "married". The only measure of central tendency applicable to the nominal scale is mode and the only applicable arithmetic operation is counting.

The ordinal measurement scale is more descriptive than the nominal scale in that the ordinal scale allows comparison between categories. Examples of variables measured on the ordinal scale are movie ratings, consumer satisfaction surveys, and the rank or order of anything. While we can compare categories of responses on the ordinal scale (e.g. "highly satisfied" indicates a higher level of satisfaction than "somewhat satisfied"), we cannot determine anything about the difference between the categories. In other words, we cannot presume that the difference between two categories is the same as the distance between two other categories. Even if the responses are in numeric form (e.g. 1 = good, 2 = fair, 3 = poor), we can presume nothing about the intervals separating the groups. Ordinal scales allow greater or less-than comparisons and the applicable measures of central tendency are range and median.

The next measurement scale is the interval scale. Interval scales are numeric scales where intervals have a fixed, uniform value throughout the scale. An example of an interval scale is the Fahrenheit temperature scale. On the Fahrenheit scale, the difference between 40 degrees and 50 degrees is the same as the difference between 70 degrees and 80 degrees. The major limitation of interval scales is that there is no fixed zero point. For example, while the Fahrenheit scale has a value of zero degrees, this assignment is arbitrary because the measurement does not represent the absence of temperature.

Because interval scales lack a true zero point, ratio comparison of values has no meaning. Thus, the arithmetic operations addition and subtraction are applicable to interval scales while multiplication and division are not. The measures of central tendency applicable to interval scales are mode, median, and arithmetic mean.

The final, and most informative, measurement scale is the ratio scale. The ratio scale is essentially an interval scale with a true zero point. Examples of ratio scales are measurement of length (meters, inches, etc.), monetary systems, and degrees Kelvin. The zero value of each of these scales represents the absence of length, money, and temperature, respectively. The presence of a true zero point allows proportional comparisons. For example, we can say that someone with one dollar has twice as much money as someone with fifty cents. Because ratios have meaning on ratio scales, we can apply the arithmetic operations of multiplication and division to the data sets.

The **t-test** is the most commonly used method to evaluate the difference in means between two groups. The t-test assesses whether the means of two groups are statistically different from each other. The formula for the t-test is a ratio. The top part of the ratio is the difference between the two means or averages. The bottom part is a measure of the variability or dispersion of the scores.

$$\frac{\text{difference between group means}}{\text{variability of groups}} = \frac{\bar{X}_T - \bar{X}_C}{SE(\bar{X}_T - \bar{X}_C)} = \text{t-value}$$

In this example T refers to a treatment group and C refers to a control group.

To compute the top part of the formula, just find the difference between the means. The bottom part of the formula is called the **standard error of the difference**. To compute it, take the variance for each group and divide it by the number of people in that group. Add these two values and then take their square root.

$$SE(\bar{X}_T - \bar{X}_C) = \sqrt{\frac{\text{var}_T}{n_T} + \frac{\text{var}_C}{n_C}}$$

The final formula for the t-test is

$$t = \frac{\bar{X}_T - \bar{X}_C}{\sqrt{\frac{\text{var}_T}{n_T} + \frac{\text{var}_C}{n_C}}}$$

Once you compute the t-value, you have to look it up in a table of significance to test whether the ratio is large enough to say that the difference between the groups is not likely to have been a chance finding. To test the significance, you need to set a risk, or alpha level, which is usually .05. You also must determine the degrees of freedom (df) for the test. In the t-test, the df is the sum of the persons in both groups minus 2. Using the t-value, the alpha level, and the df, you can look up the t-value in a standard table of significance to determine whether the t-value is large enough to be significant. If it is, you can conclude that the difference between the means for the two groups is different.

The **chi-square test** is a method of determining the odds for or against a given deviation from expected statistical distribution.

Example:

We want to determine if the odds of flipping a coin heads-up is the same as tails-up; is the coin flipped fairly? We collect data by flipping the coin 200 times. The coin landed heads-up 92 times and tails-up 108 times.

To perform a chi-square test we first must establish a null hypothesis. In this example, the null hypothesis states that the coin should be equally likely to land head-up or tails-up, every time. The null hypothesis allows us to state expected frequencies. For 200 tosses we would expect 100 heads and 100 tails.

Next, prepare a table:

	Heads	Tails	Total
Observed	92	108	200
Expected	100	100	200
Total	192	208	400

The observed values are the data gathered. The expected values are the frequencies expected, based on the null hypothesis.

We calculate chi-squared:

$$\text{Chi-squared} = \frac{(\text{observed} - \text{expected})^2}{(\text{expected})}$$

We have two classes to consider in this example, heads and tails.

$$\text{Chi-squared} = \frac{(100-92)^2}{100} + \frac{(100-108)^2}{100}$$
$$= \frac{(8)^2}{100} + \frac{(-8)^2}{100}$$
$$= 0.64 + 0.64$$
$$= 1.28$$

We then consult a table of critical values of the chi-squared distribution. Here is a portion of such a table:

df/prob.	0.99	0.95	0.90	0.80	0.70	0.50	0.30	0.20	0.10	0.0
1	0.00013	0.0039	0.016	0.64	0.15	0.46	1.07	1.64	2.71	3.8
2	0.02	0.10	0.21	0.45	0.71	1.39	2.41	3.22	4.60	5.9
3	0.12	0.35	0.58	1.99	1.42	2.37	3.66	4.64	6.25	7.8
4	0.3	0.71	1.06	1.65	2.20	3.36	4.88	5.99	7.78	9.4
5	0.55	1.14	1.61	2.34	3.00	4.35	6.06	7.29	9.24	11

We determine the degrees of freedom (df) by subtracting one from the number of classes. In this example we have two classes (heads and tails), so df is 1. Our chi-squared value is 1.28. In the table our value lies between 1.07 (a probability of .30) and 1.64 (a probability of .20). Interpolation gives us an estimated probability of 0.26. This value means that there is a 74% chance that the coin is biased. Because the chi-squared value we obtained is greater than 0.05 (0.26 to be exact), we accept the null hypothesis as true and conclude that the coin is fair.

To make a **bar graph** or a **pictograph**, determine the scale to be used for the graph. Then determine the length of each bar on the graph or determine the number of pictures needed to represent each item of information. Be sure to include an explanation of the scale in the legend.

Example: A class had the following grades:
4 A's, 9 B's, 8 C's, 1 D, 3 F's.
Graph these on a bar graph and a pictograph.

Pictograph

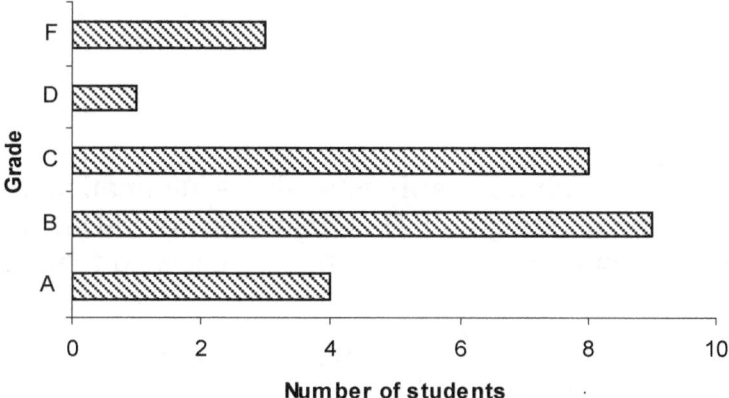

Bar graph

To read a bar graph or a pictograph, read the explanation of the scale that was used in the legend. Compare the length of each bar with the dimensions on the axes and calculate the value each bar represents. On a pictograph count the number of pictures used in the chart and calculate the value of all the pictures.

To make a **line graph**, determine appropriate scales for both the vertical and horizontal axes (based on the information to be graphed). Describe what each axis represents and mark the scale periodically on each axis. Graph the individual points of the graph and connect the points on the graph from left to right.

Example: Graph the following information using a line graph.

The number of National Merit finalists/school year

	90-'91	91-'92	92-'93	93-'94	94-'95	95-'96
Central	3	5	1	4	6	8
Wilson	4	2	3	2	3	2

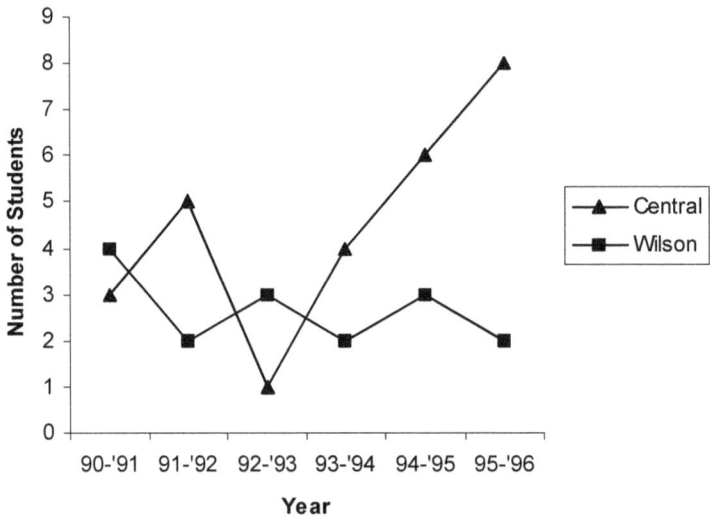

To make a **circle graph**, total all the information that is to be included on the graph. Determine the central angle to be used for each sector of the graph using the following formula:

$$\frac{\text{information}}{\text{total information}} \times 360° = \text{degrees in central } \angle$$

Lay out the central angles to these sizes, label each section and include its percent.

Example: Graph this information on a circle graph:

Monthly expenses:

> Rent, $400
> Food, $150
> Utilities, $75
> Clothes, $75
> Church, $100
> Misc., $200

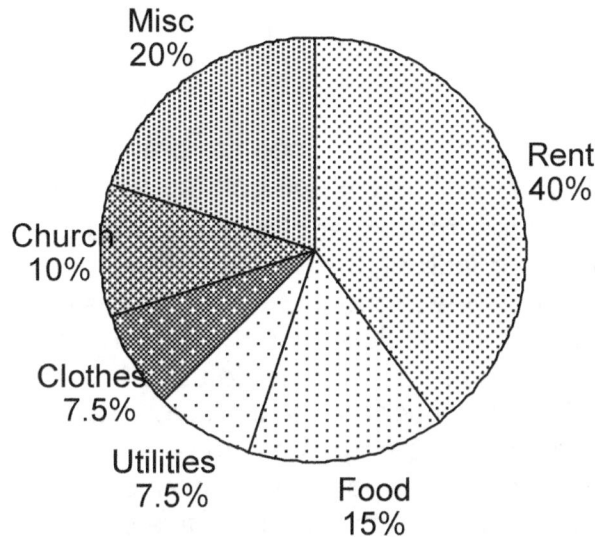

To read a circle graph, find the total of the amounts represented on the entire circle graph. To determine the actual amount that each sector of the graph represents, multiply the percent in a sector times the total amount number.

Correlation is a measure of association between two variables. It varies from -1 to 1, with 0 being a random relationship, 1 being a perfect positive linear relationship, and -1 being a perfect negative linear relationship.

The **correlation coefficient** (r) is used to describe the strength of the association between the variables and the direction of the association.

Example:

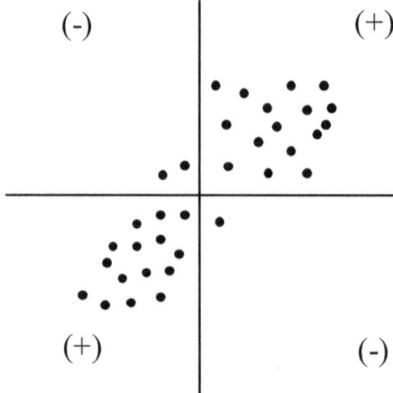

Horizontal and vertical lines are drawn through the point of averages which is the point on the averages of the x and y values.

This divides the scatter plot into four quadrants. If a point is in the lower left quadrant, the product of two negatives is positive; in the upper right, the product of two positives is positive. The positive quadrants are depicted with the positive sign (+). In the two remaining quadrants (upper left and lower right), the product of a negative and a positive is negative. The negative quadrants are depicted with the negative sign (-). If r is positive, then there are more points in the positive quadrants and if r is negative, then there are more points in the two negative quadrants.

Regression is a form of statistical analysis used to predict a dependent variable (y) from values of an independent variable (x). A regression equation is derived from a known set of data.

The simplest regression analysis models the relationship between two variables using the following equation: $y = a + bx$, where y is the dependent variable and x is the independent variable. This simple equation denotes a linear relationship between x and y. This form would be appropriate if, when you plotted a graph of x and y, you tended to see the points roughly form along a straight line.

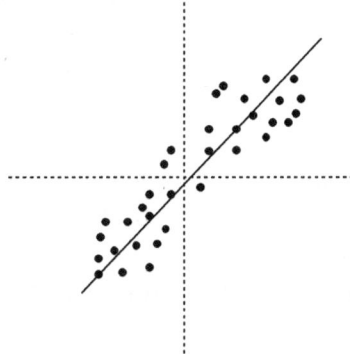

The line can then be used to make predictions.

If all of the data points fell on the line, there would be a perfect correlation ($r = 1.0$) between the x and y data points. These cases represent the best scenarios for prediction. A positive or negative r value represents how y varies with x. When r is positive, y increases as x increases. When r is negative y decreases as x increases.

Competency 17   Understand the theory of probability and probability distributions.

In probability, the **sample space** is a list of all possible outcomes of an experiment. For example, the sample space of tossing two coins is the set {HH, HT, TT, TH}, the sample space of rolling a six-sided die is the set {1, 2, 3, 4, 5, 6}, and the sample space of measuring the height of students in a class is the set of all real numbers {R}.

When conducting experiments with a large number of possible outcomes it is important to determine the size of the sample space. The size of the sample space can be determined by using the fundamental counting principle and the rules of combinations and permutations.

The **fundamental counting principle** states that if there are m possible outcomes for one task and n possible outcomes of another, there are
($m \times n$) possible outcomes of the two tasks together.

A **permutation** is the number of possible arrangements of items, without repetition, where order of selection is important.

A **combination** is the number of possible arrangements, without repetition, where order of selection is not important.

Permutations and combinations are covered in detail in Skill 9.4.

Examples:

1. Find the size of the sample space of rolling two six-sided die and flipping two coins.

    Solution:
    List the possible outcomes of each event:
    each dice: {1, 2, 3, 4, 5, 6}
    each coin: {Heads, Tails}

    Apply the fundamental counting principle:
    size of sample space = 6 x 6 x 2 x 2 = 144

2. Find the size of the sample space of selecting three playing cards at random from a standard fifty-two card deck.

Solution:
Use the rule of combination –
$$_{52}C_3 = \frac{52!}{(52-3)!3!} = 22100$$

Sample Probabilities

Odds are defined as the ratio of the number of favorable outcomes to the number of unfavorable outcomes. The sum of the favorable outcomes and the unfavorable outcomes should always equal the total possible outcomes.

For example, given a bag of 12 red and 7 green marbles compute the odds of randomly selecting a red marble.

$$\text{Odds of red} = \frac{12}{19}$$

$$\text{Odds of not getting red} = \frac{7}{19}$$

In the case of flipping a coin, it is equally likely that a head or a tail will be tossed. The odds of tossing a head are 1:1. This is called even odds.

Dependent events occur when the probability of the second event depends on the outcome of the first event. For example, consider the two events (A) it is sunny on Saturday and (B) you go to the beach. If you intend to go to the beach on Saturday, rain or shine, then A and B may be independent. If however, you plan to go to the beach only if it is sunny, then A and B may be dependent. In this situation, the probability of event B will change depending on the outcome of event A.

Suppose you have a pair of dice, one red and one green. If you roll a three on the red die and then roll a four on the green die, we can see that these events do not depend on the other. The total probability of the two independent events can be found by multiplying the separate probabilities.

$$P(A \text{ and } B) = P(A) \times P(B)$$
$$= 1/6 \times 1/6$$
$$= 1/36$$

Many times, however, events are not independent. Suppose a jar contains 12 red marbles and 8 blue marbles. If you randomly pick a red marble, replace it and then randomly pick again, the probability of picking a red marble the second time remains the same. However, if you pick a red marble, and then pick again without replacing the first red marble, the second pick becomes dependent upon the first pick.

P(Red and Red) with replacement = P(Red) $\times$ P(Red)
$= 12/20 \times 12/20$
$= 9/25$

P(Red and Red) without replacement = P(Red) $\times$ P(Red)
$= 12/20 \times 11/19$
$= 33/95$

The absolute probability of some events cannot be determined. For instance, one cannot assume the probability of winning a tennis match is ½ because, in general, winning and losing are not equally likely. In such cases, past results of similar events can be used to help predict future outcomes. The **relative frequency** of an event is the number of times an event has occurred divided by the number of attempts.

Relative frequency = $\dfrac{\text{number of successful trials}}{\text{total number of trials}}$

For example, if a weighted coin flipped 50 times lands on heads 40 times and tails 10 times, the relative frequency of heads is 40/50 = 4/5. Thus, one can predict that if the coin is flipped 100 times, it will land on heads 80 times.

Example:

Two tennis players, John and David, have played each other 20 times.

John has won 15 of the previous matches and David has won 5.
(a) Estimate the probability that David will win the next match.
(b) Estimate the probability that John will win the next 3 matches.

Solution:

(a) David has won 5 out of 20 matches. Thus, the relative frequency of David winning is 5/20 or ¼. We can estimate that the probability of David winning the next match is ¼.

(b) John has won 15 out of 20 matches. The relative frequency of John winning is 15/20 or ¾. We can estimate that the probability of John winning a future match is ¾. Thus, the probability that John will win the next three matches is ¾ x ¾ x ¾ = 27/64.

Permutations and Combinations

Probability is the study and quantification of the likelihood of an event. We use combinations and permutations to determine the number of possible outcomes of a given selection of objects. The key difference between combinations and permutations is that we use combinations when the order of the objects chosen does not matter and permutations when the order does matter. In addition, geometric probability describes the likelihood of events involving shapes and measures.

Permutations are the number of possible arrangements of objects when the order of the objects matters. For example, we can find the number of 3 letter arrangements we can make from the first ten letters of the alphabet by determining the number of permutations of size 3 taken from a set of 10. We represent this situation symbolically as $_{10}P_3$. The general formula for determining the value of a permutation is

$$_nP_r = \frac{n!}{(n-r)!},$$

where n is the number of objects in the set and r is the number of objects chosen. Thus, the number of possible three-letter arrangements chosen from the first 10 letters of the alphabet is

$$_{10}P_3 = \frac{10!}{(10-3)!} = \frac{10!}{7!} = 10 \times 9 \times 8 = 720.$$

Combinations are the number of possible groups of objects when the order of the objects does not matter. For example, we can determine the number of different 4 card hands we can deal from a deck of 52 cards by determining a combination, because the order of the cards is not important.

We present this situation symbolically as $_{52}C_4$. The general formula for determining the value of a combination is

$$_nC_r = \frac{n!}{r!(n-r)!},$$

where n is the total number of objects and r is the number of objects chosen. Thus, the number of possible four-card hands in a 52-card deck is

$$_{52}C_4 = \frac{52!}{4!(52-4)!} = \frac{52!}{4!(48!)} = \frac{52 \times 51 \times 50 \times 49}{4 \times 3 \times 2 \times 1} = 270725.$$

Geometric probability describes situations that involve shapes and measures. For example, given a 10-inch string, we can determine the probability of cutting the string so that one piece is at least 8 inches long. If the cut occurs in the first or last two inches of the string, one of the pieces will be at least 8 inches long.

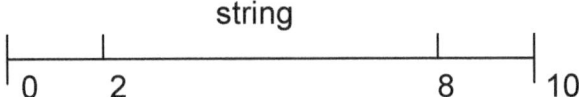

Thus, the probability of such a cut is $\frac{2+2}{10} = \frac{4}{10} = \frac{2}{5}$ or 40%.

Other geometric probability problems involve the ratio of areas. For example, to determine the likelihood of randomly hitting a defined area of a dartboard (pictured below) we determine the ratio of the target area to the total area of the board.

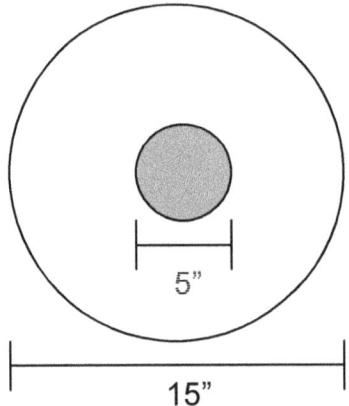

Given that a randomly thrown dart lands somewhere on the board, the probability that it hits the target area is the ratio of the areas of the two circles. Thus, the probability, P, of hitting the target is

$$P = \frac{(2.5)^2 \pi}{(7.5)^2 \pi} \times 100 = \frac{6.25}{56.25} \times 100 = 11.1\%$$

The **binomial distribution** is a sequence of probabilities with each probability corresponding to the likelihood of a particular event occurring. It is called a binomial distribution because each trial has precisely two possible outcomes. An **event** is defined as a sequence of Bernoulli trials that has within it a specific number of successes. The order of success is not important.

Note: There are two parameters to consider in a binomial distribution:

1. p = the probability of a success
2. n = the number of Bernoulli trials (i.e., the length of the sequence).

Example:

Toss a coin two times. Each toss is a Bernoulli trial as discussed above. Consider heads to be success. One event is one sequence of two coin tosses. Order does not matter.

There are two possibilities for each coin toss. Therefore, there are four (2·2) possible subevents: 00, 01, 10, 11 (where 0 = tail and 1 = head).

According to the multiplication rule, each subevent has a probability of $\frac{1}{4}\left(\frac{1}{2} \cdot \frac{1}{2}\right)$.

One subevent has zero heads, so the event of zero heads in two tosses is
$$p(h=0) = \frac{1}{4}.$$
Two subevents have one head, so the event of one head in two tosses is
$$p(h=1) = \frac{2}{4}.$$
One subevent has two heads, so the event of two heads in two tosses is
$$p(h=2) = \frac{1}{4}.$$

So the binomial distribution for two tosses of a fair coin is:

$$p(h=0) = \frac{1}{4}, \quad p(h=1) = \frac{2}{4}, \quad p(h=2) = \frac{1}{4}.$$

A **normal distribution** is the distribution associated with most sets of real-world data. It is frequently called a **bell curve**. A normal distribution has a **random variable** X with mean μ and variance σ^2.

Example:

Albert's Bagel Shop's morning customer load follows a normal distribution, with **mean** (average) 50 and **standard deviation** 10. The standard deviation is the measure of the variation in the distribution. Determine the probability that the number of customers tomorrow will be less than 42.

First convert the raw score to a **z-score**. A z-score is a measure of the distance in standard deviations of a sample from the mean.

The z-score = $\dfrac{X_i - \overline{X}}{s} = \dfrac{42-50}{10} = \dfrac{-8}{10} = -.8$

Next, use a table to find the probability corresponding to the z-score. The table gives us .2881. Since our raw score is negative, we subtract the table value from .5.

$$.5 - .2881 = .2119$$

We can conclude that $P(x < 42) = .2119$. This means that there is about a 21% chance that there will be fewer than 42 customers tomorrow morning.

Example:

The scores on Mr. Rogers' statistics exam follow a normal distribution with mean 85 and standard deviation 5. A student is wondering what the probability is that she will score between a 90 and a 95 on her exam.

We wish to compute $P(90 < x < 95)$.

Compute the z-scores for each raw score.

$$\dfrac{90-85}{5} = \dfrac{5}{5} = 1 \quad \text{and} \quad \dfrac{95-85}{5} = \dfrac{10}{5} = 2.$$

Now we want $P(1 < z < 2)$.

Since we are looking for an occurrence between two values, we subtract:

$$P(1 < z < 2) = P(z < 2) - P(z < 1).$$

We use a table to get :

$P(1 < z < 2) = .9772 - .8413 = .1359.$ (Remember that since the z-scores are positive, we add .5 to each probability.)

We can then conclude that there is a 13.6% chance that the student will score between a 90 and a 95 on her exam.

A **Bernoulli trial** is an experiment whose outcome is random and can be either of two possible outcomes, called "success" or "failure." Tossing a coin would be an example of a Bernoulli trial. We make the outcomes into a random variable by assigning the number 0 to one outcome and the number 1 to the other outcome. Traditionally, the "1" outcome is considered the "success" and the "0" outcome is considered the "failure." The probability of success is represented by p, with the probability of failure being $1-p$, or q.

Bernoulli trials can be applied to any real-life situation in which there are just two possible outcomes. For example, concerning the birth of a child, the only two possible outcomes for the sex of the child are male or female.

Competency 18   Understand principles of discrete mathematics.

The difference between permutations and combinations is that in permutations all possible ways of writing an arrangement of objects are given while in a combination a given arrangement of objects is listed only once.

Given the set {1, 2, 3, 4}, list the arrangements of two numbers that can be written as a combination and as a permutation.

Combination	Permutation
12, 13, 14, 23, 24, 34	12, 21, 13, 31, 14, 41, 23, 32, 24, 42, 34, 43
six ways	twelve ways

Using the formulas given below the same results can be found.

$$_nP_r = \frac{n!}{(n-r)!}$$

The notation $_nP_r$ is read "the number of permutations of n objects taken r at a time."

$$_4P_2 = \frac{4!}{(4-2)!}$$

Substitute known values.

$$_4P_2 = 12$$

Solve.

$$_nC_r = \frac{n!}{(n-r)!r!}$$

The number of combinations when r objects are selected from n objects.

$$_4C_2 = \frac{4!}{(4-2)!2!}$$

Substitute known values.

$$_4C_2 = 6$$

Solve.

Proofs by mathematical induction.

Proof by induction states that a statement is true for all numbers if the following two statements can be proven:

1. The statement is true for $n = 1$.
2. If the statement is true for $n = k$, then it is also true for $n = k+1$.

In other words, we must show that the statement is true for a particular value and then we can assume it is true for another, larger value (k). Then, if we can show that the number after the assumed value ($k+1$) also satisfies the statement, we can assume, by induction, that the statement is true for all numbers.

The four basic components of induction proofs are: (1) the statement to be proved, (2) the beginning step ("let $n = 1$"), (3) the assumption step ("let $n = k$ and assume the statement is true for k, and (4) the induction step ("let $n = k+1$").

Example:

Prove that the sum all numbers from 1 to n is equal to $\frac{(n)(n+1)}{2}$.

Let $n = 1$.	Beginning step.
Then the sum of 1 to 1 is 1.	
And $\frac{(n)(n+1)}{2} = 1$.	
Thus, the statement is true for $n = 1$.	Statement is true in a particular instance.

Assumption

Let $n = k + 1$
$k = n - 1$

Then $[1 + 2 + \ldots + k] + (k+1) = \frac{(k)(k+1)}{2} + (k+1)$	Substitute the assumption.
$= \frac{(k)(k+1)}{2} + \frac{2(k+1)}{2}$	Common denominator.
$= \frac{(k)(k+1) + 2(k+1)}{2}$	Add fractions.
$= \frac{(k+2)(k+1)}{2}$	Simplify.
$= \frac{(k+1)+1)(k+1)}{2}$	Write in terms of $k+1$.

For $n = 4$, $k = 3$

$= \frac{(4+1)(4)}{2} = \frac{20}{2} = 10$

Conclude that the original statement is true for $n = k+1$ if it is assumed that the statement is true for $n = k$.

Proofs on a coordinate plane

Use proofs on the coordinate plane to prove properties of geometric figures. Coordinate proofs often utilize formulas such as the Distance Formula, Midpoint Formula, and the Slope Formula.

The most important step in coordinate proofs is the placement of the figure on the plane. Place the figure in such a way to make the mathematical calculations as simple as possible.

Example:

1. Prove that the square of the length of the hypotenuse of triangle ABC is equal to the sum of the squares of the lengths of the legs using coordinate geometry.

Draw and label the graph.

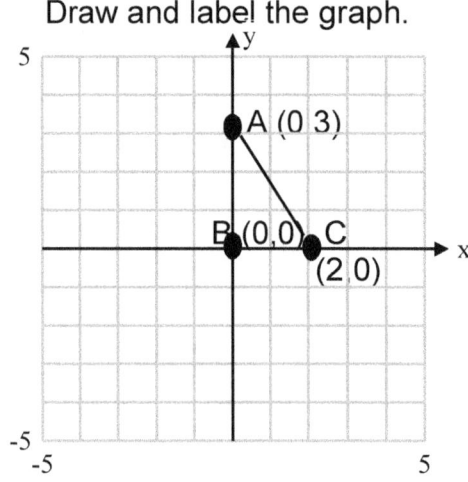

Use the distance formula to find the lengths of the sides of the triangle.

$$d = \sqrt{(x_2 - x_1)^2 + (y_2 - y_1)^2}$$

AB = $\sqrt{3^2} = 3$, BC = $\sqrt{2^2} = 2$, AC = $\sqrt{3^2 + 2^2} = \sqrt{13}$

Conclude

$(AB)^2 + (BC)^2 = 3^2 + 2^2 = 13$
$(AC)^2 = (\sqrt{13})^2 = 13$

Thus, $(AB)^2 + (BC)^2 = (AC)^2$

TEACHER CERTIFICATION STUDY GUIDE

Answer Key to Practice Problems

COMPETENCY 1, *page 5*

Question #1   The Red Sox won the World Series.
Question #2   Angle B is not between 0 and 90 degrees.
Question #3   Annie will do well in college.
Question #4   You are witty and charming.

COMPETENCY 4,

page 37

Question #1 $\dfrac{{}^-12x^5z^5}{y}$

Question #2 $25a^4 + 15a^2 - 7b^3$

Question #3 $100x^{20}y^8 + 8x^9y^6$

page 42

Question #1 $\begin{pmatrix} 11 & 7 \\ 11 & 1 \end{pmatrix}$

Question #2 $\begin{pmatrix} 0 & 3 \\ -10 & 13 \\ 5 & 0 \end{pmatrix}$

page 43

Question #1 $\begin{pmatrix} -4 & 0 & -2 \\ 2 & 4 & -8 \end{pmatrix}$

Question #2 $\begin{pmatrix} 18 \\ 34 \\ 32 \end{pmatrix}$

Question #3 $\begin{pmatrix} -12 & 16 \\ -4 & -2 \\ 0 & 6 \end{pmatrix}$

page 45

Question #1 $\begin{pmatrix} -7 & 0 \\ -12 & -3 \\ 6 & 5 \end{pmatrix}$

Question #2 $\begin{pmatrix} 3 & \frac{47}{4} \\ 3 & 7 \end{pmatrix}$

Question #3 a = -5 b= -1 c = 0 d = -4 e = 0 f = -10

page 46

Question #1 $\begin{pmatrix} -15 & 25 \\ -1 & -13 \end{pmatrix}$

Question #2 $\begin{pmatrix} 5 & -5 & -10 \\ 5 & 5 & 0 \\ 1 & 8 & 7 \\ -9 & 13 & 22 \end{pmatrix}$

COMPETENCY 5, *page 57*

Question #1 $S_5 = 75$

Question #2 $S_n = 28$

Question #3 $S_n = -\dfrac{-31122}{15625} \approx ^-1.99$

COMPETENCY 6, *page 62*

Question #2 a, b, c, f are functions
Question #3 Domain = $^-\infty, \infty$ Range = $^-6, \infty$
Question #4 Domain = 1,4,7,6   Range = -2
Question #5 Domain = $x \neq 2, ^-2$
Question #6 Domain = $^-\infty, \infty$ Range = -4, 4
           Domain = $^-\infty, \infty$ Range = $2, \infty$
Question #7 Domain = $^-\infty, \infty$ Range = 5
Question #8 (3,9), (-4,16), (6,3), (1,9), (1,3)

page 66

Question #1

Question #2

page 79,

Question #1

Question #2

Question #3

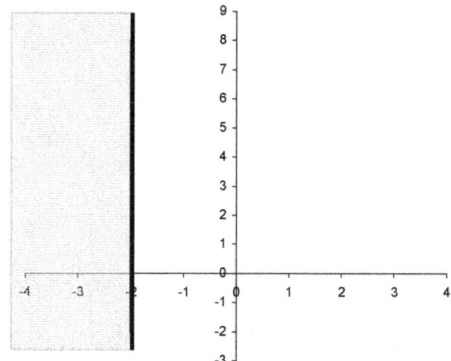

page 80,

Question #1   x-intercept = -14   y-intercept = -10   slope = $-\dfrac{5}{7}$

Question #2   x-intercept = 14   y-intercept = -7   slope = $\dfrac{1}{2}$

Question #3   x-intercept = 3   y-intercept = none

Question #4   x-intercept = $\dfrac{15}{2}$ y-intercept = 3   slope = $-\dfrac{2}{5}$

page 81,

Question #1 $y = \dfrac{3}{4}x + \dfrac{17}{4}$

Question #2 $x = 11$

Question #3 $y = \dfrac{3}{5}x + \dfrac{42}{5}$

Question #4 $y = 5$

page 93,

Question #1 $\begin{pmatrix} x \\ y \end{pmatrix} = \begin{pmatrix} 3 \\ 1 \end{pmatrix}$

Question #2 $\begin{pmatrix} x \\ y \\ z \end{pmatrix} = \begin{pmatrix} 4 \\ 4 \\ 1 \end{pmatrix}$

page 103,

Question #1   The sides are 8, 15, and 17

Question #2   The numbers are 2 and $\dfrac{1}{2}$

COMPETENCY 8, *page 109*

Question #1 $9xz^5$

Question #2 $\dfrac{3x+2y}{x^2+5xy+25y^2}$

Question #3 $\dfrac{x^2+8x+15}{(x+2)(x+3)(x-7)}$

page 112

Question #1   It takes Curly 15 minutes to paint the elephant alone
Question #2   The original number is 5/15
Question #3   The car was traveling at 68mph and the truck was traveling at 62mph

MATHEMATICS (Secondary)

TEACHER CERTIFICATION STUDY GUIDE

page 114

  Question #1 $(6x-5y)(36x^2+30xy+25y^2)$
  Question #2 $4(a-2b)(a^2+2ab+4b^2)$
  Question #3 $5x^2(2x^9+3y)(4x^{18}-6x^9y+9y^2)$

page 118

  Question #1 $\dfrac{8x+36}{(x-3)(x+7)}$

  Question #2 $\dfrac{25a^2+12b^2}{20a^4b^5}$

  Question #3 $\dfrac{2x^2+5x-21}{(x-5)(x+5)(x+3)}$

page 119

  Question #1 $x=7,\ x=^-5$
  Question #2 $x=\dfrac{13}{8}$

page 120

  Question #1 $5\sqrt{6}$
  Question #2 $-5\sqrt{3}+6\sqrt{5}=\sqrt{15}-30$
  Question #3 $-3\sqrt{2}-9\sqrt{3}-3\sqrt{6}-12$

page 122

  Question #1 $17\sqrt{6}$
  Question #2 $84x^4y^8\sqrt{2}$
  Question #3 $\dfrac{5a^4\sqrt{35b}}{8b}$
  Question #4 $-5\left(3+\sqrt{3}+2\sqrt{5}\right)$

page 124

  Question #1 $x=11$
  Question #2 $x=17$

page 125

      Question #2 $x = 9$
      Question #3 $x = 3$ or $x = 6$
      Question #4   1

COMPETENCY 9, *page 136*

      Question #1   49.34
      Question #2   1

page 138

      Question #1 ∞
      Question #2   -1

page 164

      Question #1 $\cot \theta = \dfrac{x}{y}$

$$\frac{x}{y} = \frac{x}{r} \times \frac{r}{y} = \frac{x}{y} = \cot \theta$$

      Question #2 $1 + \cot^2 \theta = \csc^2 \theta$

$$\frac{y^2}{y^2} + \frac{x^2}{y^2} = \frac{r^2}{y^2} = \csc^2 \theta$$

page 166

      Question #1 $t(0) = -24$ m/sec
      Question #1 $g(x) = -20 \sin x + c$

COMPETENCY 13, *page 231*

Question # 1

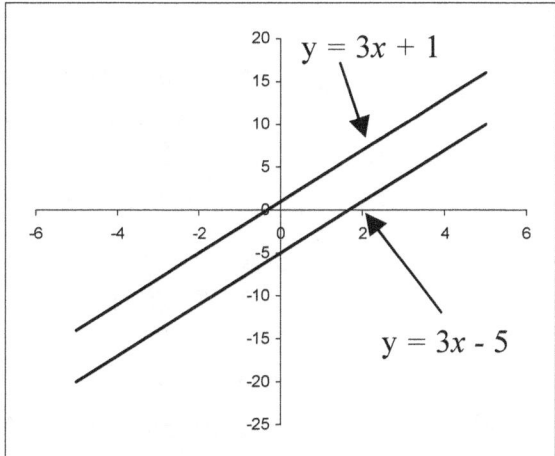

The locus is a parallel line between two lines, on line: $y = 3x - 2$.

Sample Test

Directions: Read each item and select the best response.

1. Change $.\overline{63}$ into a fraction in simplest form.

   A) 63/100
   B) 7/11
   C) 6 3/10
   D) 2/3

2. Which of the following sets is closed under division?

   I) {½, 1, 2, 4}
   II) {-1, 1}
   III) {-1, 0, 1}

   A) I only
   B) II only
   C) III only
   D) I and II

3. Which of the following illustrates an inverse property?

   A) a + b = a - b
   B) a + b = b + a
   C) a + 0 = a
   D) a + (-a) = 0

4. $f(x) = 3x - 2$; $f^{-1}(x) =$

   A) $3x + 2$
   B) $x/6$
   C) $2x - 3$
   D) $(x+2)/3$

5. What would be the total cost of a suit for $295.99 and a pair of shoes for $69.95 including 6.5% sales tax?

   A) $389.73
   B) $398.37
   C) $237.86
   D) $315.23

6. A student had 60 days to appeal the results of an exam. If the results were received on March 23, what was the last day that the student could appeal?

   A) May 21
   B) May 22
   C) May 23
   D) May 24

7. Which of the following is always composite if x is odd, y is even, and both x and y are greater than or equal to 2?

   A) $x + y$
   B) $3x + 2y$
   C) $5xy$
   D) $5x + 3y$

8. Which of the following is incorrect?

   A) $(x^2 y^3)^2 = x^4 y^6$
   B) $m^2 (2n)^3 = 8m^2 n^3$
   C) $(m^3 n^4)/(m^2 n^2) = mn^2$
   D) $(x + y^2)^2 = x^2 + y^4$

9. Express .0000456 in scientific notation.

   A) $4.56 x 10^{-4}$
   B) $45.6 x 10^{-6}$
   C) $4.56 x 10^{-6}$
   D) $4.56 x 10^{-5}$

10. Compute the area of the shaded region, given a radius of 5 meters. 0 is the center.

    A) 7.13 cm²
    B) 7.13 m²
    C) 78.5 m²
    D) 19.63 m²

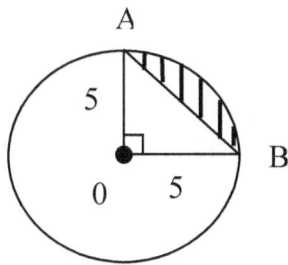

11. If the area of the base of a cone is tripled, the volume will be

    A) the same as the original
    B) 9 times the original
    C) 3 times the original
    D) 3 π times the original

12. Find the area of the figure pictured below.

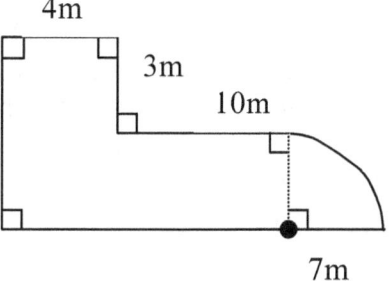

    A) 136.47 m²
    B) 148.48 m²
    C) 293.86 m²
    D) 178.47 m²

13. The mass of a Chips Ahoy cookie would be to

    A) 1 kilogram
    B) 1 gram
    C) 15 grams
    D) 15 milligrams

14. Compute the median for the following data set:

    {12, 19, 13, 16, 17, 14}

    A) 14.5
    B) 15.17
    C) 15
    D) 16

15. Half the students in a class scored 80% on an exam, most of the rest scored 85% except for one student who scored 10%. Which would be the best measure of central tendency for the test scores?

A) mean
B) median
C) mode
D) either the median or the mode because they are equal

16. What conclusion can be drawn from the graph below?

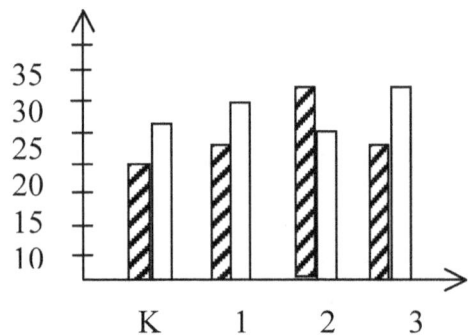

MLK Elementary
Student Enrollment   Girls Boys

A) The number of students in first grade exceeds the number in second grade.
B) There are more boys than girls in the entire school.
C) There are more girls than boys in the first grade.
D) Third grade has the largest number of students.

17) State the domain of the function $f(x) = \dfrac{3x-6}{x^2-25}$

A) $x \neq 2$
B) $x \neq 5, -5$
C) $x \neq 2, -2$
D) $x \neq 5$

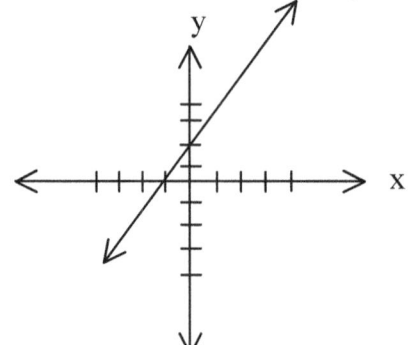

18. What is the equation of the above graph?

A) $2x + y = 2$
B) $2x - y = -2$
C) $2x - y = 2$
D) $2x + y = -2$

19. Solve for v_0: $d = at(v_t - v_0)$

A) $v_0 = atd - v_t$
B) $v_0 = d - atv_t$
C) $v_0 = atv_t - d$
D) $v_0 = (atv_t - d)/at$

20. Which of the following is a factor of $6 + 48m^3$

A) (1 + 2m)
B) (1 - 8m)
C) (1 + m - 2m)
D) (1 - m + 2m)

21. Which graph represents the equation of $y = x^2 + 3x$?

A)   B)

C)   D)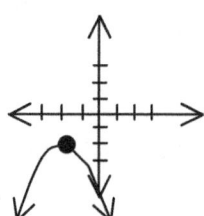

22. The volume of water flowing through a pipe varies directly with the square of the radius of the pipe. If the water flows at a rate of 80 liters per minute through a pipe with a radius of 4 cm, at what rate would water flow through a pipe with a radius of 3 cm?

   A) 45 liters per minute
   B) 6.67 liters per minute
   C) 60 liters per minute
   D) 4.5 liters per minute

23) Solve the system of equations for x, y and z.

$$3x + 2y - z = 0$$
$$2x + 5y = 8z$$
$$x + 3y + 2z = 7$$

   A) (−1, 2, 1)
   B) (1, 2, −1)
   C) (−3, 4, −1)
   D) (0, 1, 2)

24. Solve for x: $18 = 4 + |2x|$

   A) $\{-11, 7\}$
   B) $\{-7, 0, 7\}$
   C) $\{-7, 7\}$
   D) $\{-11, 11\}$

25. Which graph represents the solution set for $x^2 - 5x > -6$?

   A)
   -2   0   2

   B)
   -3   0   3

   C)
   -2   0   2

   D)
   -3   0   2 3

26. Find the zeroes of
    $f(x) = x^3 + x^2 - 14x - 24$

   A) 4, 3, 2
   B) 3, -8
   C) 7, -2, -1
   D) 4, -3, -2

27. Evaluate $3^{1/2}(9^{1/3})$

   A) $27^{5/6}$
   B) $9^{7/12}$
   C) $3^{5/6}$
   D) $3^{6/7}$

28. Simplify: $\sqrt{27} + \sqrt{75}$

   A) $8\sqrt{3}$
   B) 34
   C) $34\sqrt{3}$
   D) $15\sqrt{3}$

29. Simplify: $\dfrac{10}{1+3i}$

   A) $-1.25(1-3i)$
   B) $1.25(1+3i)$
   C) $1+3i$
   D) $1-3i$

30. Find the sum of the first one hundred terms in the progression.
    (-6, -2, 2 . . .)

   A) 19,200
   B) 19,400
   C) -604
   D) 604

31. How many ways are there to choose a potato and two green vegetables from a choice of three potatoes and seven green vegetables?

   A) 126
   B) 63
   C) 21
   D) 252

32. What would be the seventh term of the expanded binomial $(2a+b)^8$?

   A) $2ab^7$
   B) $41a^4b^4$
   C) $112a^2b^6$
   D) $16ab^7$

33. Which term most accurately describes two coplanar lines without any common points?

   A) perpendicular
   B) parallel
   C) intersecting
   D) skew

34. Determine the number of subsets of set K.
    K = {4, 5, 6, 7}

   A) 15
   B) 16
   C) 17
   D) 18

35. What is the degree measure of an interior angle of a regular 10 sided polygon?

   A) 18°
   B) 36°
   C) 144°
   D) 54°

36. If a ship sails due south 6 miles, then due west 8 miles, how far was it from the starting point?

   A) 100 miles
   B) 10 miles
   C) 14 miles
   D) 48 miles

37. What is the measure of minor arc AD, given measure of arc PS is 40° and $m<K=10°$?

   A) 50°
   B) 20°
   C) 30°
   D) 25°

38. Choose the diagram which illustrates the construction of a perpendicular to the line at a given point on the line.

   A)

   B)

   C)

   D)

39. When you begin by assuming the conclusion of a theorem is false, then show that through a sequence of logically correct steps you contradict an accepted fact, this is known as

   A) inductive reasoning
   B) direct proof
   C) indirect proof
   D) exhaustive proof

40. Which theorem can be used to prove $\triangle BAK \cong \triangle MKA$?

   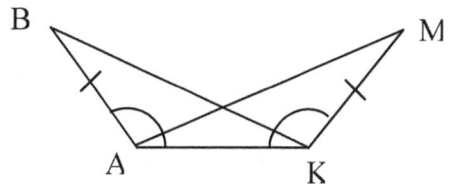

   A) SSS
   B) ASA
   C) SAS
   D) AAS

41. Given that QO⊥NP and QO=NP, quadrilateral NOPQ can most accurately be described as a

   A) parallelogram
   B) rectangle
   C) square
   D) rhombus

42. Choose the correct statement concerning the median and altitude in a triangle.

    A) The median and altitude of a triangle may be the same segment.
    B) The median and altitude of a triangle are always different segments.
    C) The median and altitude of a right triangle are always the same segment.
    D) The median and altitude of an isosceles triangle are always the same segment.

43. Which mathematician is best known for his work in developing non-Euclidean geometry?

    A) Descartes
    B) Riemann
    C) Pascal
    D) Pythagoras

44. Find the surface area of a box which is 3 feet wide, 5 feet tall, and 4 feet deep.

    A) 47 sq. ft.
    B) 60 sq. ft.
    C) 94 sq. ft
    D) 188 sq. ft.

45. Given a 30 meter x 60 meter garden with a circular fountain with a 5 meter radius, calculate the area of the portion of the garden not occupied by the fountain.

    A) 1721 m²
    B) 1879 m²
    C) 2585 m²
    D) 1015 m²

46. Determine the area of the shaded region of the trapezoid in terms of x and y.

    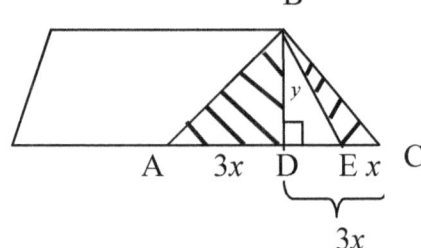

    A) $4xy$
    B) $2xy$
    C) $3x^2 y$
    D) There is not enough information given.

47. Compute the standard deviation for the following set of temperatures.
    (37, 38, 35, 37, 38, 40, 36, 39)

    A) 37.5
    B) 1.5
    C) 0.5
    D) 2.5

48. Find the value of the determinant of the matrix.

$$\begin{vmatrix} 2 & 1 & -1 \\ 4 & -1 & 4 \\ 0 & -3 & 2 \end{vmatrix}$$

A) 0
B) 23
C) 24
D) 40

49. Which expression is equivalent to $1-\sin^2 x$?

A) $1-\cos^2 x$
B) $1+\cos^2 x$
C) $1/\sec x$
D) $1/\sec^2 x$

50. Determine the measures of angles A and B.

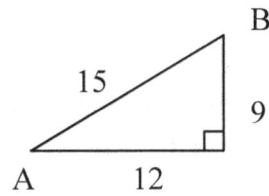

A) A = 30°, B = 60°
B) A = 60°, B = 30°
C) A = 53°, B = 37°
D) A = 37°, B = 53°

51. Given $f(x)=3x-2$ and $g(x)=x^2$, determine $g(f(x))$.

A) $3x^2-2$
B) $9x^2+4$
C) $9x^2-12x+4$
D) $3x^3-2$

52. Determine the rectangular coordinates of the point with polar coordinates (5, 60°).

A) (0.5, 0.87)
B) (-0.5, 0.87)
C) (2.5, 4.33)
D) (25, 150°)

53. Given a vector with horizontal component 5 and vertical component 6, determine the length of the vector.

A) 61
B) $\sqrt{61}$
C) 30
D) $\sqrt{30}$

54. Compute the distance from (-2,7) to the line $x = 5$.

A) -9
B) -7
C) 5
D) 7

55. Given $K(-4, y)$ and $M(2,-3)$ with midpoint $L(x,1)$, determine the values of x and y.

   A) $x=-1, y=5$
   B) $x=3, y=2$
   C) $x=5, y=-1$
   D) $x=-1, y=-1$

56. Find the length of the major axis of $x^2 + 9y^2 = 36$.

   A) 4
   B) 6
   C) 12
   D) 8

57. Which equation represents a circle with a diameter whose endpoints are $(0,7)$ and $(0,3)$?

   A) $x^2 + y^2 + 21 = 0$
   B) $x^2 + y^2 - 10y + 21 = 0$
   C) $x^2 + y^2 - 10y + 9 = 0$
   D) $x^2 - y^2 - 10y + 9 = 0$

58. Which equation corresponds to the logarithmic statement: $\log_x k = m$?

   A) $x^m = k$
   B) $k^m = x$
   C) $x^k = m$
   D) $m^x = k$

59. Find the first derivative of the function: $f(x) = x^3 - 6x^2 + 5x + 4$

   A) $3x^3 - 12x^2 + 5x = f'(x)$
   B) $3x^2 - 12x - 5 = f'(x)$
   C) $3x^2 - 12x + 9 = f'(x)$
   D) $3x^2 - 12x + 5 = f'(x)$

60. Differentiate: $y = e^{3x+2}$

   A) $3e^{3x+2} = y'$
   B) $3e^{3x} = y'$
   C) $6e^3 = y'$
   D) $(3x+2)e^{3x+1} = y'$

61. Find the slope of the line tangent to $y = 3x(\cos x)$ at $(\pi/2, \pi/2)$.

   A) $-3\pi/2$
   B) $3\pi/2$
   C) $\pi/2$
   D) $-\pi/2$

62. Find the equation of the line tangent to $y = 3x^2 - 5x$ at $(1,-2)$.

   A) $y = x - 3$
   B) $y = 1$
   C) $y = x + 2$
   D) $y = x$

63. How does the function $y = x^3 + x^2 + 4$ behave from $x = 1$ to $x = 3$?

    A) increasing, then decreasing
    B) increasing
    C) decreasing
    D) neither increasing nor decreasing

64. Find the absolute maximum obtained by the function $y = 2x^2 + 3x$ on the interval $x = 0$ to $x = 3$.

    A) −3/4
    B) −4/3
    C) 0
    D) 27

65. Find the antiderivative for $4x^3 - 2x + 6 = y$.

    A) $x^4 - x^2 + 6x + C$
    B) $x^4 - 2/3x^3 + 6x + C$
    C) $12x^2 - 2 + C$
    D) $4/3x^4 - x^2 + 6x + C$

66. Find the antiderivative for the function $y = e^{3x}$.

    A) $3x(e^{3x}) + C$
    B) $3(e^{3x}) + C$
    C) $1/3(e^x) + C$
    D) $1/3(e^{3x}) + C$

67. The acceleration of a particle is dv/dt = 6 m/s². Find the velocity at t=10 given an initial velocity of 15 m/s.

    A) 60 m/s
    B) 150 m/s
    C) 75 m/s
    D) 90 m/s

68. If the velocity of a body is given by v = 16 - t², find the distance traveled from t = 0 until the body comes to a complete stop.

    A) 16
    B) 43
    C) 48
    D) 64

69. Evaluate: $\int (x^3 + 4x - 5)dx$

    A) $3x^2 + 4 + C$
    B) $\frac{1}{4}x^4 - 2/3x^3 + 6x + C$
    C) $x^{4/3} + 4x - 5x + C$
    D) $x^3 + 4x^2 - 5x + C$

70. Evaluate $\int_0^2 (x^2 + x - 1)dx$

    A) 11/3
    B) 8/3
    C) -8/3
    D) -11/3

71. Find the area under the function $y = x^2 + 4$ from $x = 3$ to $x = 6$.

   A) 75
   B) 21
   C) 96
   D) 57

72. -3 + 7 = -4   6(-10) = -60
    -5(-15) = 75   -3+-8 = 11
    8-12 = -4   7- -8 = 15

   Which best describes the type of error observed above?

   A) The student is incorrectly multiplying integers.
   B) The student has incorrectly applied rules for adding integers to subtracting integers.
   C) The student has incorrectly applied rules for multiplying integers to adding integers.
   D) The student is incorrectly subtracting integers.

73. About two weeks after introducing formal proofs, several students in your geometry class are having a difficult time remembering the names of the postulates. They cannot complete the reason column of the proof and as a result are not even attempting the proofs. What would be the best approach to help students understand the nature of geometric proofs?

   A) Give them more time; proofs require time and experience.
   B) Allow students to write an explanation of the theorem in the reason column instead of the name.
   C) Have the student copy each theorem in a notebook.
   D) Allow the students to have open book tests.

74. What would be the shortest method of solution for the system of equations below?

   $$3x + 2y = 38$$
   $$4x + 8 = y$$

   A) linear combination
   B) additive inverse
   C) substitution
   D) graphing

75. **Identify the correct sequence of subskills required for solving and graphing inequalities involving absolute value in one variable, such as $|x+1| \leq 6$.**

    A) understanding absolute value, graphing inequalities, solving systems of equations
    B) graphing inequalities on a Cartesian plane, solving systems of equations, simplifying expressions with absolute value
    C) plotting points, graphing equations, graphing inequalities
    D) solving equations with absolute value, solving inequalities, graphing conjunctions and disjunctions

76. **What would be the least appropriate use for handheld calculators in the classroom?**

    A) practice for standardized tests
    B) integrating algebra and geometry with applications
    C) justifying statements in geometric proofs
    D) applying the law of sines to find dimensions

77. **According to Piaget, what stage in a student's development would be appropriate for introducing abstract concepts in geometry?**

    A) concrete operational
    B) formal operational
    C) sensori-motor
    D) pre-operational

78. **A group of students working with trigonometric identities have concluded that $\cos 2x = 2\cos x$. How could you best lead them to discover their error?**

    A) Have the students plug in values on their calculators.
    B) Direct the student to the appropriate chapter in the text.
    C) Derive the correct identity on the board.
    D) Provide each student with a table of trig identities.

79. Which of the following is the best example of the value of personal computers in advanced high school mathematics?

    A) Students can independently drill and practice test questions.
    B) Students can keep an organized list of theorems and postulates on a word processing program.
    C) Students can graph and calculate complex functions to explore their nature and make conjectures.
    D) Students are better prepared for business because of mathematics computer programs in high school.

80. Given the series of examples below, what is 5¢4?

    4¢3=13   7¢2=47
    3¢1=8   1¢5=-4

    A) 20
    B) 29
    C) 1
    D) 21

Answer Key

1)	B	21)	C	41)	C	61)	A
2)	B	22)	A	42)	A	62)	A
3)	D	23)	A	43)	B	63)	B
4)	D	24)	C	44)	C	64)	D
5)	A	25)	D	45)	A	65)	A
6)	B	26)	D	46)	B	66)	D
7)	C	27)	B	47)	B	67)	C
8)	D	28)	A	48)	C	68)	B
9)	D	29)	D	49)	D	69)	B
10)	B	30)	A	50)	D	70)	B
11)	C	31)	A	51)	C	71)	A
12)	B	32)	C	52)	C	72)	C
13)	C	33)	B	53)	B	73)	B
14)	C	34)	B	54)	D	74)	C
15)	B	35)	C	55)	A	75)	D
16)	B	36)	B	56)	C	76)	C
17)	B	37)	B	57)	B	77)	B
18)	B	38)	D	58)	A	78)	C
19)	D	39)	C	59)	D	79)	C
20)	A	40)	C	60)	A	80)	D

TEACHER CERTIFICATION STUDY GUIDE

Rationales for Sample Questions

1. Let N = .636363.... Then multiplying both sides of the equation by 100 or 10^2 (because there are 2 repeated numbers), we get 100N = 63.636363... Then subtracting the two equations gives 99N = 63 or N = $\frac{63}{99} = \frac{7}{11}$. **Answer is B**

2. I is not closed because $\frac{4}{.5} = 8$ and 8 is not in the set.

   III is not closed because $\frac{1}{0}$ is undefined.

   II is closed because $\frac{-1}{1} = -1, \frac{1}{-1} = -1, \frac{1}{1} = 1, \frac{-1}{-1} = 1$ and all the answers are in the set. **Answer is B**

3. **Answer is D** because a + (-a) = 0 is a statement of the Additive Inverse Property of Algebra.

4. To find the inverse, $f^{-1}(x)$, of the given function, reverse the variables in the given equation, y = 3x – 2, to get x = 3y – 2. Then solve for y as follows: x+2 = 3y, and y = $\frac{x+2}{3}$. **Answer is D.**

5. Before the tax, the total comes to $365.94. Then .065(365.94) = 23.79. With the tax added on, the total bill is 365.94 + 23.79 = $389.73. (Quicker way: 1.065(365.94) = 389.73.) **Answer is A**

6. Recall: 30 days in April and 31 in March. 8 days in March + 30 days in April + 22 days in May brings him to a total of 60 days on May 22. **Answer is B.**

7. A composite number is a number which is not prime. The prime number sequence begins 2,3,5,7,11,13,17,.... To determine which of the expressions is <u>always</u> composite, experiment with different values of x and y, such as x=3 and y=2, or x=5 and y=2. It turns out that 5xy will always be an even number, and therefore, composite, if y=2. **Answer is C.**

8. Using FOIL to do the expansion, we get $(x + y^2)^2 = (x + y^2)(x + y^2) = x^2 + 2xy^2 + y^4$. **Answer is D.**

9. In scientific notation, the decimal point belongs to the right of the 4, the first significant digit. To get from 4.56×10^{-5} back to 0.0000456, we would move the decimal point 5 places to the left. **Answer is D.**

MATHEMATICS (Secondary)

10. Area of triangle AOB is .5(5)(5) = 12.5 square meters. Since $\frac{90}{360} = .25$, the area of sector AOB (pie-shaped piece) is approximately $.25(\pi)5^2$ = 19.63. Subtracting the triangle area from the sector area to get the area of segment AB, we get approximately 19.63-12.5 = 7.13 square meters. **Answer is B.**

11. The formula for the volume of a cone is $V = \frac{1}{3}Bh$, where B is the area of the circular base and h is the height. If the area of the base is tripled, the volume becomes
$V = \frac{1}{3}(3B)h = Bh$, or three times the original area. **Answer is C.**

12. Divide the figure into 2 rectangles and one quarter circle. The tall rectangle on the left will have dimensions 10 by 4 and area 40. The rectangle in the center will have dimensions 7 by 10 and area 70. The quarter circle will have area $.25(\pi)7^2$ = 38.48.
The total area is therefore approximately 148.48. **Answer is B.**

13. Since an ordinary cookie would not weigh as much as 1 kilogram, or as little as 1 gram or 15 milligrams, the only reasonable answer is 15 grams. **Answer is C.**

14. Arrange the data in ascending order: 12,13,14,16,17,19. The median is the middle value in a list with an odd number of entries. When there is an even number of entries, the median is the mean of the two center entries. Here the average of 14 and 16 is 15. **Answer is C.**

15. In this set of data, the median (see #14) would be the most representative measure of central tendency since the median is independent of extreme values. Because of the 10% outlier, the mean (average) would be disproportionately skewed. In this data set, it is true that the median and the mode (number which occurs most often) are the same, but the median remains the best choice because of its special properties. **Answer is B.**

16. In Kindergarten, first grade, and third grade, there are more boys than girls. The number of extra girls in grade two is more than made up for by the extra boys in all the other grades put together. **Answer is B.**

17. The values of 5 and −5 must be omitted from the domain of all real numbers because if x took on either of those values, the denominator of the fraction would have a value of 0, and therefore the fraction would be undefined. **Answer is B.**

18. By observation, we see that the graph has a y-intercept of 2 and a slope of 2/1 = 2. Therefore its equation is y = mx + b = 2x + 2. Rearranging the terms gives 2x − y = -2. **Answer is B.**

19. Using the Distributive Property and other properties of equality to isolate v_0 gives $d = atv_t - atv_0$, $atv_0 = atv_t - d$, $v_0 = \dfrac{atv_t - d}{at}$. **Answer is D.**

20. Removing the common factor of 6 and then factoring the sum of two cubes gives
$6 + 48m^3 = 6(1 + 8m^3) = 6(1 + 2m)(1^2 - 2m + (2m)^2)$. **Answer is A.**

21. B is not the graph of a function. D is the graph of a parabola where the coefficient of x^2 is negative. A appears to be the graph of $y = x^2$. To find the x-intercepts of
$y = x^2 + 3x$, set $y = 0$ and solve for x: $0 = x^2 + 3x = x(x + 3)$ to get $x = 0$ or $x = -3$. Therefore, the graph of the function intersects the x-axis at $x=0$ and $x=-3$.
Answer is C.

22. Set up the direct variation: $\dfrac{V}{r^2} = \dfrac{V}{r^2}$. Substituting gives $\dfrac{80}{16} = \dfrac{V}{9}$. Solving for V gives 45 liters per minute. **Answer is A.**

23. Multiplying equation 1 by 2, and equation 2 by –3, and then adding together the two resulting equations gives $-11y + 22z = 0$. Solving for y gives $y = 2z$. In the meantime, multiplying equation 3 by –2 and adding it to equation 2 gives $-y - 12z = -14$. Then substituting 2z for y, yields the result $z = 1$. Subsequently, one can easily find that $y = 2$, and $x = -1$. **Answer is A.**

24. Using the definition of absolute value, two equations are possible: $18 = 4 + 2x$ or $18 = 4 - 2x$. Solving for x gives $x = 7$ or $x = -7$. **Answer is C.**

25. Rewriting the inequality gives $x^2 - 5x + 6 > 0$. Factoring gives $(x - 2)(x - 3) > 0$.

The two cut-off points on the number line are now at $x = 2$ and $x = 3$. Choosing a random number in each of the three parts of the number line, we test them to see if they produce a true statement. If $x = 0$ or $x = 4$, $(x-2)(x-3)>0$ is true. If $x = 2.5$, $(x-2)(x-3)>0$ is false. Therefore the solution set is all numbers smaller than 2 or greater than 3. **Answer is D.**

26. Possible rational roots of the equation $0 = x^3 + x^2 - 14x - 24$ are all the positive and negative factors of 24. By substituting into the equation, we find that -2 is a root, and therefore that $x+2$ is a factor. By performing the long division $(x^3 + x^2 - 14x - 24)/(x+2)$, we can find that another factor of the original equation is $x^2 - x - 12$ or $(x-4)(x+3)$. Therefore the zeros of the original function are -2, -3, and 4. **Answer is D.**

27. Getting the bases the same gives us $3^{\frac{1}{2}}3^{\frac{2}{3}}$. Adding exponents gives $3^{\frac{7}{6}}$. Then some additional manipulation of exponents produces $3^{\frac{7}{6}}=3^{\frac{14}{12}}=\left(3^2\right)^{\frac{7}{12}}=9^{\frac{7}{12}}$. **Answer is B**.

28. Simplifying radicals gives $\sqrt{27}+\sqrt{75}=3\sqrt{3}+5\sqrt{3}=8\sqrt{3}$. **Answer is A.**

29. Multiplying numerator and denominator by the conjugate gives
$\dfrac{10}{1+3i}\times\dfrac{1-3i}{1-3i}=\dfrac{10(1-3i)}{1-9i^2}=\dfrac{10(1-3i)}{1-9(-1)}=\dfrac{10(1-3i)}{10}=1-3i$. **Answer is D**.

30. To find the 100th term: t_{100} = -6 + 99(4) = 390. To find the sum of the first 100 terms: S = $\dfrac{100}{2}(-6+390)=19200$. **Answer is A.**

31. There are 3 slots to fill. There are 3 choices for the first, 7 for the second, and 6 for the third. Therefore, the total number of choices is 3(7)(6) = 126. **Answer is A.**

32. The set-up for finding the seventh term is $\dfrac{8(7)(6)(5)(4)(3)}{6(5)(4)(3)(2)(1)}(2a)^{8-6}b^6$ which gives 28(4a^{2}b^6) or 112a^{2}b^6. **Answer is C.**

33. By definition, parallel lines are coplanar lines without any common points. **Answer is B.**

34. A set of n objects has 2^n subsets. Therefore, here we have 2^4 = 16 subsets. These subsets include four which each have 1 element only, six which each have 2 elements, four which each have 3 elements, plus the original set, and the empty set. **Answer is B.**

35. Formula for finding the measure of each interior angle of a regular polygon with n sides is $\dfrac{(n-2)180}{n}$. For n=10, we get $\dfrac{8(180)}{10}=144$. **Answer is C.**

36. Draw a right triangle with legs of 6 and 8. Find the hypotenuse using the Pythagorean Theorem. $6^2 + 8^2 = c^2$. Therefore, c = 10 miles. **Answer is B.**

37. The formula relating the measure of angle K and the two arcs it intercepts is $m\angle K=\dfrac{1}{2}(mPS-mAD)$. Substituting the known values, we get $10=\dfrac{1}{2}(40-mAD)$. Solving for mAD gives an answer of 20 degrees. **Answer is B.**

38. Given a point on a line, place the compass point there and draw two arcs intersecting the line in two points, one on either side of the given point. Then using any radius larger than half the new segment produced, and with the pointer at each end of the new segment, draw arcs which intersect above the line. Connect this new point with the given point. **Answer is D**.

39. By definition this describes the procedure of an indirect proof. **Answer is C**.

40. Since side AK is common to both triangles, the triangles can be proved congruent by using the Side-Angle-Side Postulate. **Answer is C**.

41. In an ordinary parallelogram, the diagonals are not perpendicular or equal in length. In a rectangle, the diagonals are not necessarily perpendicular. In a rhombus, the diagonals are not equal in length. In a square, the diagonals are both perpendicular and congruent. **Answer is C**.

42. The most one can say with certainty is that the median (segment drawn to the midpoint of the opposite side) and the altitude (segment drawn perpendicular to the opposite side) of a triangle may coincide, but they more often do not. In an isosceles triangle, the median and the altitude to the base are the same segment. **Answer is A.**

43. In the mid-nineteenth century, Reimann and other mathematicians developed elliptic geometry. **Answer is B**.

44. Let's assume the base of the rectangular solid (box) is 3 by 4, and the height is 5. Then the surface area of the top and bottom together is 2(12) = 24. The sum of the areas of the front and back are 2(15) = 30, while the sum of the areas of the sides are 2(20)=40. The total surface area is therefore 94 square feet. **Answer is C**.

45. Find the area of the garden and then subtract the area of the fountain: $30(60) - \pi(5)^2$ or approximately 1721 square meters. **Answer is A**.

46. To find the area of the shaded region, find the area of triangle ABC and then subtract the area of triangle DBE. The area of triangle ABC is .5(6x)(y) = 3xy. The area of triangle DBE is .5(2x)(y) = xy. The difference is 2xy. **Answer is B.**

47. Find the mean: 300/8 = 37.5. Then, using the formula for standard deviation, we get

$$\sqrt{\frac{2(37.5-37)^2 + 2(37.5-38)^2 + (37.5-35)^2 + (37.5-40)^2 + (37.5-36)^2 + (37.5-39)^2}{8}}$$

which has a value of 1.5. **Answer is B.**

48. To find the determinant of a matrix without the use of a graphing calculator, repeat the first two columns as shown,

```
2   1   -1    2    1
4   -1   4    4   -1
0   -3   2    0   -3
```

Starting with the top left-most entry, 2, multiply the three numbers in the diagonal going down to the right: 2(-1)(2)=-4. Do the same starting with 1: 1(4)(0)=0. And starting with –1: -1(4)(-3) = 12. Adding these three numbers, we get 8. Repeat the same process starting with the top right-most entry, 1. That is, multiply the three numbers in the diagonal going down to the left: 1(4)(2) = 8. Do the same starting with 2: 2(4)(-3) = -24 and starting with –1: -1(-1)(0) = 0. Add these together to get -16. To find the determinant, subtract the second result from the first: 8-(-16)=24.
Answer is C.

49. Using the Pythagorean Identity, we know $\sin^2 x + \cos^2 x = 1$. Thus $1 - \sin^2 x = \cos^2 x$, which by definition is equal to $1/\sec^2 x$. **Answer is D.**

50. Tan A = 9/12=.75 and $\tan^{-1} .75$ = 37 degrees. Since angle B is complementary to angle A, the measure of angle B is therefore 53 degrees.
Answer is D.

51. The composite function $g(f(x)) = (3x-2)^2 = 9x^2 - 12x + 4$. **Answer is C.**

52. Given the polar point $(r,\theta) = (5, 60)$, we can find the rectangular coordinates this way: $(x,y) = (r\cos\theta, r\sin\theta) = (5\cos 60, 5\sin 60) = (2.5, 4.33)$. **Answer is C.**

53. Using the Pythagorean Theorem, we get v = $\sqrt{36+25} = \sqrt{61}$. **Answer is B.**

54. The line x = 5 is a vertical line passing through (5,0) on the Cartesian plane. By observation the distance along the horizontal line from the point (-2,7) to the line x=5 is 7 units. **Answer is D.**

55. The formula for finding the midpoint (a,b) of a segment passing through the points (x_1, y_1) and (x_2, y_2) is $(a,b) = (\frac{x_1+x_2}{2}, \frac{y_1+y_2}{2})$. Setting up the corresponding equations from this information gives us $x = \frac{-4+2}{2}$, and $1 = \frac{y-3}{2}$. Solving for x and y gives x = -1 and y = 5. **Answer is A.**

56. Dividing by 36, we get $\dfrac{x^2}{36}+\dfrac{y^2}{4}=1$, which tells us that the ellipse intersects the x-axis at 6 and –6, and therefore the length of the major axis is 12. (The ellipse intersects the y-axis at 2 and –2). **Answer is C.**

57. With a diameter going from (0,7) to (0,3), the diameter of the circle must be 4, the radius must be 2, and the center of the circle must be at (0,5). Using the standard form for the equation of a circle, we get (x-0)² + (y-5)² = 2². Expanding, we get
$x^2 + y^2 - 10y + 21 = 0$. **Answer is B.**

58. By definition of log form and exponential form, $\log_x k = m$ corresponds to $x^m = k$. **Answer is A.**

59. Use the Power Rule for polynomial differentiation: if y = ax^n, then y'=nax^{n-1}. **Answer is D.**

60. Use the Exponential Rule for derivatives of functions of e: if y = ae$^{f(x)}$, then y' = f'(x)ae$^{f(x)}$. **Answer is A.**

61. To find the slope of the tangent line, find the derivative, and then evaluate it at
x = $\dfrac{\pi}{2}$. y' = 3x(-sinx)+3cosx. At the given value of x,
y' = $3(\dfrac{\pi}{2})(-\sin\dfrac{\pi}{2})+3\cos\dfrac{\pi}{2}=\dfrac{-3\pi}{2}$. **Answer is A.**

62. To find the slope of the tangent line, find the derivative, and then evaluate it at x=1.

y'=6x-5=6(1)-5=1. Then using point-slope form of the equation of a line, we get y+2=1(x-1) or y = x-3. **Answer is A.**

63. To find critical points, take the derivative, set it equal to 0, and solve for x. f'(x) = 3x² + 2x = x(3x+2)=0. CP at x=0 and x=-2/3. Neither of these CP is on the interval from x=1 to x=3. Testing the endpoints: at x=1, y=6 and at x=3, y=38. Since the derivative is positive for all values of x from x=1 to x=3, the curve is increasing on the entire interval. **Answer is B.**

64. Find CP at x=-.75 as done in #63. Since the CP is not in the interval from x=0 to x=3, just find the values of the functions at the endpoints. When x=0, y=0, and when x=3, y = 27. Therefore 27 is the absolute maximum on the given interval. **Answer is D.**

65. Use the rule for polynomial integration: given ax^n, the antiderivative is $\dfrac{ax^{n+1}}{n+1}$. **Answer is A.**

66. Use the rule for integration of functions of e: $\int e^x dx = e^x + C$. **Answer is D.**

67. Recall that the derivative of the velocity function is the acceleration function. In reverse, the integral of the acceleration function is the velocity function. Therefore, if a=6, then v=6t+C. Given that at t=0, v=15, we get v = 6t+15. At t=10, v=60+15=75m/s. **Answer is C.**

68. Recall that the derivative of the distance function is the velocity function. In reverse, the integral of the velocity function is the distance function. To find the time needed for the body to come to a stop when v=0, solve for t: v = 16 – t^2 = 0. Result: t = 4 seconds. The distance function is s = 16t - $\dfrac{t^3}{3}$. At t=4, s= 64 – 64/3 or approximately 43 units. **Answer is B.**

69. Integrate as described in #65. **Answer is B.**

70. Use the fundamental theorem of calculus to find the definite integral: given a continuous function f on an interval [a,b], then $\int_a^b f(x)dx = F(b) - F(a)$, where F is an antiderivative of f.

$\int_0^2 (x^2 + x - 1)dx = (\dfrac{x^3}{3} + \dfrac{x^2}{2} - x)$ Evaluate the expression at x=2, at x=0, and then subtract to get 8/3 + 4/2 – 2-0 = 8/3. **Answer is B.**

71. To find the area set up the definite integral: $\int_3^6 (x^2 + 4)dx = (\dfrac{x^3}{3} + 4x)$. Evaluate the expression at x=6, at x=3, and then subtract to get (72+24)-(9+12)=75. **Answer is A.**

72. The errors are in the following: -3+7=-4 and –3 + -8 = 11, where the student seems to be using the rules for signs when multiplying, instead of the rules for signs when adding. **Answer is C.**

73. **Answer is B.**

74. Since the second equation is already solved for y, it would be easiest to use the substitution method. **Answer is C.**

MATHEMATICS (Secondary)

75. The steps listed in answer D would look like this for the given example: If $|x+1| \leq 6$, then $-6 \leq x+1 \leq 6$, which means $-7 \leq x \leq 5$. Then the inequality would be graphed on a number line and would show that the solution set is all real numbers between –7 and 5, including –7 and 5. **Answer is D.**

76. There is no need for calculators when justifying statements in a geometric proof. **Answer is C.**

77. By observation the **Answer is B**.

78. **Answer is C.**

79. **C is the best answer.**

80. By observation of the examples given, $a \not\subset b = a^2 - b$. Therefore, $5 \not\subset 4 = 25 - 4 = 21$. **Answer is D**.

Good luck to all of you. May you have many happy years teaching.

The end.

XAMonline, INC. 21 Orient Ave. Melrose, MA 02176

Toll Free number 800-509-4128

TO ORDER Fax 781-662-9268 OR www.XAMonline.com

MICHIGAN TEST FOR TEACHER EXAMINATION - MTTC - 2007

PO#   Store/School:
Address 1:

Address 2 (Ship to other):

City, State Zip

Credit card number_____-_____-_____-_____   expiration_____

EMAIL _____

PHONE   FAX

ISBN	TITLE	Qty	Retail	Total
978-1-58197-968-8	MTTC Basic Skills 96		$27.95	
978-1-58197-954-1	MTTC Biology 17		$59.95	
978-1-58197-955-8	MTTC Chemistry 18		$59.95	
978-1-58197-974-9	MTTC Early Childhood Education 82		$73.50	
978-1-58197-966-4	MTTC Elementary Education 83		$28.95	
978-1-58197-950-3	MTTC English 02		$59.95	
978-1-58197-959-6	MTTC French 23		$15.00	
978-1-58197-965-7	MTTC Guidance Counselor 51		$59.95	
978-1-58197-972-5	MTTC Integrated Science 94		$59.95	
978-1-58197-963-3	MTTC Library Media 48		$59.95	
978-1-58197-958-9	MTTC Mathematics 22		$59.95	
978-1-58197-962-6	MTTC Physical Education 44		$59.95	
978-1-58197-871-1	MTTC Physics 19		$59.95	
978-1-58197-952-7	MTTC Political Science 10		$34.95	
978-1-58197-951-0	MTTC Reading 05		$59.95	
978-1-58197-960-2	MTTC Spanish 28		$59.95	
978-1-58197-9732	MTTC Special Education- Emotionally Impaired 59		$59.95	
978-1-58197-953-4	MTTC Learning Disabled 63		$59.95	
978-1-58197-970-1	MTTC Social Studies 84		$59.95	
			SUBTOTAL	
			Ship	$8.25
			TOTAL	

www.ingramcontent.com/pod-product-compliance
Lightning Source LLC
Chambersburg PA
CBHW080535300426
44111CB00017B/2730